HIGH

CONFESSIONS OF AN INTERNATIONAL
DRUG SMUGGLER

BRIAN O'DEA

DISCARD

OTHER PRESS
NEW YORK

Published by arrangement with Random House Canada,
a division of Random House of Canada Limited. Originally
published in Canada by Random House Canada, Toronto, in 2006.

Other Press edition 2009
Production Editor: Yvonne E. Cárdenas

This book was set in Janson MT by Alpha Design & Composition
of Pittsfield, NH.

10 9 8 7 6 5 4 3 2 1

Library of Congress Cataloging-in-Publication Data
O'Dea, Brian.
High : confessions of an international drug smuggler / by Brian O'Dea.
p. cm.
Originally published: Random House Canada Limited : Toronto, 2006.
ISBN 978-1-59051-310-1 (hardcover)—ISBN 978-1-59051-331-6
(e-book) 1. O'Dea, Brian. 2. Drug dealers—United States—Biography.
3. Drug traffic. 4. Drug traffic—United States. 5. Recovering addicts—
Biography. I. Title.
HV5805.O34A2 2008
364.1'3365092—dc22
[B]
2008050764

This is a work of nonfiction. Some of the events in this story took
place many years ago; consequently, the conversations quoted, and
the events surrounding the conversation, and their order, are to the
best of my recollection and convey, at the very least, the flavor of the
moments depicted herein. Some of the names have been changed to
protect the unindicted and the innocent.

Susannah, Wife, Lover, Best Friend, and Giver of Everything, without whom these words would still be rattling around inside me, I love you.

COME, COME, *whoever you are, wanderer, worshipper, lover of leaving; it doesn't matter ours is not a caravan of despair. Come, even if you have broken your vow a thousand times. Come, yet again, come, come.*

—Rumi

PROLOGUE

THERE'S NOTHING SPECIAL about us kids except that we're John O'Dea's kids, and he owns the Newfoundland Brewery. We live up on Lawler's farm on Cherry Hill Road, and you know the sort of place it is. It's that big sort of farmhouse with two stories and a basement and a really big kitchen, a huge kitchen with a table made of wood that's as long as anything you've ever seen, as long as maybe a Chevrolet, maybe not quite.

This house is right on top of Cherry Hill, and when I was a really little kid it was all fields there, but later, when I was eleven, for instance, when this story happens, there were plenty of other houses being built around. There's a long, long driveway up from Cherry Hill Road to our house, and boy, you don't want your father to tell you and your brother Johnny to shovel snow out of that driveway. Not Saturday morning, you don't. And Chris, who's about a year younger than me, he never got told until he was about twelve. I don't know why. Lucky.

There's two barns, too, on the farm, a big one and a little one, and there used to be a garage, but a kid burned it down by accident two years ago. A kid used to steal cigarettes from his mom, and there was a sort of double wall inside the garage, and the kid would drop the cigarette package down there and fish it out with a garden rake. One time, the kid couldn't get the pack out, and he lit a piece of paper with a match and dropped it down the wall so he could see the pack. Boy, that burned, and the kid ran and got a watering can, but no use and the kid ran way down the lane to Cherry Hill Road and pulled the fire alarm and hid. After the fire trucks came, the kid came up the lane like he wanted to see what was going on.

When I was eleven, Dad had a blue '53 Chevy and Mom had an olive and yellow '57 Chevy. They had my two sisters too, Eileen and Judy, who was Johnny's twin, but all this isn't about them.

I went to Winterton School until I was eleven. It was a nice school for little kids. The main problem was red blazers and red and green striped ties and gray short pants, which were the worst part, and gray knee socks. And the teachers were women, which was embarrassing for you when you got older. I can tell you, I couldn't wait to get to St. Bon's, where Johnny and the older boys went.

Where we live, in St. John's, Newfoundland, everybody's pretty religious. Whatever church you go to on Sunday morning, that's the kind of school you go to for the rest of the week and the hockey team you play on in the winter and the baseball team you play on in the summer and the scout troop. It's a big thing, a big deal, your religion. I don't know why. We kids and Mom and Dad are Catholics.

Every day at about seven in the morning, Dad would start pushing and rocking us and calling at us kids to get up. There were five big bedrooms, and everybody had their own except Mom and Dad and also Chris and me. Dad would say, "All right now, all right. There's nothing more to be had from sleeping when you've slept enough," and stuff like that. We'd all get up and pee and wash, and it was cold in winter upstairs, I'll tell you. We'd all brush our teeth and get dressed and go downstairs. Mom made breakfast, not Dad, and sometimes it was bacon and eggs, which I liked, and sometimes it was brewis, which you've probably heard about. You know there's lots of salt fish in St. John's, lots of cod, and Mom would soak this hard salt fish overnight in water and then rinse it off real careful in the morning. She'd heat up the frying pan and crisp up little pieces of fatback pork and put in the fish, and she'd soak these little pieces of hard old bread too, and when they were just right, in they'd go and she'd mix it all around. That was how Mom made brewis, anyway, and we'd have porridge sometimes and homemade bread and jam. If us kids were real lucky, we'd sometimes get toutons, which Mom made by frying up bread dough in grease and covering it over in syrup or molasses. All this time, the CBC radio would be yacking away on the shelf. Then we always had to give India her food. She was a big Newfoundland dog. You could see her picture on the label of Dad's beer. She was a good old water dog, India, except, like a fool, she kept thinking she was pregnant when she wasn't usually. She'd dig these funny holes in the ground and lie there in them. I don't know what her problem was. Lonely.

When I was eleven, it was a fairly good summer. It wasn't as bad as most. There wasn't as much rain, drizzle, and fog— "RDF" everybody called it, but it wasn't that bad that summer. Weekends Dad and Mom and us kids would ride out to the Greens' summer house way out on Oliver's Pond, maybe eight miles or so. The Greens were friends of Dad and Mom's. There were blueberries, plenty of them, up on the barrens. You could just go out and pick, and we'd also have a picnic sometimes by the water, the sea, that is. They had a platform that floated in the water near the shore, and we'd dive off seems like all day. On the way home, we'd say the rosary, all of us, because we were good Catholics, and then we'd pull into Cherry Hill Road, which was still dirt, and right there at the bottom of our driveway, right there every time, would be this old Plymouth and there'd be these two old ladies in it looking out at the sunset. Somebody might say they were ghosts. I don't know. Maybe they were saying their rosary. It gave me a spooky feeling, but a good spooky feeling, like they were old guardians waiting for us to come home, keeping it safe for us.

We'd all run upstairs, us kids, and get washed and changed for bed. Sometimes I was last, and halfway up, the stairs turned and went the other way and you could see under a radiator and past the radiator was the upstairs hallway. I just had to look under that radiator every time, just to make sure there were no ghosts there, but I think there were anyway. I don't know for sure.

There was a niche in the wall in the upstairs hallway and there we had an altar and that's where the blessed Virgin Mary was. We'd all of us, even Mom and even Dad, get on our knees there every evening and say the rosary. I was afraid of God, like all of us. And the demons in hell, where we'd burn. I was very afraid. But the Blessed Virgin understood about that. The Blessed Virgin would always be there to listen, no matter. That's what was good about her.

Of course, I was eleven that summer. That fall, all the little kids got to stay at Winterton School and I got to go to St. Bonaventure's College for Boys and Chris got to go there too. Mom took us out to Ayre's two weeks before, got us our blue blazers and our long gray pants and the blue and gold striped ties. I put mine on twice on the Saturday before school started and just looked in the mirror and saw how I was no little kid now.

I was excited that first morning, I'll tell you. Chris and me and Johnny got in Dad's Chevy, and Dad said things were getting easier now he could take all his boys to one school.

Along Cherry Hill Road we passed the spot where we played street hockey, and it was getting to be the time again. School and leaves falling and then the street hockey gets going good. Bull Cook and Andy Wells and Harry Warford and Dave Pope and Derek Blandford and Herbie Compton and Danny Breen. Hockey's a big thing for kids.

Across the field, past the woods, you could see Mount Cashel Orphanage. It was a big old place. Kids went there who lost their moms and dads. I don't know how, but they didn't have them anymore. These kids went to school there and lived there too, and the Brothers looked after them and taught them and stuff. I knew a couple of these kids, Freddie Gough for one. Sometimes we'd play guns in the woods, me and some of these kids. They seemed serious, sort of. Billy Wilson told me some Brothers pretended these kids were girls and did stuff to them. I didn't believe him. You know the kind of kid Billy was, generally a liar.

We drove over the bridge that crosses Rennie's River, past Sliding Rock, and boy was it fun to play around there, though your mother said you couldn't go near it, and oops, you'd just slide in accidentally. The water was dirty.

Dad stopped outside the brewery. "All right, boys, off you go then and have a good day. Do what the Brothers tell you. Johnny, you keep an eye out for Chris and Brian."

"Bye, Dad!" we all called. We got out and started up Mullock Street. I was so excited my heart was pounding.

"Okay," Johnny said. "That's George's. Don't go in there."

"Why not?"

"Why not? 'Cause that's where the St. Pat's boys hang out. They'll beat you for sure. They beat Ricky Lamey in the spring. You want to be beaten? They got a pool table in there."

Chris's and my eyes sort of bugged out as we passed the door of George's. How could we have known? We didn't want trouble.

"This is Jim's," Johnny said. "Let's go in for candy."

Jim's wasn't like George's. It seemed a St. Bon's kid was safe at Jim's. I looked back toward the brewery, but Dad had long disappeared. I was glad I had an older brother to steer me. We went in and bought a pocketful each of jujubes—three for a cent—and a bunch of hard-candy–covered spearmint jelly balls. I loved jelly balls.

"Don't let the Brothers see them," warned Johnny. "That's the strap for sure."

We got to the gates of St. Bon's. Two boys were smoking cigarettes there.

"Hi, Johnny," they said.

"Hi, Rick. Hi, Al."

"Those your brothers?" Al asked.

"Yeah."

"What's their names?"

"Brian and Chris."

"Yeah."

"Hey," said Rick. "Look out. It's Brother James."

A Christian Brother and a man in a suit came out from the school. They weren't walking too fast. Rick and Al flicked the ash off their cigarettes and cupped the cigarettes in their hands, then stuck their hands in their pockets. I'd never seen that.

Brother James and the man in the suit walked out the gate and right by us, talking. Then all of a sudden Brother James sort of wheeled around and came back and came up to Rick and didn't say a word and smacked Rick's pocket right where his hand was. Then he went over and smacked Al's pocket too. He went right off, talking to the man. I looked at Rick and Al, and their eyes seemed like they were watering some. After a minute they took their hands out. Their cigarettes were destroyed.

"Ow! Ow!" they said. They held their hands and walked around in circles, sort of. They held out their hands and looked at them, and they were both burned. I could see the red.

"Damn it!" Al said, but he was sort of smiling.

"Damn it!" Rick said.

"Shit!" Al said.

"Shit!" Rick said.

We went in. A person can be awful proud of his uniform, even when everybody else has the same one. And I was scared, but I don't know why. Maybe the Christian Brothers. You know how tall they look, and their robes are black, and they don't smile, ever. But you know, at Winterton School, the teachers all liked me, and these Brothers would like me too. They would know I was a good Catholic and my dad owned the Newfoundland Brewery.

I found my classroom and said good-bye to Chris and Johnny. I went in. There were about thirty-five boys in there. I sat down. I didn't say anything because I didn't know anybody. A lot of them were running around and talking. Not me. I was starting a new year in a new school with a new uniform.

Then I could sort of feel the Brother outside the door. Everybody got real quiet. My heart started pounding. The door opened and he came in. He was tall and thin. His eyes were funny, sort of sunk down and shadowy. His skin looked like my grandmother's after she died. He went fast up to the front and dropped his books on the desk with a bang. We were all real quiet. He looked around, and he didn't smile a bit. I don't know why. His eyes were like a bird's.

"Well," he said. "Boys, we have a Little Lord Fauntleroy with us this year."

We all looked around for this lord, but we didn't see any. I even looked behind me.

"O'Dea! Come up here!"

I felt a thing like an electric shock.

"Up here!"

I got up. My knees were shaking. I went up to the Brother. Maybe somebody had told him about how good I was at arithmetic at Winterton.

"Hold them out," the Brother said. He still wasn't smiling. He looked mad.

"I beg your pardon, Brother?" I said. Then I understood. I had to show my nails, like at Winterton. How was a person to know they did this at St. Bon's? My hands were clean. I held them out.

"Turn them over!"

I turned my hands over. They were clean. The Brother reached out and grabbed my wrist with his hand. It was bony. He pulled a black thing from his cassock. He lifted it over his head and brought it down hard on my hand. I made some kind of squeal, not loud. No grown person had ever hit me. He lifted the thing and hit me maybe eight times. Then he grabbed my other hand and held my wrist and hit that hand hard eight times more. When he stopped, I didn't feel right. I didn't feel real. I didn't hear sounds, and then I heard some boys. They were snickering, sort of. I looked down, and my new gray pants were soaking wet. I was a kid who pissed his pants, and everybody saw.

From far off I heard the Brother say, "This isn't Winterton School anymore, O'Dea. Now get out of here until you can control yourself!"

I felt these tears. I couldn't stop them. They just poured out like the pee. I went down the aisle. The pee was already getting cold on my legs. I heard more boys making noises, like sort of snickering. I went out the door and just stood around in the hall, you know, the way little kids do when they're scared and there's nobody around and they don't know what's going on. I just kept standing there in the hallway, crying.

Then this man came around the corner. I didn't know who he was, just another Christian Brother. I was so scared I stopped crying, but the tears were still coming down my face because you can't stop tears like that when you're a kid. He wasn't a very big man, and he was sort of fat and his face sort of round. He smiled and he took hold of my hand. His own was soft.

"Well, now, what's happening here?" he asked.

I wanted to tell him, but I couldn't. He looked at me, real worried, and I knew he wasn't going to hit me or anything. I went to say something, I don't know what, but out came this big sort of sob. There was snot running out of my nose, and it made a salty taste in my mouth.

"My goodness, this isn't right," he said. "This isn't right."

He took me by the hand and led me into another room. It was his office. He put his arms around me.

"There, there," he said.

He got out a big handkerchief and dried my tears and wiped my nose.

"Let's get you out of those wet pants," he said. "We'll dry them off."

He took off my new gray pants and he took off my underpants. He put them on the radiator in his office. He gave me a towel. I knew the Brother who'd hit me had made a big mistake. I was glad it was all right now. I was glad this man was my friend. I knew he'd tell that Brother about the big mistake he'd made. He'd tell him I was a good boy. He wouldn't let him hit me anymore.

"Stand up," the man said. He patted my leg. It was still a bit wet.

"Oh, you're still a bit wet," he said.

He patted my bum with his soft hands and then he patted my penis with one hand and he kept that hand on it.

"Cold," he said.

He put his fingers around my penis and squeezed it.

"Cold," he said.

He kept squeezing it and then pulling on it. I didn't want him to do that, because that was what DJ did to me, but DJ was just a bit older than my brother Johnny, and DJ always said if I told anybody what he did and what he made me do he'd beat the shit out of me. I didn't want the Brother to beat me, and I didn't want him to do that because it's a mortal sin, but he kept doing it. I didn't know what to do, and the Brother kept doing it until it happened.

He took his hand away then and left me there standing by the chair. He talked to somebody on the telephone and he sat at his desk. I felt awful bad. I knew for sure God had seen me just then and seen me make a mess. God knew I was bad and I was sorry, I was so sorry, because now I'd have to burn in hell forever and nobody would ever be able to come and help me and I didn't understand how all this had happened. I had wanted to be good, and now I would be always burning when I died, which would be soon. God, please don't kill me, I started saying, real quiet to myself. Don't kill me, please.

The Brother got up and felt my pants on the radiator.

"They're quite dry," he said. "You put them on now and go out for recess with the other boys."

I put on my pants. They were still a bit wet.

"Don't cry now," the man said.

That was my first day. I don't know about other kids. I guess the Brother didn't call any other kids to come in that day. I didn't cry so much later on. I got beat some more, but not so much, and everybody got beat and some of them pretty hard and they screamed and screamed because some Brothers used the real hard straps that would make big bruises. I got called to come to that man's office pretty often, maybe once a week, and he'd make me take my pants off because he'd say he wanted to see if my penis was still okay, and then he'd do it. I wouldn't cry though, not around him. I started talking all the time to the Blessed Virgin. I'd tell her I was sorry, and I'd ask her if she could talk to God for me and see if maybe I could not die and burn because I'd always been a good kid before. I'd talk to her up at our shrine in the upstairs hall, but I also talked to her on the street and when I was out playing and even sometimes when I was with the Brother. I talked and talked to her all that year, and the man kept calling me to his office and sometimes he'd call other boys too, so it wasn't always me.

The next year he went away and there was a new man in his office, and he didn't ever call me. I talked to the Virgin less, because I didn't want to think about it. A kid can't think about the burning all day, because it's not good for him. After a while, I didn't think about it so much, and I didn't think about the Virgin or the Christian Brother. I didn't think about school much, really. I guess I was scared.

I'm a bit older now.

ONE

THE DAWN OF AN OLD DAY

SANTA BARBARA, CALIFORNIA. Eight o'clock in the morning, 1990. I lay in bed, thinking about the hospital. A heroin addict named Danny had come in the night before. I could still feel the pressure of his head on my shoulder as he sobbed his wretched heart out. I'd started to work with him, then left about midnight. I wanted to go back that morning, see how he was doing. Poor old bastard.

A hard knock on the door. Just from the knock, I knew this day was my day.

I got up, put on the bathrobe my friend Molly had made for me—a black and white thing—and went to open the door. There were venetian blinds on the windows. They were partly closed, but through the slats I could just see the hands and the handguns. I felt a strong desire to disappear. I opened the door. One guy held up a badge with one hand—a Drug Enforcement Agency star.

"My name is Gary Annunziata, and I'm with the Drug Enforcement Agency," he said. "Your name Brian O'Dea?"

"I wish it wasn't, but it is."

He nodded almost imperceptibly. "May we come in?"

"You've got the gun."

"That's right. You got any guns in there, Mr. O'Dea?"

"No."

"You sure about that?"

"I'm positive."

They came in.

"You know why we're here?"

"No, I don't."

The other cop, the bad cop, Doug, laughed. "Don't bullshit us, O'Dea," he said.

"I'm not into bullshitting anymore."

Doug snorted. "Let's get this straight, O'Dea. We know what you do. We know you work with drunks and dopers at the hospital. We know you do good. But this ain't about change or rehabilitation. This is about crushing your life, motherfucker. Now do the right thing."

Something rumbled deep in my gut. "The rightest thing I can think is to call my lawyer."

Doug laughed outright. "Listen, asshole, I wouldn't be calling your lawyer, because he's fucking next, and so is every other lawyer down at that fucking Main Street law office."

So that was it, then. My whole law thing was out of the bag.

"Brian," said Gary, the good cop, "we're going to have a couple of people come down here. Do you mind?"

"No, no. Knock yourself out."

They got on the radio, and in two minutes there were eight cops in my apartment on the side of the hill in the Riviera district of Santa Barbara. They started to tear my place apart right away.

I asked to go to the bathroom. They checked it out and said, yeah, go. I shut the door, and after a minute I had a terribly thorough bowel movement. I flushed and imagined following it down, down, and out, out of everything that was happening here.

There was a knock on the bathroom door. "You still in there, O'Dea?"

"Oh yeah."

"Just about done, are you?"

"Oh yeah."

I had a glassed-in pool room out on the deck that overlooked the town. This Gary guy and I went out there.

"I guess you must have thought we'd never come," he said. "I mean, you working in hospitals with dopers and all."

"Listen," I explained. "I've got nothing to say. Honest to God, I don't. I've got absolutely nothing to say. Please don't try to trick me into answering questions. But you know what? I'll just talk to you. We'll talk about the weather, about sports, about girls, about drinking. We'll have a game of pool, and we'll let them do what they need to do. That'll be fine."

Gary drank a beer and we shot pool and talked. Weather, sports, girls. The crew was there for a few hours, and they finally found my storage shed receipt. I had a storage shed in downtown Santa Barbara, and they said they had to go down and search it, and oh, by the way, they weren't going to arrest me that day, but I should get ready because they'd be coming back to get me someday soon. There was an indictment coming for me, so I should be prepared.

"Fine," I said.

"Oh, and by the way," said Doug, "this woman right here, Sergeant Smith, she's with the Santa Barbara County Police. Soon as we're done at your storage shed, she's going to arrest you and take you to Santa Barbara County Jail."

"You can't do that," I said. "That county jail is known to be one of the worst places on the planet."

Doug smiled. "It seems, O'Dea, you owe a fine of $500 for driving without a license."

"Jeez. I forgot about that. What can I do about it, guys?"

"Talk to Sergeant Smith," Gary suggested.

Sergeant Smith came over. She was a nice-enough-looking woman, small, dark-haired. I recommended she overlook this peccadillo.

"No," she said. "I got to take you there and fingerprint you and book you, but if you pay the fine then and there, you can leave right away."

I phoned my girlfriend, Susannah, a textile designer I'd met only recently. She worked nearby. Susannah didn't know a whole lot about my life. She did know I'd had a life.

"Honey, can you come down to my storage shed?"

"Hmm. Well, I suppose so, yes."

"And would you mind grabbing $500 from the bank for me on your way? Be down there in, say, about five minutes."

"Okay, Brian," she said. "I'm working on something, but I'll meet you there in about forty minutes."

"Susannah, honey, uh . . . I can't tell you how important this is. The police are here with me, quite a few of them, and I'm going to my storage shed. Meet me there in five minutes."

In five minutes, Susannah pulled up. Eight cops and I were standing outside the storage shed.

"Oh, Jesus," she said. She handed me the money and got back in her car.

They ripped my storage shed apart, and then I hopped in the back of a Santa Barbara County Sheriff's car and went and got booked and paid $500 and got out.

Everybody said I should flee the scene.

"Run for it, Bri," they said. "Go, baby."

In fact, I couldn't run anymore. One guy I knew had been in the Bastille Day Parade in Paris when he was picked up by the DEA and Interpol. Another friend of mine was arriving from the South Pole, pulling into the southernmost port in Chile, just getting off his boat. The DEA were waiting for him on the dock. There was nowhere to go, not a safe place in the world for people like me. Anyway, that wasn't why I couldn't run. What was I going to do instead? Sober as I was, I couldn't go back to dealing. Anyway, that wasn't why I couldn't run. I just couldn't run. This was my chance to get this thing done. I had to get it done with. This shit had been crawling all over me for years, even though it hadn't been showing its face.

When I got back home from my booking at the county jail, I went straight off to an AA meeting. I'd been going three times a day since I'd gotten sober eighteen months earlier. I went to the AA meeting, and I stood up in the AA meeting, and I said, for the first time in my life, I need help. "The wreckage of my past has finally caught up with me. The police are telling me I'm looking at thirty to life."

The room was quiet.

"If any of you know me and have watched me for the past few years, here in Santa Barbara, I'd appreciate it if you could write a letter on my behalf."

A guy in the back stood up. He was going to say he felt my pain, right?

"Brian," he said. "You always look so fucking good. I'm so glad to see you're finally deciding to save your ass instead of your face. Because, Brian, you know what they say? They say a man can't save his face and his ass at the same time."

He sat down. That was the first time I'd heard that little ditty, but it made perfect sense to me. I'd always wanted everybody to believe that I was an island, that I could handle anything. Asking for help was like climbing Everest.

After the meeting, I called my lawyer in Santa Monica and gave him the news, especially the warning that I shouldn't use anybody from his firm because they were all next. My lawyer was exceptionally distressed. His partners were important people in the California legal community. They, too, were distressed. It was supposed to be their clients who got in trouble. In pretty short order, they got me another lawyer named Brendan O'Neil, a great-spirited young man. This was a good thing, because it had just begun to occur to me that I might be running out of money.

There had been many of us involved, and a month later we were all charged. We had to go up to Seattle to be indicted, because this case was in the Western District of Washington, Ninth Circuit. We had to plead not guilty and put up bail. Brendan paid for my ticket. Through my share in a fishing company, I owned an island in Alaska and some boats, the fishing business, and property in LA and Lake Nacimiento. My bail was a quarter million, and I put up my assets and got out.

Fifty-five men were indicted with me, and the DA offered half-time to everybody who debriefed. Debriefing was to be part of our repentance. In the end, fifty-three did. Two did not: me and our mechanic, Frank Graf. In retaliation, the feds confirmed that I was looking at thirty years to life.

Two weeks after the indictment, the authorities held a hearing to determine the source of the bail. The Seattle district attorney, Mark Bartlett, stood up in front of a magistrate. He was an elegant young man.

"Your honor," he said, "the crime this man is charged with committing is punishable by either life in prison or the death penalty."

I went weak all over. My name and the death penalty in the same sentence?

The court decided my gains were ill-gotten. They seized everything—the island, the boats, the properties. Three million dollars worth of real estate gone for good, and that was the last three million. Now I had no bail. They locked me up in the Snohomish County Jail. I hated jail. I needed another quarter million to get out. All I had were quarters for the telephone.

I couldn't find anyone who could spare me this kind of change. Everyone was afraid the feds might somehow take their money. My ex-wife and my mother-in-law had property in Chatsworth, California, that I'd paid for with my own hard-earned cash, but—no surprise—they wouldn't put it up. My stash of quarters was looking thin.

I called my buddy Dave Richo, a psychologist, at his office.

"Brian," Dave said, "I love you, but I have a policy: I never put my house up for anything."

"I understand, Dave."

"But my partner, Regina, wants you to call her."

"I don't know Regina that well."

"Call her. Maybe she has an idea."

I called.

"I hear you need some money to get out of prison," she said.

"Yeah. A quarter of a million bucks, that's all."

"I'd like to help somehow."

"I'm not quite sure what you can do, but thanks, Regina."

"I have a house in Taos that's worth about $600,000. I've been holding on to it so it can support me when I have a child. But I have this thing about human freedom. Would that house do it?"

I couldn't think of anything to say.

"Why would you do that?" I finally asked.

"I can just tell it's the right thing to do."

A couple of days later, I was out of the Snohomish County Jail and back on the streets of Santa Barbara.

I spent the next year doing exactly what I was doing before the DEA arrived. I went to three AA meetings every day, I hung out with Susannah, I read, I ran, I worked out, I counseled and consoled drug addicts and drunks at the hospital.

I shared my strength and hope with them. They, sadder and more desperate than I was, gave me strength and hope in return. I stayed sober.

I had asked the people at AA for help. I asked everyone I met for help. I needed references, I explained. Good references. Letters arrived from people in the community, from lawyers, from a judge, from movie stars, from regular joes, from psychologists. I sent copies to seventeen different people, including the president of United States, the vice president, the attorney general, the congressman from my district, one of the two senators from my state, the state assemblyman, the mayor, even the judge in my forthcoming trial and the district attorney, Mark Bartlett, who may have been seeking my death, for all I knew.

The Shaffer brothers, my former colleagues, were still out there. The cops made them an offer. Come in and cough it all up, and we'll give you three years, and we won't charge anyone else. We'll let everybody else go. The Shaffers said no, but they finally did give it up when almost everybody was cooperating against them and they knew there was nowhere left to hide. They could have given fifty-three guys a ride but, as it was, everybody was to get more time than the Shaffers were offered.

I met with Bartlett, the district attorney. I told him I accepted full responsibility, but I had nothing to say about anyone else. The response from the community appeared to have persuaded him I wasn't kidding. I was not going to say anything.

There was no trial. About twelve of us out of the fifty-five indicted—we were the management—struck our separate deals and went to court together to change our pleas to guilty. That day, in March 1991, a terrible ice storm struck

Seattle. Everything was stopped, not a car on the highway, which was a sheet of glass. Getting to the courthouse was as life threatening as anything I'd experienced on the Bering Sea.

There was nobody in the courthouse but us. The hallways were empty and silent. Judge John C. Coughenhour was up at the front of the courtroom in a big plaid mackinaw shirt under his robe, and we noticed he was wearing his gum boots. One at a time, we changed our pleas to guilty. I had a real hard time saying the words and making my statement. I could hardly get them out. I saw the DA looking at me strangely.

Afterward we stood around in the courthouse, having a chat with our lawyers, and the judge came out from his chambers and joined in the circle of about thirty, because he knew a few of the lawyers personally. We were all talking. A curious mixture: a dozen men who would be spending years of their lives locked in cages as a result of this day, their lawyers, the judge, two court marshals, the FBI, the two DEA guys.

Suddenly, Bartlett, the DA, came through the circle and walked up to me.

"Good luck, Brian," he said. He extended his hand and I took it. It was a slender hand, but firm. A sort of chill ran through me. What did this hand have to offer me? What was the man holding behind the gesture? I shook the hand. He turned and walked out.

I looked around. The other men stared in silence. I'd received the kiss of Judas. Every one of them now believed I had something going on with this guy, something no one else knew about and something better than they had managed. The color drained from my face, but there was nothing I could say.

The others received sentences of anywhere from six months to ten years. I received ten years.

———

Six months passed. Susannah, this brainy six-footer from an accomplished artistic family, this woman who had plunged into an affair with a man she barely knew, a man whose life promptly dropped off a cliff, this woman should have been gone, long gone. But she was not.

I acted out, I screamed, I raged, I slammed doors, I left skid marks on driveways, I bullied, and I loved. She quailed. Cherishing her own well-being, she did leave. Then, miraculously, she returned. Surely this was a sign.

The 29th of June, 1991. I was to report the following morning to begin my ten-year sentence at Terminal Island, the prison in Los Angeles Harbor, connected by bridge to Long Beach. I looked around and realized I was supposed to be in prison the next day—not jail, but prison—and there was no way that could happen. I hadn't made a single preparation. Every table, chair, lamp, towel, and bedsheet was still in place, as though life would go on tomorrow very much like today. I had a truck in the driveway, and I would need a week to pack it and get it safely stored. What was I going to do? I had to do something. My lawyer was away, and I couldn't reach him. I picked up the phone.

"Office of the district attorney."

"Hi. I'd like to talk to Mark Bartlett."

"One moment, please."

"Bartlett speaking."

"Mark, it's Brian O'Dea."

"I can't talk to you, Mr. O'Dea. We're required to communicate through your lawyer."

"I realize I'm not supposed to talk to you, but I have to talk to you. I'm supposed to be in prison tomorrow, and Brendan isn't available. I can't get hold of him and, quite frankly, Mark, I'm not ready."

"What do you mean, you're not ready?"

"You know, Mark, I just had a look around my house here, and my house looks like I'm not going anywhere, and I guess I've just been in denial about all of this till this moment, and I realize I'm supposed to be in fucking prison for ten years as of tomorrow, and I'm not ready to go. But, Mark, I promise you, if you give me a month, I'll be ready and I'll show up."

"I can't do that."

"Mark, honestly, I'm not trying to cause trouble. I've done everything according to my bail conditions. I'm not going anywhere. I'm going to go up, but I've been in denial about this, and honestly I will go. I'm just not ready at this . . . this moment."

There was a lengthy pause.

"Call me back in half an hour."

I called him back in half an hour.

"Okay. I talked to Judge Coughenhour. July 30, but not a day later."

"Thanks, Mark."

Now I acted like I was leaving. I got in touch with every creditor I had and said, hey, sorry, I'm going to prison but I'll be back in ten years. If you want to keep the bill, I'll pay you then. They all said they'd write it off, all except one: the phone company.

"Will you pay us when you get out?" the phone guy asked.

"Oh, yes," I said. "I certainly will."

"Okay," he said. "I'll make a note of it."

"Thanks."

The 29th of July. A beautiful day. My friends threw a beach party for me. There were maybe fifty people there. Somebody painted a banner that read "Brian celebrates change, babe." That was nice. Doug Miller, my original AA sponsor, who was in the band on stage, went to the microphone and reminded everyone that this was a celebration, a celebration of change. When he was offstage, he told someone that was the saddest moment for him, when he said that. He knew and I knew that the state didn't think this was about change. It was about crushing my life.

But I'd beaten them to it by years. They didn't know this, but the old life just hadn't worked. Since I'd faced my addiction, I'd been nothing for almost two years, and nothing was a great thing to be. When I'm nothing, other people are something. When other people are something, I can be sober. When I'm sober, my spirit can continue its journey.

The next morning my buddy Rodney Utt picked up Susannah and me in a van. We had breakfast at the Hilton—bacon and eggs, though I was a vegetarian. It seemed like the thing to do. Back in the van, I shed a tear. We drove over the bridge to Terminal Island and got out. Rodney and I shook hands and hugged. I kissed Susannah once or twice and then again. It had been fifteen months since the DEA had knocked on my door. Now there was only a hundred-yard walk down the road to the tower. I heaved my suitcase over my back and set off, and only looked back once.

TWO

I'M SLEEPING IN a hallway on a bunk with a plastic mat as a mattress. The freeway, they call it. The cells are stacked in tiers on both sides, and the ceiling of the freeway is three tiers of cells high. Chain-link extends to the top of tier three. In front of the cells on the other tiers is a walkway, and men look down from there onto the freeway. My neighbors are Spanish. Drug offense, drug offense, drug offense. Twenty-, thirty-, forty-year sentences. Twelve hundred men stacked like rats in a rat catcher's sack in a place built for four hundred and two. One toilet for thirty. One shower for sixty.

I arrived here with new sneakers and sweats under my arm but the guards took them away from me and handed me filthy rags in return. No pillow, no toothbrush, no comb, no soap, no shampoo, no toilet paper. I was taken to the entrance of the freeway, where I stared in at this vast stew of men, muscles, tattoos, noise. My stomach twisted in fear. By the entrance to the toilet, I found a scrap of paper and a pencil. They, and the breakfast I had this morning, are my possessions. I began to write.

Let go, let go of every big and little thing. Tonight: lettuce, bread, cauliflower, and a potato. Let go.

There are beds in every walkway, under every stairwell. Each area is its own community. Guys jockey for position, switch bunks so they can be with their own: Colombians under the easternmost stairwell; Mexicans without connections on second-floor stairwells; American-Mexican gangsters on the second floor in cells; bikers and Aryans on the third floor, opposite me.

I used to know a guy we called Bad Billy. He was a friend of my ex, Suzi. Like a lot of bandits, he lived up at the end of Box Canyon, just off the old Wells Fargo stagecoach line. He was so crazy even the Hell's Angels didn't want him, except to make their bombs. Anyway, he's here. He comes to take me on a tour of the yard, introduce me to the heavies, give me a pair of gray sweats, very used tennis shoes, brown T-shirt. The stuff I was issued is rags, falling off me, no crotch, paint splattered all over. Billy doesn't want me looking like a fish. Wants to give me everything. The price will be steep, I know.

"Count! Count! Recount! Recount!"

"Stupid bastards!"

Shouts from every side, anger reverberating off the iron.

"Learn to count, asshole!"

"Rookie!"

"Recount! Recount! Let's go, people!"

"Go back to school!"

Walk five miles with José, fifteen years for coke. Meet Mike, twenty-five years, banks, and Pat, ten years, banks, and John and Steve, twenty years each. I don't ask.

"The time goes faster than you think, man."

"Them motherfuckers, man."

Jail, prison, penitentiary, federal correctional institution, lock up, lock down, up, down, out.

"Ain't never had no motherfuckin' father, man. Just me and my brothers and sisters and mother, man. Know what

I'm sayin', man? Dig, bro? Know what I'm sayin', homes? I stole every motherfuckin' thing I had."

"Pruitt, Frank! Pruitt? Pruitt? Pruitt?"

Silence.

"Man missing! No movement! Recount!"

A voice behind me as we stand waiting for the count: "Jack Daniel's, man—like water. I get out, we get together, man, then we gonna get some Jack Daniel's, then we gonna get some weed, then we gonna run outta that an'—who knows, man? Who knows?"

The Cubans are loud. According to Bad Billy, the noise of fourteen whites equals seven Mexicans equals four blacks equals one Cuban.

Billy wants to give me more shit, old and dirty sneakers, towels. Can't afford to say no to anything at the moment. A Cuban who lives across from me can't keep his eyes off me. Saw a guy with breasts today and then several others like him. TV screaming Spanish at one end of the hall, TV screaming English at the other. The noise, the noise.

Morning. Billy talks Jesus as Lord. He's spirit-filled, born again. Quotes the Bible to us in the morning's lesson on acceptance. Talks bombs, submachine guns with silencers and killing with a smile. Who is this Lord of his, this God of destruction he knows so intimately? They're shipping him out for a week or two. Some court case.

"Morgan! Where's Morgan? Morgan!"

The guards are as loud as anyone who calls this place home.

The toilet area is just beside me, and in one corner is a large cardboard box for garbage. Mostly missed.

A Mexican rolls over in his bunk and looks at me. "Hey, where'd you come from, man?"

"Santa Barbara."

"Yeah? Where at there?"

"Alameda Padre Sierra."

"No shit, man, I was born on APS, went to McKinley. How much time'd ya get?"

"Ten years for '86 pot they didn't get a joint of. Surrendered yesterday. O'Dea, Brian."

"Vasquez, Ricardo."

"Nice to meet you, Ricardo."

"You did better than me, man. First offense, thirty years."

"Coke?"

"Yeah. Never in trouble before." Amazing, the warmth of his eyes. "Hey. We got some good guys from Santa Barbara here. Introduce you when you're ready."

"Thanks. Whoa, who's that creepy-looking dude? Looks like Fagin."

"Who?"

"Fagin. Guy in a book."

"That's Sam, man."

A skinny white man, big afro hair, slinks quickly from cell to cell like a spider running to suck prey. Tattoos from the top of his forehead to the bottom of his feet.

Ricardo sniffs. "Sam's a junk man. Real junkie. Been in and out of prison forever."

"Fucking scary."

The color of everything is welfare green. In the wall directly above my bunk is a huge window of glass block, each block about six inches square. Through this window I saw the top of a cruise ship today, passengers gawking in our direction as they docked directly alongside.

Spanish is becoming my second language. My neighbor Patricio has a body full of Spanish tattoos.

"This place is a fuckin' kindergard, man," he tells me. "A fuckin' kindergard."

———

More clothes are supposed to be issued at 10 a.m. Billy intends to be there. "Be first in the crowd. Good stuff, man."

Clothes get issued at 1 p.m. instead. They ship Billy out.

"Stand down! Count! Stand down!"

We're so crowded together it's hard to get an accurate count.

"Hey, Brian! Brian!"

"Yeah. Who's calling?"

"Here! Over here! Pierre!"

"Hey, Pierre. What's up?"

"Did Billy leave today?"

"Yeah."

"You movin' up?"

"No, he'll be back in a week or so. They're keeping his cell for him."

Two things I've wanted since I got here: Billy to leave me to myself and candy and ice cream. Now Billy's gone. Time to find my own way around. Head pounds relentlessly. Still haven't sat down to shit in front of all these guys. Headache. Probably constipation and coffee withdrawal. I climb on my bunk and nap until dinner. Dreaming of candy and ice cream. George, ten years for one kilo of cocaine, gets his weekly chance to go to the commissary and brings me a pint of Cherry Garcia, gummy bears, a Snickers bar, and cookies. I inhale the whole lot in ten minutes and decide I want to be released right away.

Find a way to be with what this is. Not diminished but enlightened. Enhanced. Welcome to Karma Kleaners. We're in business for you. Find a way to be with what this is.

"Hey, Jimmy, how ya doing?"

"Wanna walk the track, Brian?"

"Sure. How long you been in jail, Jimmy?"

"Fourteen years."

"How old are you?"

"Twenty-eight. Been in prison since I was fourteen."

"Oh yeah?"

"Killed a U.S. marshal when I was runnin' some stolen government weapons. Then I've had two murder counts since I've been inside. Trouble with some guys. My dad told me if I didn't kill them, they'd kill me."

"You inside with your father?"

"Yeah. He's in Leavenworth now. I'm tryin' to get there to be with him."

"How'd you kill those guys?"

"Jus' came up behind the two of them with a double strand of piano wire. They died."

You're never going to leave here, son.

"I don't hang with nobody, man, just business associates. But I'll walk with you, 'cause you got somethin', man. People respect me, man. They don't fuck with me, ever."

"Count time! Count time!"

Everybody is willing to share everything: shampoo, deodorant, soap.

"Still counting! B Range, no movement!"

"Recount!"

"Hey, Doug."

"Hey, Brian."

"Hey, Patricio."

"Hey, Brian."

Night. Day.

Across the freeway is the cell of spidery Sam, the man with tattoos from head to foot. The hardest-looking men in the place come and go there. I pass him a few times and he looks at me closely, rubs his nose, slinks by. Don't want to attract his attention.

THREE

I ENTER VARIOUS TRADES AND FIND ONE TO MY LIKING

MY GOD was a hefty god and, from what I knew of him, not usually in a very good mood. This same God kept an inferno brewing for all eternity, specifically designed to roast rule-breakers. The Blessed Virgin, on the other hand, was as compassionate as any mother could be, though reticent in conversation. After tireless years of one-sided negotiation with these higher beings, I grew weary. Given the alternative, I wanted them to like me but, frankly, how was a boy to know whether they did? People, on the other hand, especially my friends, liked me quite a lot. After some time, I stopped thinking about currying the favor of God's family and His representatives in the St. John's area. I concentrated instead on currying the favor of the guys who hung out around Jim's candy store and responded appropriately to my gifts.

At eleven, I started taking nickels and dimes from Mom's purse and Dad's trousers. So effortless was this siphoning of my parents' wealth that I graduated by degrees to pilfering thousands of dollars over a number of years. Abandoning all restraint, I stole my brother Chris's Newfoundland coin collection. For myself, I bought Mexican-hat jujubes, which continued to be three or four for a penny, and bull's-eyes, a

Newfoundland molasses confection stirred up in the back rooms of candy stores, and I consumed these in solitary consolation. But the larger part of the loot went to a sort of philanthropy. All I asked in return was affection.

Gentle Tom Healy, the sales manager of Dad's Newfoundland Brewery Company, took me on one of his sales trips. I was sixteen, and this was my introduction to the world outside St. John's. In Montreal, Tom took a group of us to nightclubs where beautiful women in evening gowns would come up and ask to sit with you, even ask you to buy them a drink. They drank only champagne. One woman obviously liked me a lot, and Tom bet me I didn't have the nerve to ask her to dance. Of course I did, and I was certainly surprised when she turned out to have an erect penis under her gown. We left the club right after that.

We went on to Labrador City and Wabush, isolated iron-ore mining company towns, accessible only by permit and airplane. The two places owned between them a three-mile stretch of connecting road and a total of eighteen miles of streets—after that, wilderness. It looked to me like every adult male citizen possessed a Sting Ray, a big Mustang, or a 442 Oldsmobile. So this was adulthood. Well, well.

I finished high school at seventeen, and my father got me a job interview with the boss of the mining company. The obstacles, such as they were for me, were the minimum age requirement of eighteen and an eye exam that I wouldn't be able to pass because of some weakness in my left eye. The woman who gave the eye exam explained that you had to look in this machine and tell her what box the dots were in. I asked her for a Kleenex and when she went to get one, I moved my right eye over to the left side, memorized the first five boxes and then returned the left eye to position and rattled them off to her.

"Where's your birth certificate?" she asked. She seemed a little suspicious, but I was a pretty stout liar by this point, not quick to show the flag.

"I brought it the last time I was here and I gave it to you," I said, allowing just a tinge of disappointment and resentment to enter my tone.

Anyway, she knew I was an O'Dea.

They paid me $3.48 an hour as a janitor. It was 1965, and women were working in St. John's for fifty cents an hour and taking home $17 for a forty-hour week. I worked overtime every day and got my first taste of real money. It was also my first taste of real work. My job was to keep the bunkhouse spotless, a bunkhouse that warehoused a thousand men. They came out of the Ashawanabe pit, black from head to toe, just their teeth and eyes visible, drank themselves stupid, stumbled back to the bunkhouses, threw up, and washed up. There were a hundred sinks in every bathroom, and every sink and all the floors were black. I was the only English-speaking janitor; the rest were Portuguese. I lasted two months.

That fall I went to university in Halifax, Nova Scotia, where my brother Johnny was already enrolled. We seldom crossed paths, though: he gravitated naturally to intellectual friends, Bass Weejuns penny loafers, madras shirts, the Brothers Four, the Kingston Trio, barbershop haircuts, and "Michael, Row Your Boat Ashore." I was drawn to—or fell on, as we say—a different sort of ground, a stonier ground.

I managed to get through my first year on the money Dad had given me. For my second year, the year of Canada's centennial and the cresting wave of the counterculture, I moved into an apartment with Cam, a giant red-headed guy from Sudbury, Ontario, who was on the football team; Tony, whose father owned liquor stores in Boston; and Brian from

Waterloo, Quebec. We spent every night in the draft bars and sort of dozed around the apartment during the day.

One afternoon in January 1967, two long-haired guys dropped by. I vaguely knew them from Murray's Restaurant under the Lord Nelson Hotel. Big coffee drinkers. They produced a small bag of fragrant vegetation and some cigarette papers, then rolled us a funny kind of cigarette. The opportunity to put something in my body that would alter my consciousness, that would literally change my mind, was good, as far as I was concerned. Like uncounted thousands of young people before me and millions after me, I went to the fridge and painted peanut butter on a piece of bread. Fascinating. And delicious. I went out on the street. Everything was moving slowly past me. I could tell that everybody was looking at me, knew I was screwed up, knew I liked it.

Such a transformation could have only one response: I stopped doing anything other than smoking dope. With Mom and Dad far away, I had no access to daily infusions of cash, but I quickly flushed through my tuition money and my food money, though I drastically curtailed my drinking. I distributed the dope I bought to my friends, who liked me for that every bit as much as those in earlier years had liked me for candy. I dropped out of school to better taste the heady pleasures of freedom. When the school year was over, I returned to Newfoundland.

Now I had something to do. Having discovered that I could buy weed, I found I could also sell it. I broadened my world with a trip to Toronto, and the place made an agreeable impression on me. There were people there who would sell me sizable amounts for less than people in St. John's would pay for it.

I could not, of course, be seen to be relying on this delightful trade for my livelihood. By 1969 Dad was growing uneasy at my hanging around, apparently doing nothing, and he referred me to his friend Billy Forde. From my perspective, though Billy was close to Dad's age, he was refreshing, even astonishing, because he smoked dope, a fact he didn't share with my father. He'd come to Newfoundland with a carnival business he owned, and he had dope in his possession long before anyone else in that province. He stayed on and sold the carnival and became a successful real estate guy. With Billy and I linked in so many ways, it was inevitable I should start working for him in real estate. Unfortunately, I couldn't see myself as a salesman, at least not of products that required persuasion. I took to studying the view out the office window and was engaged one morning in that study while listening to a man called Ron Pumphrey do a talk show. This Pumphrey had taken the entire morning market away from every other radio station in St. John's.

"Shit," I said to Billy, "I could do that."

Billy was filling out a contract. He glanced up. "You could do what?"

"I could go get a job up at CJON doing that and take that guy on."

"Could you?" Billy said, but he didn't bother to look up this time. "How's that?"

"Look, all you need's a mouth and an opinion. I got those."

He finished writing. "Have to agree, Brian," he said. Now he looked up. "Tell you what. Here's twenty bucks says you can't."

Twenty bucks. That was twenty bucks more than I'd made in real estate. I called the station. A man named Colin Jaimeson was the boss there. Since my name was O'Dea and this was Newfoundland, he agreed to see me immediately. I went down the following morning, Friday, and was shown into the office. A conservative-looking fellow in his forties, white shirt and tie carefully in place, sat behind a desk. I thought it wise not to show hesitation of any sort.

"Look, Colin, I know you're losing the morning audience here, and so does everyone else. I'm your man to take back the mornings."

There was a silence while Jaimeson shifted gears from whatever he'd been thinking about. "What makes you think you can do that?" he finally asked.

"Anyone can do that."

"You think so, do you?"

"I do, sir."

"That's very bold of you, Brian. What's say you let us set up a closed-circuit broadcast right here at the station?"

"Of course."

"We'll set up a mock talk show for you. How's that? We'll give you a topic to deal with, and I'll have people call you from all over the station, and we'll listen to you and we'll see."

"You will," I said.

He led me to an announcer's booth. The desk in front of me sat against a glass wall that gave me a view of the producer. On my desk was a set of headphones, a button that could kill my mike—a cough button, they called it—and a multiline telephone. I felt instantly at home.

The test was piped throughout the building, and anyone working there could hear me and call the extension. Jaimeson opened the microphone and explained the setup to the staff. The topic, he said, would be the condition of the Smallwood leadership of the Liberal Party—a political issue, of course. Newfoundlanders are hugely political and have a lot of time to talk about it.

"All right, Brian," he said. "It's all yours."

He gave me a cryptic smile. I was, after all, a kid, not a political correspondent, and the staff members were for the most part diehard Smallwoodians. I smiled back. Thank you, Colin, I thought.

Not many years before, the Americans had pulled their air force base out of an impoverished district of Newfoundland called Stephenville. The economy had promptly died. My father, who had been in the brewery business all his life, had then made a deal with the Newfoundland government to build a brewery in Stephenville. It had all been done on a handshake from Premier Joey Smallwood—that was Joey's style. The new brewery was to be a state-of-the-art operation, and the government would supply the land and the infrastructure, and rebate to the brewing company all the sales tax for the first three years. Dad built the brewery and got the business underway. By the third year, however, he was struggling with cash flow and needed the promised tax rebate. That was all just before my debut as a radio host.

I cleared my throat. The engineer gave me the high sign.

"Welcome to *Open Line*. My name's Brian O'Dea, and beginning today, we'll bring you two hours of the day's hottest topics, two hours for you to have your own say on the matters of the day. Now, just for starters, how about that Joey? Does the man know when to quit gracefully? Let's hear from you."

The board lit.

"Hi, you're on *Open Line*."

The caller didn't bother to identify himself, he was so thirsty for blood. "Hello, Brine, is that you, b'y? Listen, b'y, I knew you when you were just a tom cod, and that wasn't too long ago. What makes you think you're old enough to know anything about this?"

"What does my age have to do with whether or not Mr. Smallwood's time has finally come—what did you say your name was?"

"George. George's my name, and I knew your father, and his father, two good men, and I can tell by your approach you are going to hurt their good name."

"Okay, George, I'm going to tell you what. Just like my age, my father and my long-dead grandfather have nothing to do with my opinion—thankfully—or with the facts. Next caller. Go ahead, you're on *Open Line.*"

"Yes, Mr. O'Dea, my name is Vera, and I wonder what you have to say about the free university education you've been getting thanks to our good premier? And the actual salary the government pays you kids for going to those classes? And the hospitals and paved roads, what about them? It never would have happened without Mr. Smallwood."

"Yeah, Vera. We're all very thankful for these things that Mr. Smallwood does and that every government should do. And we're so grateful to Mr. Smallwood for the shocking Churchill Falls giveaway, for the oil refinery fiasco and for the surrender of all our natural resources and money to American swindlers. Thank you, Joey, thank you. Next caller!"

That was Friday. I did my first live show on Monday: *Open Line with Knowledgeable O'Dea.* The time slot was from nine to eleven in the morning, with a break at ten for a newscast.

Smallwood had recently attempted to revitalize his party by bringing into the cabinet younger men with considerable talent, guys like John Crosbie, Clyde Wells, and Edward Roberts. Few of these potential rivals remained in his cabinet for long. Meanwhile, his economic development program was stumbling, and his Liberals had lost seats in the 1968 federal election and in a provincial by-election in Gander. Smallwood announced his retirement in 1969, but he just could not bring himself to relinquish power, particularly to the front-runner, Crosbie, who had earlier resigned from the caucus. So Smallwood was running for the leadership again, and a bitter contest pitted the younger generation, which supported Crosbie, against an older generation of Smallwood loyalists.

There was an air of imminent change. Everyone was talking about the first cracks appearing in the Smallwood wall. The old Smallwood loyalists were huddled in a corner, protecting their holdings. The young and vibrant Crosbie supporters were all over the place. It was only a matter of time before they came to power.

My father was a member of the House of Assembly for the poorest district in Newfoundland. His tendency was to give his money away to the impoverished people in his district. My uncle, Dr. Fabian A. O'Dea, though he failed to hide his personal distaste for my young career, was the lieutenant governor. So we knew politics in our house, and by 1969 I had become the demonstrations manager for Crosbie's campaign. I was too young to appreciate that nothing changes quickly in politics.

I had Joey on my show right away, in September. We were just about to break for the ten o'clock news, and he was talking about his triumphs.

"Excuse me, Mr. Smallwood," I interrupted. "We're going to break for the news right now, Mr. Smallwood, but before we go, I just want to say that if I had a vote at that convention to select the new leader for the Liberal Party—and I appreciate everything you've done for Newfoundland, you've done so much—my vote would not be for you. I think it's time for a change. Break for news and be right back." Click.

Smallwood looked at me. "Listen," he growled. "Listen to me, you little son of a bitch. Whether that brewery in Stephenville wins or loses, it's my say so. My say so!" I glanced at the engineer through the window. He was sipping coffee.

"Mr. Smallwood, with all due respect, sir, fuck you. That brewery has nothing to do with me. That's my father's business, and the government owes him money for setting that business up."

"You'll see," he said.

He got up and walked out. We filled the remaining hour with telephone callers.

The promised tax relief for my father's brewery never materialized. The government eventually seized the brewery, and Joey sold it for a dollar to John C. Doyle, an international investment pirate and fraudster on the run in Panama and unable to return to the United States. Doyle ultimately sold the operation to Labatt for a fortune.

Open Line alternated between the number one and number two spots in the Newfoundland market. I did not, however, allow it to interfere with my dope smoking, and it was at this time that I discovered acid. I stayed up through the night with the guys, and at a quarter to nine I'd rouse myself to drive to the station for the nine o'clock air time. After six months, they fired me. It turns out the work was interfering with my drug use.

I was lamentably free of guilt. I suggested to a few friends on the student council at Memorial University that I could centralize the selling of advertisements for all student-run publications—for the radio station, for concert flyers, and, needless to say, for special brewery promotions—and efficiently organize it all in one office in the student center, an office staffed by myself. I felt a 20 percent consideration was not unreasonable, and all were in accord. Our agreement did not mention that I would also be free to merchandise mind-altering substances from that office.

FOUR

GUMS HURT. Can't afford any problems inside my mouth, or in any part of my body. The doctors they have here are questionable at best.

"Hi, Mike."

"Hi, Brian."

"Nice shirt."

"Yeah. I'll introduce you to my tailor. You want any decent clothes, you give him a couple of bucks for each item. I got this shirt and a visiting shirt and pants and these tennis shoes and some socks for nine bucks. Hang with me, I'll introduce you. You get a jacket?"

"No."

"Ya see, you gotta buy that shit. Used to get jackets when you came in, but somehow, now, if you want them, you gotta buy them. Was your underwear issue new?"

"No."

"Ya see, you're supposed to get all new underwear, socks, T-shirts, shoes, pants, shirts, every fuckin' thing. In Phoenix the whole issue was new."

I can see through the pants and shirt I got from Billy.

I think of Susannah. I think of my children, whose father I so often wasn't. I think of my loyal friends and family. How I love them all. But my freedom is an inside job. I will be here until I am that freedom. My bed is uncomfortable, the food is bad, and yet I am not so unhappy. Not me. But a weight of injustice presses down on me and is all around me.

Mike is a tall, lanky guy, a scar on his face. He smiles. I smile back.

"How long have you been here?" I ask.

"Six weeks here. And twelve years Lompoc. The Walls. Terrible place. It was okay in the early eighties, but they're doubling up there and everybody's crazy. Guys get out of there now and kill people just to get even. It's not about makin' money anymore, it's about evens. Every twenty minutes there, you get locked down. The dogs are always goin' through your house. It's fucked. Trouble happens, and everyone's out in the yard all day. It's fucked. The system's gonna blow. All fuckin' over, man, the system's gonna blow."

A week into my sentence, I shit. Getting settled somewhat. Head pounding subsides somewhat. Lettuce and cauliflower and bean sprouts are the fresh foods for a vegetarian. For me, a little cauliflower goes a long way.

Gene arrived when I did.

"But I've been in the system since '83."

"Since 1983?"

"Yeah, for three hundred pounds of pot."

"You've been down since '83?"

"Yeah. I got fifteen years. Should get out in a couple."

"Four o'clock! Stand down! Count B Range! Stand down, you assholes! Counting!"

Brian Daniels. Family man, generous and kind. Uncle Bri to the children of the guy who rolled him up. Six-million-dollar fine and twenty-five years for conspiracy to distribute marijuana. He was one of our contacts in Southeast Asia. Under the

new sentencing guidelines—the new law, they call it—he'll do
85 percent of that. A gentle man in every way.

"Excuse me. Are you Brian Daniels?"

"Yeah."

"Hey, BD, I'm Brian O'Dea. I worked with the Shaffer
brothers."

"No shit. Those pricks owe me millions."

"I guess you're not alone."

"When'd you get here, O'Dea?"

"Couple of days ago. Self-surrender. Ten years. Sentenced by
the same judge as you. We have a lot of friends in common."

We talk.

"You want to see this out, O'Dea? Three things you stay
away from: gambling, drugs, fags."

The tailor comes by, and I order pants and shirt, three bucks.
But even the tailor can't get me a jacket.

On the way to the shower, I pass a little round face that
looks up from the last bunk.

"Hey, man, you're not goin' to the shower like that, man.
You use shower shoes. Here, man, use mine. I'm Louie."

"Thanks, Louie. I'm Brian."

"Any time you need them, man, they're under here."

"Thanks, Louie, thanks a lot, man."

The first day, a group of us were gathered in a holding cell,
milling around, nervous, not looking each other in the eye. We
all had the same fear of one another. Now, a week later, we're
neighbors and share what little we have.

The flushing toilet is the Muzak of the freeway, night and
day. It's across from my bunk, and above my bunk is the open
window that draws the air from the toilet.

"Hey, mang, let me get you a new mattress, mang."

"Yeah, and how much will that cost me?"

"Nothing, mang, for you I do that for free."

———

Beautiful sunny day. I spend the afternoon talking with Brian Daniels outside the rec shack. This is where most of the pot smugglers at Terminal Island find work, dispensing recreational equipment to prisoners on the south yard.

"I'm not going to introduce you to anyone I don't know about, Brian. Right now, I want you to meet Cornbread. Cornbread, meet Brian, good man from my field."

Cornbread—short, goatee, deep Texan drawl—is in shorts and sneakers. He's just finished playing tennis in the middle yard with Chuck, another major pot smuggler.

"Hey, Brian, if BD says it's true, it's true. A pleasure."

A smiling California boy stands beside him.

"Brian, this is Bobby."

"Hi, Bobby."

"Nice to meet you, man. How long you gonna be able to stay with us?"

"Oh, about ten years, I guess."

"New law or old?"

"Old."

"All right, man. That means six and change. I've got two left, man, on the same time and beef as you. I'm stoked. I'm workin' outside the yard for the Coast Guard."

"Fuck them, Bobby. They chase people like us."

"Oh yeah, they most certainly do. But it's sure good to get out of here. They've got a beautiful ship out there with fourteen marijuana leaves and three coke leaves painted on the bow."

"Bastards."

"Stand down! Four o'clock count!"

"Stand down! Nine o'clock count! You motherfuckers play cards any more when I'm tryin' to count ya, I'll lock you motherfuckers down."

"Yeah, ya fat prick. You couldn't get another job anywhere."

"You want trouble, ya fat motherfucker, jus' lock us down."

The warehoused, the forgotten. Thirty years, thirty years, twenty-five years consecutive with twenty-five, twenty-eight–twenty-six, twenty-five–twenty, and on and on. Who do these judges and legislators think they are? BD says we must always create hope through putting our plans in action, through making the best of this.

New pants arrive from the tailor. Commissary tonight.

Saturday morning. Nobody works Saturday morning. Seething humanity.

Tall, disheveled guy comes up to me. "Excuse me?"

"What's up, man?"

"I feel like doin' somethin' crazy, man. Don't know what."

"Take it easy, man."

"Hey, Springfield! Get the fuck over here, man, you crazy fuck! Clean this fuckin' place up, motherfucker!"

Springfield lopes back to his cell. He's named for the federal psychiatric institution. His real name is Billy Witherall, the guy who was stealing those rare Abraham Lincoln manuscripts and books a few years back. He's one of those unwashed, untidy, unkempt genius types. Gets a lot of abuse and smiles.

"D'you take a fuckin' shower yet, Springfield?"

"No. Next week I will, though."

"What the fuck's Springfield doin' in that fuckin' bathroom, man? He's been in there twenty fuckin' minutes."

"He's readin' the fuckin' 'cyclopedia, man."

"Hey, motherfucker, get the fuck outta there, man."

"Leave me alone."

"Get the fuck outta that bathroom, man!"

No refuge anywhere.

FIVE

I GO ABROAD

MY PRACTICE flourished from my new offices in the student center at Memorial University in St. John's. My supply runs reached as far west as Toronto, but in due course the charms of Toronto began to wear thin. At this point, I stiffed my poor, loyal, loving brother Chris, who'd cosigned for my car, and left the car and St. John's for Montreal, where I met a young man named Colin K. He had the compulsion of counting his fingers. I hadn't encountered this particular compulsion before and, on reflection, I haven't since. He moved his lips while he counted.

"Five four three two one two three four five four three two one two three four five four three two one."

As he recited each number, often in the course of conversation, he used an as-yet-uncounted finger to tap the finger that corresponded to that number—a sort of digit-for-digit Tourette's, not quite a dactylonomist, but close.

Together, Colin and I dressed in North African robes, dropped acid, and walked the streets of Montreal. We marveled at the melding of the real and the questionably real as the sacred and the profane ran like rivers through those streets. Montreal became a fluid city, transformed by the chemical percolating through our skulls. We wandered, oblivious to questioning eyes or disapproving glances, read each other's minds, used words only occasionally to punctuate a silent conversation that never stopped. We mulled the universal questions, saw answers in geometric patterns that formed freely on the faces of passersby, on the walls of buildings or in thin air. We wordlessly conveyed to one another our visions and the understanding that accompanied them: mind-sharing, mind-melding, the silence loaded with presence. We would end up at the top of Mount Royal, lying on the ground in a circle with other friends, holding hands, feeling the earth—or something—move.

As distracting as Colin's counting was for others, I recognized him as the possessor of a massive brain—and a brain with splendid contacts on Telegraph Avenue in Berkeley. We began to travel together to California, flying back to Vermont with a quart or two of liquid LSD in a shopping bag. In Vermont, we'd rent a car and drive to Lake Champlain. There we'd find a boat hidden in the bushes, a boat Colin would use to cross the lake to Canada with our cargo. I would return home by a conventional route. Colin's parents owned a cottage on the Canadian side of the lake, and by the time I arrived at that cottage, Colin would already be there. The tabbing machine would be humming, and he would be counting his way to heaven finger by finger, already lifted into another dimension from handling the goods. Acid tabs would be falling off the assembly line like aspirin, and as soon as a few bags were full, I was out the door for Newfoundland. As I had discovered, the market there had an insatiable appetite for more of just about anything intoxicating.

From acid, we expanded the product line to include mescaline, peyote, and psilocybin. Unfortunately, Colin's curious mentality drifted further and further off-center. Eventually I felt compelled to say so long to my counting friend and take up residence in a rooming house on rue Sainte-Famille. My fellow roomers were Jim from Austin and his group of small-time, hippie, tarot-reading dope dealers from Texas. We middled small amounts of pot and hash and anything else we could get our hands on. Our customers were a college crowd from the neighborhood.

One evening a well-referenced kid, maybe twenty years old—long, long red hair, very cool—showed up looking for hash. I'd just made a coke connect in Ottawa. Cocaine was the most exotic of substances, treated with care and reverence. I'd sampled it myself and liked it. To secure any amount of it was unique in our world. We sold him on five kilos of hash and on the coke. We set the deal up for the following day at four o'clock at our place. We immediately arranged for the five kilos of hash, and I phoned my coke guy in Ottawa. He assured me he would be at our place by two the following afternoon.

At noon the next day the kid, Red, called. Jim picked up the phone.

"How's it looking for today, Jimmy?"

"Great," said Jim. "Gonna have the dirt in a minute and the cleaning powder in a couple of hours. Can't see why four won't work."

"Okay, man, see you then. Au revoir."

Jim and I and a tough, hot chick named Michelle waited. Forty-five minutes later, there was a knock on the door. I opened it a tad, and the muzzle of a nine-millimeter pistol was pressed firmly against that place right between my eyes.

Someone said, "Back up slowly, little dog."

I backed up. A man came in, a short man with a stylish haircut, dark complexion, dark moustache, dark suit, dark tie. Five more men just like him were right behind. In Newfoundland, these guys would be cops, but there was something not quite right here.

"You, and you, over fucking here," said the man. "You too," he said to Michelle. "Get the fuck over here."

We got over.

"Okay, listen to me, you fucks. They call me the Syrian. One fucking little tiny fucking problem, and I'm gonna personally shoot you. You understand that? I won't fuck around. You understand?"

Wise enough even in my youth to recognize a rhetorical question when I heard one, I let him go on.

"You're expecting five keys of hash and a couple of ounces of cocaine here at four. Who the fuck do you think you are, you fucks? Nobody deals hash and coke in this part of town without the Syrian. Who the fuck do you think you are? Before my friends and me leave here, I want fifty keys of hash and a pound of coke. You understand?"

No problem.

"Now, take off all your clothes and kneel right there in the middle of the room while we have a look around."

Michelle and Jim and I looked at one another in horror.

"I said, take off your clothes, little dogs."

We stripped immediately. I had not previously noticed how impressive Michelle's tits were, but I didn't feel tempted. This was not true of the Syrian's guys. One of them put his paw on her ass.

"Can we fuck this one, Donny?" he asked.

"Shut up and get away from that bitch," Donny snarled. "And my name's the Syrian, not Donny."

At least chivalry wasn't entirely dead.

We knelt in the middle of the room and the Syrian threw stuff around. He found Jim's address book in about two minutes.

"Come here, little boy," he ordered. Jim shuffled across the floor while ineffectively covering his dick with his hand. "Get on this fucking phone and start calling these friends of yours. Tell them you've got hash here at two hundred less for a key than you were going to sell it to us for."

By this means, twenty guys were persuaded to arrive at our door with their pockets stuffed with cash, and the Syrian greeted each of them with his nine-mill. Between noon and four he was able to fill the room with twenty-three naked, worried, very pissed-off guys, all kneeling around holding their dicks but otherwise empty-handed. One of the last guys in, Brant, was especially indignant.

"You don't know who I am?" he shouted. "My brother works for the Mafia. Let me outta here now!"

The Syrian, whose mob connections seemed to be just as good, whacked Brant alongside the head with his pistol. Then, feeling he'd done a good day's work, he bid us adieu.

"Remember," he said, "you work for me now."

They retired to their Lincolns. Everyone immediately began hopping around, pulling on their underwear and cursing Jim and me and Michelle.

"I had to call," Jim protested. "He had a gun to my head!"

"Why didn't you let him shoot ya?" Brant wanted to know.

Within an hour of the Syrian leaving, I'd packed up and left Montreal, not to return for years. I learned later that the Syrian was somebody called Donny Murray, a friend of Michelle's mother.

I headed back to Newfoundland, from where I made occasional trips to Toronto or Ottawa for supplies. This proved financially prohibitive. The Toronto dealers took advantage of me and my trading colleagues, exhibiting a traditional bias by charging us Newfies a premium. From time to time, a Texan acquaintance would show up in St. John's in a VW camper, the paneled walls stuffed with Mexican reefer, but there was rarely enough for commercial purposes.

In 1971 I was still working by day at the university, booking groups and selling ads. In this way, I met an English blues singer named PD, who had gigged with the Sopwith Camel, a well-known British group. I became a kind of de facto manager for PD's new band, and two days prior to his concert, I drove him out to the Old Mill, the social center for any band in Newfoundland. We shared a spliff along the way.

"It's terrible, what we pay for necessities such as this," I said.

I'd already recounted the predations of the Toronto dealers. PD took a long toke and let it out slowly. "I have a couple of mates in England who might help," he said.

I took a toke. "Really?"

"Two of my mates in Brixton sell plenty of this stuff— better stuff, actually, and definitely cheaper."

I took another toke. "Yeah, but what about kilos? Ounces, quarter ounces, fine, but I admire quantity."

PD took a toke. "Bri, these guys do nothing but move dope. Maybe you could bring them some of that aspirin acid you're so famous for, make a trade. That shit sells for five times as much there as here."

I was still selling acid at this point and had so much in the market it was going for as little as five bucks a hit in singles.

"They pay that much a hit for bulk purchases in England," PD said.

"What do they sell hash for?"

"Four or five hundred dollars a key."

I turned the car around in the middle of Brookfield Road. That was half the price I was paying.

"Uh, PD, you don't mind if we run back into town for a few minutes, do you?"

"Hey, mate, whatever you like."

"We'll come back out here later today."

"Want the last of this spliff?"

"Uh, no. No, thanks."

In twenty minutes, I'd surrounded him with my ad hoc Newfoundland partners: Gary Sexton, Gary Fowler, Dick Andrews, and Will Shears. In twenty-four hours, I was on a plane for England. In thirty-five hours, an elderly woman saved my life as I stepped off the curb and looked the wrong way for oncoming traffic. In forty-eight hours, I was eating my first and last Wimpy Burger. In seventy-two hours, I was in Gander, getting off an Air Canada flight from England with five kilos taped to my legs and waist and stinking like horse-shit. They had apparently shipped the product to Europe from Afghanistan in a load of fertilizer.

I handed my passport to the Immigration officer as I entered the country. I was barely aware that I looked like a hippie dope smuggler, and I was only vaguely aware of my smell. The Immigration officer wrinkled his nose, looked at me sharply. For the first time on this trip, I thought about the consequences of my actions. My palms were suddenly damp. The officer looked at my picture and name, then at me again. I looked back and swallowed.

"Are you John's son?"

"Yes, sir, I am."

"Your father's a good man, Brian. I've known him for twenty years, more. I used to drive a delivery truck for the brewery out here. I worked for Gordon Gosse, your father's distributor for central Newfoundland."

"Gordon?" I laughed with relief. "How is he? I haven't seen him for three or four years."

"He had a stroke last year, and I don't see him much, but he's getting better."

I glanced at the man's name tag. "Jim?"

"Jim Mercer, Mr. O'Dea." He reached out and shook my hand. "Give my regards to your father. A good man, John O'Dea."

He stamped my passport.

SIX

LIBRARY FULL of jailhouse lawyers, guys working hard, poring through old law books, hoping to find the words that can cut through these bars and set them free. God help them. They do work hard.

"Hey, Brian."

"Hi, Ben, how're ya doing?"

"Okay, man, okay. D'ya ever work Colombia, Bri?"

"Oh yeah. Bogotá, Barranquilla, Riohacha, La Guajira."

"La Guajira? Yeah? Shit, they kidnapped me there for a couple of months, tried to get a million from my connect for me. They let me go, though."

"My friend there called himself the Chief of the Guajiros. His name was Billy G."

"Billy G.! It was him and his people hung on to me, man."

BD isn't saying much today. He's into his drawing and painting. Some days you just do time. Whirring typewriters clicking out futile appeal after futile appeal, but you have to do it. Part of the hope plan.

———

"Hey, Brian, what you doin', mang?"

"Writing in my book, José, writing in my book."

"Ju let me see sometime?"

"No way, man, no way."

I notice the evil-looking Fagin-like Sam is gone.

"Where's that Sam guy?"

"Hole."

"Oh yeah?"

"Tattoos."

"Everybody's got tattoos here, man. Tattoos and muscles and trouble, that's all this place is."

"No. Sam's the ink slinger, the best tattoo man in the federal system. Guy's a fuckin' artist. But they found his gun."

BD stops me.

"Hey, Brian man, where you goin' dressed like that?"

"What do you mean?"

"You can't go eat like that, man. No shorts in the north yard at all."

"Thanks, bro." Rules and regulations are a hit-and-miss thing here. I find out something is a rule when I break it. My hope is that it's always another prisoner who catches me.

I ask a guard if he can help me find a mattress.

"I'll see what I can do on Monday," he says. "They're pretty stingy over there in supply."

Who the fuck are they saving them for?

"Four o'clock! Stand down. Count B Range. Stand down. Counting!"

Tonight a guard takes half my meal off my plate and puts it back, says I'm getting too much. I have less than half that of the man in front of me. Thank God I'm me and not that guard.

I'll leave here someday, but he'll be in this system for the rest of his life.

"You want soup? I got soup over there."

"No, thanks."

"You sure?"

"Yeah, positive. Thanks."

"*Cuenta!*"

BD introduces me to Mark, a Canadian. He's been in seven years on fifty for coke. He's setting up an appointment with the consulate to work on a transfer. My Chilean neighbor, ten years for coke, has a little son who goes to the same school as my children in Chatsworth.

The captain walks through, looks at me as I'm standing in the freeway, ironing my clothes. Ironing is a big thing here.

"Hey, you! You can't have that ironing board there."

"Why not?"

"Listen, punk, get that fucking board outta there or get to SHU. Know what that is? That's the fucking hole. Clear?"

That's the daily threat—SHU, the special handling unit. But they've got it all wrong. The whole problem is the result of a love deficiency. That's clear, isn't it?

"Hey, blanco, ju steel writing, mang?"

"Yeah."

"Don' worry, mang. Soon ju run out of tings to write, mang. Soon ju stop."

"I'll run out of things to write when you run out of things to say, ese."

Mark, the Canadian, and I are talking at breakfast.

"So what was your full sentence, Mark?"

"Fifty years, with a forty-year special."

"Forty years more if you mess up on parole?"

"That's right."

"Sweet Jesus, what the fuck are they thinking about?"

Mark and I join the other amateur legal beagles and begin our journey to the border. Transfer to the Canadian system: our only hope.

"Okay, Bri, you call your lawyer and ask him if the other Canadians—Steve and Bobby—got their transfer. That'll tell us plenty. After lunch we'll meet in the library and type the letters for the consulate. Call your brother and have him get in touch with the consulate too. Put a request in to your case-worker to get your presentence report and send it along with your version to the consulate. Birth certificate too. Pour on the juice, man. Together we'll do it."

"Thanks, Mark."

"Do you know Harry Kreamer, Bri? He's a lawyer, doing ten like you."

"Hey, Harry, nice to meet you."

"Same, Brian. You look familiar, like we must've met out there. I know the Shaffer brothers, so it was probably in one of their deals. Anyway, I'm going to help you guys."

"Harry's good people, Brian, he'll be a big help."

"Great, man. Thanks, Harry."

"Hey, it's my job, man."

"All right, see you in the library after lunch. We're last out today, so we'll be late."

"Okay. No sweat."

"We won't eat till 12:30 today."

"Brian, I'm going to be here till the year 2010. Half past noon ain't going to kill me."

"Thank you, Harry. Ciao."

"Ciao."

Whirling typewriter wheels, sliding copiers, Harry and I at work on his case.

"June 4, 1987."

"Okay. Next date."

"No reduction of sentence."

"Okay, next."

Harry frowns. "Presentence report. My PSR is in connection with both cases."

"You know what I'm thinking, Harry? That was in '83. They probably have an 85/86 version in Title 5. Lemme check."

"Treaties should be under 'Title 5, treaties.' U.S. treaties. Back there, look."

"Got it. Thanks."

"You know what we left out, Bri?"

"What?"

"The correspondence regarding the denial. I know what to do about that. Hey, Bri, is *correspondence* with an *a* or an *e*?"

"An *a*."

"No, it isn't, man. It's an *e*."

"I smell pot."

José turns over in his bunk. "No way, man."

"Oh yeah? What's all that coughing about over there?"

"Yeah, I can smell it now too."

I'm off my bunk and onto the Cubanos, two bunks away. "Hey, motherfucker! I ain't had a joint in three fucking years, and I don't want a positive piss test caused by your fucking pot blowing up my nose on its way out the window. You dig? You want to smoke that shit, take it somewhere else. I'm not doing no fucking month in the hole for you. *Entiende mi, Cubano?*"

"Hey, man, I remember you from when we were checking in the other day. I'm Brian."

"Yeah, Brian. Richard."

"Hey, Richard, pleasure. What are you doin here, bra?"

"I'll be out by January, man. Got lucky. The state cops were lookin' for my son. Said he did somethin' he didn't do. They found a receipt for a shotgun in my house and turned it over to the feds. I had four priors, one murder, so they sent me back. I was a juvenile in the murder but got tried as an adult and did five."

"You got a son, Richard?"

"Yeah, he's seventeen. Got a daughter sixteen and another son, but he's deceased."

"I'm sorry, man, how'd he die?"

"He went through the window of a car. They were gang-bangin' and the car got hit on both sides and spit him out the front. Then they shot him up and beat him with a stop sign. They only got charged with manslaughter, though, 'cause they said he was dead when he got knocked out of the car."

"Shit, man, that's tough."

"Yeah. Lost my brother too. He went to a car-club dance in the wrong town and this chick set him up, told him to meet her outside. When he came down the stairs and went out the door, this punk came from behind the door and put a shotgun to his throat and blew his head off. That guy's been stabbed more than thirty times in the system, though. He's in protective at California Men's Colony now."

"That's a lot of sorrow and grief. Your mother must be broken with pain."

"My wife still cries a lot, man. She cries a lot. I ain't never gonna have another gun in my house, man."

Sounds easy.

The chief approaches.

"Hey, Brother Brian, we had a powwow today, and my brothers and I want to offer you honorary brotherhood. If you want to accept, we are going to sit in the lodge after four o'clock count on Friday, the full moon. Ask your dreams tonight, then come see us tomorrow, brother."

"Thank you, Chief, thanks."

I see a neighbor sitting on his bunk, looking through his photo album, stopping to look at this picture longer than that one, transportation to another time with softer flesh and gentler hearts.

"Brian, wha's up, bra?"

"Time, Brook, time."

"Yeah, short for me—three more weeks."

"You're here on a vacation, right?"

"Yes."

"How much time did you have left on parole when you violated?"

"One day. I did six years, four months, twenty-nine days and got stuck with a violation on the last fuckin' day, man, the last fuckin' motherfuckin' day. Bogus violation. Gave me two years. Now I gotta do sixteen months parole on the street when I get out."

"What did they do that for?"

"The parole guy had it in for me, man, I had my own companies, my own gig, man. He didn't like it. We had words, and he needed to show me he had the power. That's all I know."

"*Cuenta! Cuenta!* Counting B Range. Down, motherfuckers!"

SEVEN

I HAVE SOME CURIOUS EXPERIENCES WITH UNFAMILIAR SUBSTANCES

WHEN ACID entered my life, I abandoned drinking entirely. Certainly, during some wild runs, we'd put ten hits of acid in a bottle of wine and chug the wine, but that didn't qualify as drinking. I'd wake up at three in the morning and drop five or six tabs and go back to sleep. By seven, the place would be nicely transformed. During this period, I'd drop in on my parents for Sunday dinner, flying. By this means and others, I did over a thousand tabs over five years.

I twice hitchhiked across Canada from St. John's to Port Alberni, British Columbia. Everyone, it seemed, was on the road. I'd get up in the morning at the youth hostel and go out on the highway, and as far as the eye could see in both directions there were hitchhikers, young, excited, on the road. But each time I returned home to Newfoundland and St. John's.

My friend Derek and I were cruising the student center at Memorial University in St. John's and ran into Fred. Neither of us knew him well, but Fred was a part of the scene, and he did sell our pot and acid from time to time, and we were comfortable with him.

"Hey," Fred said. "Hey, look at this shit." He drew a small box from his pocket and opened it. Inside was a sort of greenish powder.

The objective at the time was to experience all possible experiences that could be experienced by ingesting a substance. Fear was not a factor. We had learned to ignore what we heard from the establishment about any drug, because the establishment was lying outright about marijuana and LSD and many other delightful chemicals. Apart from getting arrested if caught while making these marvels available to others, the described consequences were patently inaccurate.

I looked at the green stuff in the box. "Far out," I said.

"Yep," Fred said. "Pretty trippy stuff."

"Far out."

"Enough for two people."

"How much?"

"Gift."

"Far out. Thanks, man."

I put the box in my pocket.

For the rest of the working day, Derek and I went about our business. This consisted of sitting around drinking coffee with the crowd, making sure everyone had enough of everything, loving our lives. At the end of the afternoon, we drove over to my place on Queen's Road in Derek's Valiant. I had rented the house myself and then rented out rooms to like-minded people. There were eight of us altogether. My roommate had left that morning to hitchhike to Toronto, and I had the space to myself for the first time since moving in.

Derek parked the car and we went into the house. As usual, there was plenty going on there. We loved activity. We stopped in the kitchen to help Snippy with a joint as he and his girlfriend, Alda, were making soup. We grabbed a couple of sodas and headed to my room. We took out the small box of green powder and examined it closely. It didn't smell very good. We put small amounts of the powder on our tongues. It tasted worse than it smelled. We washed it down with soda, but we gagged and nearly threw up. Hmm. Something of a challenge. I got some bread from the kitchen, and we put the powder in a folded-over piece of bread and downed the bread with gulps of soda. Even wrapped in bread, the stuff made us gag. We persisted.

"Sure seems a lot," Derek said.

"Enough for two to get off on," I reminded him.

Several hours passed. Nothing happened.

"Bogus shit," Derek said.

"Bad tasting, though," I said, though this was not a virtue in drugs.

We called Derek's sister-in-law Leslie and asked her if she wanted to join us for coffee at the Holiday Inn. Just in case we eventually got a buzz on this stuff, we'd be wise to have a person who was in condition to drive. We spent an hour or so chatting over coffee, then decided to head on back home.

Derek felt a little nauseous when we left the Inn, and he asked Leslie to drive. I didn't feel too good either.

"Shit might make us a bit sick," I said.

"Yeah, probably," Derek said.

We passed the expansive and sloping lawns of the university. I couldn't help but notice the cleaning woman in a maid's uniform. She was on her hands and knees, scrubbing the lawn, her pail of water and scrub brush beside her. I had the sense that something was amiss, but I couldn't put my finger on it. I looked back at her, but she was still at it. I looked to the front, where everything seemed to be in order. We drove a little farther. No, something was decidedly wrong. Thousands of people had begun to fill the streets. As our car approached them, they moved away, but as we passed by, some bent over and leered at me through the window. I doubted their intentions.

"Hey, man, uh, I'm seeing a lotta people sorta looking at me. You noticed that?"

"Yeah," Derek said. He didn't sound good, and he didn't elaborate.

I was feeling too sick to be really frightened. At least Derek was there. That made me feel less frightened. Anyway, I was preoccupied with trying not to throw up.

I suggested to Leslie that perhaps the best thing to do was to drive me home. I staggered out of the car in front of the house.

"Are you okay, Brian?" Leslie asked.

I stood looking up at the gargoyles on the corners of my house. I'd never noticed those particular gargoyles before, but my God, they were no ordinary gargoyles. They were talking about me quite openly, and their faces were twisted with inexplicable malice.

"Here he comes," the one on the south corner hissed to the one on the west corner.

"Let him come," said the second one.

"Yeah. Yeah, I'm okay, Leslie. I'll see you later."

I looked at Derek, who was still sitting in the front seat of the car. He had a hideous smile frozen on his face, a smile that looked like no fun at all. Perhaps he'd overheard the gargoyles.

I hurried into the house and past the people in the hallway. How could I be sure if they were there or if I just thought they were there? I realized I was going to die. In fact, I might already have done so. I closed the door of my room and lay on the bed. Minute by minute, I became sicker. In the next room were Snippy and Alda. Alda was a nurse. She could probably help. I began to call for her. As I was doing so, I noticed the poster of Simon and Garfunkel on the wall at the end of my bed. Paul began to talk to Art.

"Wait until he shuts his eyes," Paul said.

So. The gargoyles were not the only ones. I began to scream for Alda, but no one responded. I closed my eyes, but it was even more frightening in there. I opened them again. The Mexican blanket covering my dresser began to breathe. A mobile constructed from the colors of the Mexican blanket appeared in the air next to the dresser—six pieces, two on each level—and it was breathing, throbbing, pulsating. Its obvious and insidious aura frightened me terribly. I screamed again and closed my eyes. When I opened them again a minute or so later, the thing was directly in front of my face, throbbing. I was overwhelmed by fear. I called again for Alda in the next room. Why didn't she want to help me?

The door flew open. Leslie had come from Derek's house. He was behaving strangely, she said. She stopped still. She could sense the terrific number of demons in there with me. Suddenly I knew that I had not been calling for help at all, but had only imagined I was calling for help. I started to weep at the pathos of it. I tried to speak. Nothing came out. Finally, I managed a tiny sound.

"Help," I said.

"Um, Brian, this is Leslie. I'm going to have someone sit with you, okay? I'm going to call the shrink." There was a shrink in town who was sympathetic to hippies.

Leslie left. I lay there. An eternity passed. No one came. I was unable to move off the bed. My mouth had never been as dry as it was during that endless stretch of time. I had to pry my lips off my gums with my fingers. Finally, Alda came into the room. In fact, only seconds had passed since Leslie had left. I began to weep profusely—no tears, just sounds, haunting, frightening sounds coming from inside me. I looked at Alda, my savior. She looked down at me. She smiled. She knelt. Horns sprouted from her head. Her eyes began to bleed down her cheeks. I cringed in terror. She drew close.

"Brian," she said, her voice, soft, chilling, "everything's going to be okay. Don't worry, Brian."

Fangs grew from her mouth, and blood dripped from them onto the bed. Now, at last, I understood. This was hell.

Alda drew back. "You're frightening me, Brian," she said. I shrank back from the threat. She left. Another eternity passed in hell, as I had always known it would.

Alda came back with Murray from Montreal. I had always liked Murray.

"Brian," he said.

I tried to reply, but his horns and fangs began to grow and his eyes began to bleed. Now my deal with the devil had come home to roost. I had turned my back on the Blessed Virgin and stopped bargaining with God. Now I would pay. Murray extended his claws toward me.

"I'm thirsty," I said, because I knew I was near the end.

The demon Murray disappeared and reappeared with a glass, a tall glass full of water. I reached out for it but could not take it.

"Drink the water," said the demon.

I raised my head but could not.

"Let me help you," said the demon.

"No!" I shrieked, and nothing he or anyone else could do could force that water past my parched lips.

When Derek arrived home with Leslie, a group of friends were gathered in his living room with Carol, his wife. He came into the house and took off all his clothes and got into bed. After a few minutes, he got up and walked into the living room, went to the corner of the room where a pair of his boots were resting, picked them up, moved them to the other side of the room, and went back to his room. The group was amused, but Carol was concerned.

"Derek?" she called. "What's happening?"

He didn't answer.

"It's acid, for sure," someone said.

"I guess so," said Carol. They resumed their conversation.

Ten minutes later, Derek returned to the living room. He walked directly to the wastebasket and jammed his foot into it. He stumped over to each person in the room and peered at them while he emitted a sinister cackle. All he was wearing was the wastebasket. When he had cackled at each person, he left as he had come. It was obvious to Carol that this was not LSD.

"Leslie," she said, "what's going on?"

"I don't know," Leslie said. "Maybe it's the green powder. They swallowed some green powder Fred gave them."

Carol called Fred.

"Fred, what was that green powder you gave Derek and Brian?"

"Uh, not really . . . really, like, sure."

"What do you think it was?"

"Uh . . . belladonna? Witch's brew? Like, you know, deadly nightshade?"

"Which one?"

"Hey, it's all the same shit, I think."

Carol went into the bedroom. Derek was sitting on the bed, still naked, reading an invisible magazine aloud.

"What are you reading, Derek?" she asked.

"*Scientific American,*" he said.

She listened as he read. Yes, it was *Scientific American,* an article on tectonics. It was at that point that Leslie left to look for me.

I cannot say whether I dwelled thereafter in the inferno. After the events I have recounted, all memory is erased. Friends report that I sometimes sat on the edge of my bed in conversation, especially with my roommate, Paddy Murphy, who was, in reality, stuck on the road two hundred miles from home. These conversations were apparently coherent, allowing that the witnesses could hear only my side. When addressed by friends, I would not respond. Instead, I peered at them as if they were strangers or worse.

When, at the end of the third day, I emerged, my vision was impaired and I was unable to read for a month.

The English hash source was an excellent one, but we could only pack so much on our bodies, certainly less than we could pay for. Proving again that they don't call it dope for nothing, I instructed my contact in London to mail two packages to a nonexistent person at the uninhabited house next door to where I lived.

About a month later, a package arrived at the house next door. I was delighted, as were the dozens of my fellow Newfoundlanders who got to enjoy top-quality hash at well below mainland prices. But after a month of waiting and looking and asking the postman every time I saw him, I gave up on the second package.

Another month passed. While showering one morning, I heard a knock on my door. I went to the window in time to see the postal truck pulling away from the curb. My heart leapt. I jumped into my clothes, ran to the car, and drove east in pursuit. I found the truck on Mayor Avenue and pulled in behind the guy. I knew this driver, though not personally, and he knew me.

"Hey," I panted, "were you just trying to make a delivery at my house?"

He looked at me blankly. "No."

"But I was sure I just saw you getting into your truck in front of my house. I heard someone knock on the door. I was in the shower."

"It wasn't me."

Disconcerting.

The night before, my buddy Stan and his girlfriend, Tracy, had arrived from Texas in their VW camper—two minstrel hippies with twenty pounds of pot in their bags for the good people of Newfoundland. I loved these Texan folks, but though they liked to stay with me and use my connections, there was never any room for me in their deals. It was always, "Next time, Bri. Next time it'll be cheaper. But we need to make all the money for this one so we can go back and get a bigger and better load. Then we all can make money, right?" Enough of that. This time, when they arrived, I told them they were going to have to find another place to stay. Stan made a few calls to some of the people I'd introduced them to on their last trip, and they were planning to leave that morning for a friend's house. I was out of the picture.

I went to my office at the university, where I was the advertising agent for the student newspaper and radio station, and got on with my day. About noon, I got a call from my neighbor, Mugs Malone.

"Hey, Brian, you've got about a dozen visitors, and they've got a dog. You dig?"

I knew Stan wasn't having a party for any dog fanciers, especially considering I had two fine cats, Fat Red and Truck. This could mean only one thing. I called my cousin Frank, who had recently taken a partnership in a law firm downtown. I raced through a breathless explanation, and Frank cut right away to the heart of my dilemma. He suggested I go on home as though nothing was happening, as though I wasn't wise to what was going on. He, meanwhile, would alert my family so they could brace themselves and make whatever provisions necessary to bail me out pronto, should things turn out badly.

I took a long, long time walking up the sidewalk to my door. The cops were almost falling out of the trees in front of the house as I reached for the doorknob. I opened the door and saw a package on the stairwell, a package that looked much like the one that had been delivered a month earlier. I felt a hand grip my shoulder and heard a voice from behind.

"Brian O'Dea, you are under arrest for possession of hashish for the purposes of trafficking, possession of cocaine, and possession of marijuana for the purposes of trafficking. Hands behind your back, please."

I had never even seen cocaine more than once or twice in my life, so that part was certainly news to me. I was fitted with a brand new pair of cuffs and immediately became the highest profile dope case in the short history of Newfoundland's hippie culture. Giant headlines soaked into local newsprint, and my family's name was lowered solemnly into the local mud.

My parents avoided conversation, as did I. They concerned themselves with the practical matter of raising bail and getting me out. The postman denied he was working with the cops.

Oh. Stan and Tracy. They hadn't got around to vacating my place, and the cops found the pot in their suitcases, busted them, and hauled them away before I got home. They went to trial, pleaded guilty, and both received two years in the pen. I never saw them again.

EIGHT

EVENING. I'm lying in my bunk.

"Hey, homey!"

I look up to the third tier. Vegas RJ is leaning over, holding his dick.

"Hey, homey, come on up for some of this, okay?"

All around, the buzz. So many different groups, all working, working, working.

The Vegas group taking bets—horses, dogs, the track.

"Hey, I remember when Steve Wynn told me . . ."

"Burn that motherfuckin' casino, man . . ."

The Bloods and the Crips—deadly rival black gangstas—the Aryan Brotherhood, Mexican-American *chulos*, *Cubanos*, pot smugglers, crazies, and loners. Our group comprised boat captains, pilots—every shade of pot smuggler. We are the gentle group, the live-and-let-live group.

Tonight, Mark gives me a pint of ice cream. Eight pot guys with a total of well over 250 years in sentences sit in a row, each with a pint of ice cream that Mark has bought, each enjoying the others' company, laughing and loving.

———

Ben waves me over. "Hey, here comes Brian the Newfie. Hey there, Bri. Bri, you're good, man, but we gotta watch you, man. You're a bit nuts, right? You're the one who took off with three engines and sixteen thousand pounds aboard? Am I right?"

"Don't tell me you never took any chances, Ben."

"Ha ha. Not me. Sit down, man."

"So, what are they wanting you to do, Ben?"

"Seventy motherfuckin' years, Bri."

"Seventy years?"

"Flying pot, nothing else. Sentenced in Texas."

"Brian, you know Larry?"

"No. Larry, I'm Brian O'Dea."

"Hi, Brian, Larry Layton."

Jail pallor, pasty skin, quiet, multicolor knit hat. Something about him stands out, a serious vibration. I hear the word *Jesus* come out of his mouth as I pass him by. Larry Layton. Larry Layton. Jim Jones, Jonestown, Guyana, Kool-Aid laced with cyanide. Larry Layton was one of the few who lived through it. Now he wears the scars in his aura. Where did his world go wrong? He saw the parole board the other day, and they told him to come back in fifteen years and talk to them.

Jimmy, a Mexican career criminal, leans over to me. "I made $56 workin' the past sixteen days. Pretty good, huh, Brian?"

I look at him. He's perfectly sincere. "Jimmy," I say, "they say you're a slave for the feds, man, making their fucking office furniture, saving them a fortune. They say you're shit, Jimmy, they say you're a slave. In fact, Jimmy, you're a good man. When you get out of this place, you don't come back."

"Are you thinking about killing yourself, Mr. O'Dea?"

"No, ma'am."

"Are you thinking about relapsing on drugs, then?"

"No, ma'am."

"What are you doing with your time here, Mr. O'Dea?"

"Getting a doctorate, ma'am."

"I see. Thank you, Mr. O'Dea. That will be all."

Bad night, then the thunder of sucking toilets begins at five. Got to get a proper mattress. No one seems to be able to help me with this. Offers of money. Promises from every direction. No mattress.

I'm lying on my bunk, washed by the cool, moist morning breeze that wafts through the window above me. José is cutting his toenails on my left, Ricardo's reading the paper to my right, two Cubans are sleeping in the cell in front of me. Ships' horns in the harbor behind me blare their departure, trucks rumble up and down the alley, picking up products made by prison labor for use by various departments of the federal government. Toilets flush, locker doors creep open, George crawls out of the next bunk and scratches his ass. Another day in the slam.

"What time is it, Brian?"

"Eight-fifteen, George."

"Oh shit, I gotta get to the hospital."

José, meanwhile, humps off his top bunk, slips into his pants and shoes, blows his nose, and heads off to make a deal with someone over something.

Larry Layton poses questions that relate to the future. "What's going to happen?" he asks. But the only valid destination is this instant, this holy instant. Once I truly arrive in the fullness of this instant, I am in the fullness of the One. So much to let go of, so much to discard.

The Canadian consul comes to see me. He feels that I should be able to effect a transfer in much less than a year. I'd like to stay here as long as I must be in jail. My friends are here—

outside and inside. But everyone says, "Get out of this system, man, beat it to Canada if you can."

"Thanks for coming and seeing me so promptly, Mr. Graham."

"You're welcome, Mr. O'Dea. If there is anything we can do for you, just call. We'll contact your family, whatever you need."

"Thanks. So long."

"Bye now."

Susannah visits me. All too short a stay and she's gone.

"Over here, O'Dea. All right, strip, one piece at a time. Okay, face the wall, show me the bottom of your feet. Okay, grab your cheeks, spread 'em and cough. That's enough, get dressed and get outta here."

"*Cuenta! Cuenta!* Counting B Range. Down!"

Toilets flush, people rush to stand by their bunks, keys jangle at the hack's side as he moves through the crowd.

"Forty-six, forty-seven . . ."

Another day draws its curtain down around us. We chatter and laugh, read and write, peer through photo albums, remember our loves, and pray for protection and compassion.

Billy has returned and immediately hits me up to get him some stuff at the commissary.

"Hey, man, you shopping tonight? I need a bunch of things."

"Billy, sorry, bud, but I don't have much validation left, and I've spent just about all of it. How 'bout an ice cream?"

"Nah, forget that, man."

"Hey, Billy, you want an ice cream or not?"

"Well, all right, man, whatever."

I pass the phones on the way to the commissary. I can see Freddie, a Mexican American, all red-faced in a booth.

"Hey, bitch, what time ju get home las' night? . . . Oh, 10:20, huh? An' I called at 10:30, no fuckin' answer. . . . Oh, ju were there, huh? An' I call at 11:00, still no fuckin' answer. . . . Oh yeah, that phone came unplugged again, huh? The old unplugged phone. . . . Listen to this: Fuck ju, cunt!"

He slams down the receiver and comes swaggering out of the booth, one steaming *chulo.*

"Count! C'mon, you assholes! Get by yer bunks or I'm lockin' you down."

Rumble in A unit, across the yard. Blacks versus whites. Weapons are locks in socks, swung to the head. One guy airlifted out in bad shape. The hole fills with the extras in the drama. Noisy now, general tension in the atmosphere. We are so crowded, and we have the hack Silva—he of the giant attitude—working this shift. Instead of easing the tension, he spends his entire shift talking guns with his coworker, saying any punk prick who tries to "break into my fuckin' house is a dead motherfucker." And on and on.

"Counting!"

"*Oye, Chile!*"

"*Sí, Cuba!*"

They call each other by their country of origin, screaming over bunks for ice, or jalapeños, or any food, for that matter. The Cubans don't just talk their language, they sing it.

Harry was a fugitive pot smuggler. The cops had been following him all day. Then, while he was in a motel, at about five in the morning, they went around the corner for breakfast. His car had a beeper on it, so they figured they'd know if he tried to leave. He left, but he walked. They watched that room until noon, then came in posing as the cleaning crew, but no Harry. Now he's got about a third of his time done, and he's on the downhill slide, and all of a sudden the grand jury in San Francisco is rumbling, spitting up his name.

"Didn't you get blanket coverage on your conviction, Harry? Didn't it cover everything up to and including the offense for which you were convicted?"

"Everywhere but San Francisco. Their trick is to bring it up just before you get out and nail you with a bunch more time."

"Dirty rotten motherfuckers, Harry. You shouldn't be in jail at all, man."

"Neither should you, Brian, neither should you. Hey. Nobody should be in jail. But I feel good and up tonight. Seems I'm the only one who's up today."

"I'm snapping out of it, Harry. I'm okay."

"Counting B Range! Counting!"

NINE

AN INOPPORTUNE BRIDE

THE CHURCH by the Side of the Road was out in Topsail, about twenty miles from St. John's. A tiny, old, white church of red clapboard, with a miniature square tower and seating maybe twenty people, it sat in a gentle field of ancient graves, overlooking Conception Bay. Between the main course and dessert, Ellie and I left my cousin's dinner party on July 14, 1972, drove out to Topsail to the Church by the Side of the Road, and got married.

Ellie came from a good home: a mother who loved Oral Roberts as though he were the God he claimed to represent and a father who was an accountant to the premier's millions. She had just returned from dancing in Europe and had opened her own dance school in the city. She had a beautiful, impish face and a firm, perfect body.

I met her when a couple of buddies and I walked into Ben's, a local haunt. My cousin Anne Marie called me over.

"Hi, Brian, come sit with us. You know Eleanor?"

"Hi, Eleanor, nice to meet you."

"Hi. Actually we've met before, but I was too much of a kid for you to remember. I'm not a kid anymore."

They'd been drinking.

"Come sit on me," Ellie said. She patted her lap. "I want to feel the weight of you on me."

I lowered my 180 pounds onto her.

"Oooh, yes . . . mmm," she said.

I left with the boys but arrived back at Ben's around 11:30. By then, Ellie was incapable of driving home. When she saw me, she called out, "Hey, you! Wanna drive me home?"

"Sorry, girl, no car."

"My car, silly."

She handed me the keys, and we headed to the parking lot. Halfway to the car, she spun me around to face her and licked me into an embrace that was almost consummated on the asphalt. We raced back to my apartment. She was taking off my pants on the way.

We had sex for days. Then, after my bust, we had a fight and broke it off.

That night in July, my cousin invited us both to the same dinner party, maybe just by chance. Ellie and I met by the fridge as we were putting away our wine. Neither of us had realized the other was invited, and we burst out laughing. In minutes we were chatting. In less than three hours we were husband and wife.

When we told my parents the next day, my mother put her hands in her lap and looked at us without smiling. "Oh dear," she said.

"You have just made the biggest mistake of your life, boy," said my father.

What do fathers know?

I was heartbroken and a little frightened by their reaction. "If that's how you want it to be, Dad," I said, "don't bother coming to see us, and we won't come to see you."

The next day he showed up at the house while we were out and left hundreds of dollars' worth of groceries.

———

Ellie and I were in love. During the next few months, while I was moved through the judicial process with at least two court appearances a week, our relationship took my mind off the peril of my present adventure.

My new wife's uncle was the presiding judge at my trial. The Mounties brought in evidence in the form of a one-inch-square piece of paper with a number written on it, a number that matched a registration number on the package sent from England to a nonperson at the address next door. This piece of paper, they explained deadpan to the court, they had found in an inverted lampshade in my house. In this account of a life not always characterized by perfect truthfulness, I must assure the reader of two things: one, that hash was indeed sent under my direction, and, two, I did not put such a piece of paper in my lampshade or anywhere else.

I was sentenced to nineteen months in Her Majesty's Penitentiary, down by the city's biggest lake, Quidi Vidi, and flanking the Pleasantville graveyard. The ancient prison had no running water, hence no toilets in the cells. We used buckets instead, which we emptied into the honey pit, or hopper, every morning. All 130 of us would line up and empty our buckets, but the worst job of all was being the hopper attendant, and that job was always assigned to a prisoner who was in for drugs.

But I was a married man, a newly married man, and I had Ellie waiting for me. I worked in the laundry, and the laundry door opened onto the backyard of the prison, and the backyard overlooked the lake. Every day at the same time, Ellie would drive her car to the same place on the other side of the lake, and I could see her from the laundry door. The car was easy to recognize, but I could only dimly make her out behind the wheel. It didn't matter, she was there, faithfully observing our ritual. It buoyed me up.

I was locked down nineteen hours each day, with only a half-hour recreation period, during which I got too good at Ping-Pong. The other four and a half hours I worked in the laundry. But my spirits were high. I applied for parole and was told I had a good chance of getting out after six months. Six months until Ellie and another brand new start at life. Six months seemed like six years, but at my eligibility hearing they told me I would definitely be released at the six-month mark. I was ecstatic. I was hours away from release. I could smell it, taste it.

The day before my release, I was called to the visiting room. This was a departure from routine. I'd had my regular biweekly half-hour visit the previous week. Another visit? Just before getting out? I went into the visiting room. Ellie was sitting next to Sergeant Noel, the classification officer.

There are moments of silence that are deafening. It was Ellie who broke this one.

"You're not going to like why I'm here but . . . anyway, I'm leaving you. The rent is paid until the middle of the month. I've taken Fat Red with me, and I had Truck put to sleep. I have nothing else to say. If you have any questions, you can talk to my lawyer."

The next day, the day of my release, as I stood in the lunch line, the guard handed me a piece of paper. After a moment, I looked at it. They knew Ellie was going to leave me, and they didn't want to let me out into a "maritally unstable environment." "Parole denied," the paper said.

Despite the protests of the Newfoundland Historic Society, the Church by the Side of the Road was pulled down in the late seventies.

TEN

"WHERE'S MY LAUNDRY DETERGENT, José? What'd you do with my Tide, man?"

"Hey, O'Dea. I did some laundry, man. I didn't get it back."

"What the fuck do you mean you didn't get it back, you fuck? I just bought that and used it once. Stay the fuck out of my locker, José. Don't touch any of my shit again, all right? You got lots of lines, man. You got a story for everything, but you're just a two-bit hustler, so leave my shit alone, man."

"Hey, Brian, someone on three went to the hole, man. You better go see Webb about gettin' a cell. He thinks you're okay, man. He'll give you first shot."

"Hold it, Brian, you take that cell, the other guy in it is black."

"Yeah, but does he smoke?"

"Yeah, he smokes."

"I'll wait. Thanks for telling me."

I could use some socks and some underwear that fits. These ones fit the waist, but the legs are unbelievably tight. What kind of shape was the fit model? Mark gave me two Hanes T-shirts last night.

A *Cubano* looms up. Don't know his name.

"Hey, mang, ju move, ju geev me jor locker?"

"Sure, bra, sure."

If I even have a thought of moving, it gets around in seconds. People I've never seen before want permission to scavenge my remains.

"Hey, George, understand you're moving. Cool."

"Brian, if you got a few bucks to put into it, maybe we can get a room together."

"Yes, man, I'm for it. Go see what you can do."

"See that guy, Brian? His name is Roman. He was a Miami cop. Used to kill smugglers and dealers and take their shit and sell it. He got nailed for killin' four mules. Got thirty years. He drowned them by forcin' them out of their boat at gunpoint in the ocean at night. He jokes about being the joint's swimmin' coach. He works for Father Bill in the chapel. Stay the fuck away from him. Any other joint, they'd cut him, man, cut him plenty. He's a punk, man, killin' people like you, hidin' behind a badge. Fuck him, man. Bad news."

I feel like I'm in someone else's dream today—head's spacey, can't hear well. Keep shaking my head, trying to recover, but the dream persists.

"Hey, Bri, dig the body language, man, I don't even wanna know that cat. He thinks he's John Wayne."

"It's his protection, man. He's exaggerated into a caricature of himself. He thinks it makes him look tough so no one will fuck with him. I bet he's filled with fear. Gotta love him, man."

"Maybe you, Bri, not me."

My belt finally arrived, and now my pants can stay put.

———

"Mr. Jenkins, my name is O'Dea. My counselor, Mr. Edwards, said my fiancée, Susannah Lewis, would be approved for a visit no later than Thursday. It's been six weeks since she was here on a special permission. Could you check on it for me?"

"Come back tomorrow, O'Dea."

"But it's open house now, from three to four, and I was told I could find out what I need from the counselor replacing Edwards. You're filling in for him, aren't you?"

"You some sort of wise guy, O'Dea? What didn't you understand about 'come back tomorrow'?"

Sad faces betray those who did not hear from friends. They do their time alone, a heavy burden. My friends help me carry mine through their letters and my few phone calls and fewer visits. I have it easier and better than most.

"Brian, where you are in two weeks, mentally and emotionally, took me fifteen months. You've got a great start on this. Just remember: do it one day at a time."

"Thanks, Harry, one day at a time. Where have I heard that before?"

A hot, muggy night closes a hot muggy day in jointville. The multicultural soup bubbles tonight, cigarette smoke obscures the no-smoking sign. Smoking is not allowed.

The day I arrived here, they asked me if I smoked.

"No."

"Good. Then we don't need to tell you that smoking is not permitted in the living areas."

"Good."

The smoke is unbelievable in the living areas.

Occasional wafts of illicit herb punctuate the sentences served up. Muscles are flexed. Black, white, yellow, and beige talk among themselves and separately, and Silva is "Counting B Range! Counting!"

"Get a life, asshole.".

Sounds at 9:40 p.m. Spanish, creaking bed, pattering feet, sniffing, blowing, TV English, TV Spanish, coins dropping, lockers opening, ice in plastic cups shifting, cell doors clunking, and José saying, "Move out of my way, gringo."

The guy they call Chicago stands his ground. "Hey, motherfucker, where's my fuckin' money, man?"

"I came lookin' for ju, mang. Ju weren't nowhere, mang."

"What? I gotta catch you after work or somethin', man? To get my fuckin' money? I got debts, man, an' you're startin' to make me look bad."

"Ju already look bad, mang. Now fuck off, mang. I'm talkin' to my fren', mang."

"Friend. You ain't got no friend, motherfucker, and if you don't straighten up with me, you ain't gonna have no enemy neither. Get it, Mexico? No friend, no enemy."

Chicago traces a line from port ear to starboard along his throat, and José understands.

ELEVEN

I ENJOY NEW FREEDOM AND SOON MAKE FRIENDS IN A FARAWAY COUNTRY

I THRASHED AROUND inside my cell in the Quidi Vidi, unable or unwilling to eat. I mumbled to myself, apparently incoherently. What would I do when I got out? Who would I do it with? Ellie had been my prop, my anchor, my hostage. She would have to live with my dying from starvation and a broken heart for the rest of her life. It would look good on her.

Two weeks passed. I got weaker and lighter and sorrier for myself. One evening I rolled over on my bed to reach for a book and fell to the floor between my bunk and the wall. I let myself fall: I didn't care. There was just enough room for my body. The book fell too and landed under my face on a bookmarked page. The bookmark was a business card, and on the card was scrawled the address and telephone number of a Colombian named Benny. I had met him in Montreal prior to going to prison.

"Ju come and veesit me any time, ju hear?" That's what Benny had said. "We weel do some *negocio, buen negocio* together, amigo."

Buen negocio, amigo. It ran through my head as though he'd just said it. Visions of freedom began to circulate in my impoverished brain. New energy seeped into my undernourished veins. I was going to be getting out of here in another six months. That's right, I thought. Without any doubt, I was going to be out of this toiletless hell in six months, never to return. No parole officer, no wife. Free.

Free. I crawled off the floor, rattled my cage door, demanded food. The night guard was relieved. These guys didn't want me kicking it on their shift: too much paperwork.

Six months later, September 1973, my friend Wayne picked me up outside the gates of Quidi Vidi. I was ready. I stopped by my folks' house to pack a bag and was off to the airport for Toronto. I borrowed $500 and the money for a ticket from a friend, and in three days I was on a plane for Bogotá.

I couldn't speak Spanish, but I'd learned French during holidays on the French islands of St. Pierre and Miquelon off the coast of Newfoundland. Spanish sounded similar. I'd just have to twist my French to sound kind of Mexican and add a sprinkling of *o*'s and *a*'s at the end of English and French words. I could fake it until I could make it. Besides, everywhere I'd ever been, English was the second language, if not the first.

The business card had the address of a restaurant in what was supposed to be an upscale neighborhood of Bogotá. I was to go there and ask the maître d' or the owner to find Benny, my amigo, and let him know I was in town.

Inside the El Dorado International Airport, I encountered a problem. English was nowhere in sight or sound. I took a taxi to my hotel and went to the bar. I was always comfortable in bars.

"*Bière*," I said.

The bartender looked at me with heavy-lidded eyes.

"*Bieray? Beero?*" I tried. His interest flagged further. I pointed at a bottle of beer.

"*Cerveza*," he said wearily.

A first, small lesson in the world's vastness.

It was too late in the day to be running off to the other part of Bogotá, so I meandered the streets downtown. I knew nothing of its dangers. A stranger—and by good fortune not a dangerous stranger—spotted me for what I was. He said his name was Johnny and he spoke a little English. He and his girlfriend invited me to their apartment for coke and *aguardiente*, the national drink of Colombia, a sort of fiery anise. The streets were dangerous, they explained. I must watch out for thieves and police alike. A thin line separated the two when it came to people like me, who stuck out like a sore thumb—sore and blind.

The streets were filled with roving packs of children as young as three. At first, I reached in and gave them a few pesos, but I soon began to look like the Pied Piper, with a small army of reaching hands imploring at every step. When I walked into a store, the proprietor would invariably shoo them away from the doorway, but they would hang there in wait for me, their newfound patron. Back doors became the only way out.

On my second day in Bogotá, the sun was shining as brightly as I had ever seen it, but the air was cool, around sixty degrees. I woke early and walked through the quiet streets around my hotel. Children covered in cardboard were sleeping in doorways. Police strolled by, their machine guns slung over their shoulders. Buildings cast long shadows down deserted streets. Yesterday's exhaust fumes still lingered, mopping up the already limited oxygen in the thin air.

At about ten, I hailed a taxi and showed the now well-worn business card to my driver. He negotiated the ten miles from downtown to the upscale north end by simply making up the traffic laws as he went along. Swanky name-brand shops dotted the streets; Mercedes-Benz and BMW automobiles cruised by. Every man seemed possessed of a tailored suit, dazzling shoes polished to perfection for a quarter on the street corner, shinily manicured fingernails, a perfect haircut.

No doubt Un Pedazo de Chile had been a nice restaurant at one time. I got out of the taxi and looked at the locked gates and boarded windows with a sinking heart. I was not going to get to taste the wonderful Chilean cuisine it advertised. I stood at the gate, clutching the business card, my forehead against the bars. There was a smaller building behind the restaurant, with a chimney on the roof that was emitting a steady stream of smoke. I shook the gates loudly and shouted "Hola, hola!" This much Spanish I had learned. A little man, bent over and apparently in his nineties, came hobbling up the drive toward me.

"*Sí, señor?*"

I held the card out with Benny's name and the name of the late lamented restaurant written on it. "Do . . . you . . . know . . . this . . . guy?" Perhaps rate of speech was the key to the language problem.

"*No le entiendo, señor. No hablo inglés.*"

"Benny D. You . . ."—I pointed at his chest—"know . . ." —I pointed at my eyes and head—"Benny?"

"*Lo siento, señor, no hablo inglés.*"

Ay-yi-yi. My mind was working furiously. I had someone here who could lead me to my friend, I knew it, and I wasn't about to let him go. He shrugged his shoulders and turned to walk back down the drive.

"Wait!" I shouted, and he stopped. I rummaged through my pockets for a pen and scribbled my name, hotel, and room number on a scrap of paper. "If . . . you . . . see . . . Benny . . . give . . . him . . . this. Okay?"

"*Sí, señor.*" He looked at the paper held firmly in his hand, scratched his head and headed down the drive to his little shack. A lot of things happen when you're in prison for a year: restaurants close, people move on, things change.

It was not even noon. A cab back to the hotel would only take me back to that room to watch a television I couldn't understand. I decided to walk and, misled by the cool peaks of the mountains beyond the city, sustained one of the worst sunburns of my life. The streets were filled with vendors of all kinds, selling everything under this cool, deceptive sun. The language, the smells and colors, my novelty as a long-haired blond *turista*, all this took my mind off my quandary. For three hours I walked and walked until finally I arrived at my hotel. A couple of beers, a whiskey and—with the help of a few lines and a joint or two from the street—all was well with the non–English-speaking world.

I sat on my bed, smoking one Lucky Strike after another, a *Bonanza* rerun educating me in Spanish, a half-finished bottle of Irish whiskey on the bedside table. There was a knock on the door.

A portly, well-manicured and carefully mustachioed Colombian with a disturbing resemblance to Hercule Poirot stood in the doorway, peering over my shoulder into the room behind me. In one hand was my scribbled note, in the other a crumpled-up newspaper. "Ju?" he said, gesturing toward the card.

"Yes, that's me. Do you know Benny?"

"Jes, jes, Benny, jes."

That was the extent of his English. He motioned for me to move into the room. I did. He assured himself that there was nothing threatening and dropped his newspaper on the table. It landed with a clunk, and the butt end of a .38 revolver backed out of the paper.

Thus did I embark on a sixteen-year slide into an abyss darker than any I had previously known or imagined, though the first part of that slide was as delightful as a roller coaster ride.

This was Juan, my newest and best friend. He made it clear to me, in the brokenest of English, that I wasn't to leave. He was coming back with an interpreter.

Eighteen hours later, a second knock on my door. It was Juan with Roberto, who spoke perfect English with a New York accent. Yes, Juan knew Benny. As a matter of fact, Benny worked for Juan, who was, in fact, a Chilean. Anything I wanted to do with Benny, Juan could and would take care of it, as Benny was out of touch for the moment. Busy.

"Well, as a matter of fact, Benny told me that any time I cared to come to Colombia, he would set me up with some coke. I just got out of prison, and it seemed that this was the best time to begin, um, anew."

"Juan wishes to know what you have in mind."

"I want to get some coke, take it back to Canada and come back for more once that's gone."

"Juan needs to know how much money you have to purchase this *mercancía.*"

"Tell Juan that Benny was going to front it to me, whatever amount, but I have $500 Canadian with me."

Juan fell to laughing. "*Señor, usted es un hombre con huevos muy grandes.*"

He agreed to take my $500 and bring me fifty grams of coke the next day. He said that, if I made it back to Colombia with a few more dollars next time, we would do "*un negocio muy grande.*"

I had been thinking along the lines of a pound or a kilo. But fifty grams it was. Later the next day, Juan was back with the fifty grams and a handshake.

Now, how would I carry this stuff out of Colombia, into the United States and then on to Canada? I would, of course, do it as I had seen it done in a movie. I found a street vendor and bought a pack of Marlboros, king-size. In my room, I heated a pin with my lighter. With this hot pin, I melted the glue of the cellophane wrapping surrounding the cigarette package and removed the pack without breaking the seal. I took the smokes from the pack and squeezed the fifty grams down inside, stopping only long enough to do the requisite few lines. I slipped the now "bearded" pack of smokes back into the cellophane, reglued it, and felt great.

Moments later, I did not feel great. Cocaine creates the perfect mental atmosphere for second-guessing. In fact, I realized, I was totally vulnerable. I began to panic. I should go out and buy a carton, remove the cellophane as I did from the pack, place the pack in the middle of the carton, and put the entire lot back in the cellophane. Surely the customs agents, the cops, anyone who might be observing me—I looked around the room—would be less likely to open the carton. I did this. Okay, bags packed, I called a cab for the airport.

On the ride to the airport, I panicked again, decided to remove the pack from the carton and put it in my pocket with the pack I had opened and was smoking from.

As I was going through departure, two men in jeans and casual shirts beckoned to me to follow them. What a civilized country. They even have people to show you to the gate.

We entered a room marked "*Policía Judicial.*"

Despite my many and vociferous protestations, they got my suitcase from the plane and insisted I remove all my clothes from it. My God, I realized, my number's up already. At that moment, some angel or devil whispered in my ear, "Take the coke package from your pocket and put it in your hand, then put the pack you are smoking from on top of it, remove a cigarette, light it and offer these guys one too."

This I obediently did. The cops graciously accepted the cigarettes and apologized profusely for the inconvenience as I gave them a light from my lighter. Piece by piece they examined my clothing and handed it back to me as they finished their search. As soon as they handed me a shirt that had a pocket, in went the coke. Twenty minutes later, these guys were doing what I thought they were going to do in the first place: they were showing me to the gate.

I cut the fifty grams so it became one hundred. It took me a month to sell it, and I was back to Bogotá to meet Juan with $5,000 in my pocket. The man was astonished. "*Qué huevos, mi amigo el Zorro!*"

He took me to the restaurant, the one that was boarded up and out of business. He unlocked the chain around the gates and slipped his car out of sight behind what was once the restaurant. The little old man came out and smiled a broad and toothless grin at me when he saw that I was with *el patrón*. He rattled on in Spanish as he let us into the building I'd seen smoke coming from six weeks earlier. The place smelled of solvent, and I could see half a dozen people putting together American Tourister luggage. "What an unusual place for a suitcase factory," I thought, my thought processes slowed, perhaps, by the joint I had smoked before the ride. What, I wondered, was Juan doing knocking off American Tourister luggage? I knew these Colombians were capable of duplicating just about anything, given ten minutes alone with it, but why suitcases, for Christ's sake? How could he possibly make any money, or enough to make it worthwhile? Then one of the *indio* workers reached into a barrel and pulled out a large, flat plastic envelope filled with white powder.

"*Ah, Zorro, te gusta la mercancía ...*" Juan laughed. He even laughed like Hercule Poirot.

The working man laid this envelope, which contained a kilo of coke, inside the suitcase, then laid another and another until he had done this five times. He placed a few protective layers of plastic over the *mercancía*, then took a sheet of steel, covered one side of it with glue, and laid it over the perfectly flat layer of cocaine. He applied a press that held the panel in place until the glue dried, then fitted fabric into the suitcase. It looked like the real thing to me. If you didn't lift it, you would think it was empty—it looked empty, though it weighed ten pounds more than it should have. This was a suitcase factory indeed.

Through Roberto, Juan assured me that I had proved myself beyond question, and he was going to front me one of these suitcases, a carry-on holding two kilos. He would accept the modest sum of five grand as a down payment.

I was staying at the same hotel as the first time. Suits and ties were always stationed outside the hotel and on every floor. They represented security for guests in a dangerous land and were always prepared to help, to make arrangements for taxis and so on. They were also a direct conduit to downtown police HQ. But I was naive and felt myself to be invulnerable. I lived in a cloud of invincibility—not arrogant, just unquestioning. I met a couple in a club near my hotel. They saw me sitting alone and invited me home with them for a couple of lost days of snorting coke and smoking multiple *bocadillos de queso*—literally "cheese sandwiches"—of marijuana, tobacco, cocaine paste, cocaine, and hash. I gave no thought to the danger this represented. It was all splendidly exotic and enjoyable, blissful and invigorating. Coke was fun and delicious.

I took a taxi to the airport. As I was going through departure, the same two guys in the same two madras short-sleeve shirts met me. I couldn't tell if they recognized me. Again, after they'd showed me a laminated card that basically told me in English what they were saying in Spanish, they escorted me to the now familiar room with *Policía Judicial* engraved above the entryway. I had the carry-on bag in hand, and my heart was pounding. I went over my plan in my mind and realized I didn't have one. I had nothing but terror as I crossed the threshold into what I feared to be a series of doorways, each one leading ever farther from my origins. Off with my clothes. They went through every last stitch and seam while smoking the cigarettes I once again passed around.

"*Tenemos que revisar la maleta pequeña,*" they said, gesturing toward the small suitcase. I'd already developed a sense of the Colombian style and made great flourishing macho protestations. These guys appreciated that sort of response, and I hoped it distracted them as I held the lid of the suitcase and threw out item after item, protesting with each one until I was down to the empty bag,

"See? Come on, amigos. Again, I have nothing you may be looking for. Enough of this! I have a plane to catch!"

But they insisted on waiting for my checked suitcase to be brought from the plane for a thorough examination. Holy Mother of God, how much more of this could I take? Nonetheless, as I sat there with them, awaiting the baggage guy, I felt a certain sense of victory interspersed with my stark terror. Five minutes later, millions of apologies and an escort to the gate for Miami. The cops carried my bags.

I sat in first class and a young American sat next to me. He was being deported from Colombia for reasons he didn't discuss, but it must have taken considerable money to spring him from jail. We drank his *aguardiente* and, somewhere before Miami, I passed out. I came to in a moving wheelchair. U.S. Customs and Immigration? I looked over my shoulder. I was being pushed by a cop. The jig was up, and my heart and stomach raced for my throat.

"Whas goin' on?" I muttered.

"Boy, ah thank it's about time y'all got up an' walked by yourself," said my man. I felt a spurt of something—blood? adrenaline? relief?—and rose from the chair to greet my future. What smuggler, Customs and Immigration officials must have assumed, would be stupid enough to pass out dead drunk on a flight into the United States?

"Thank you, sir. I'm just staying here," I said. I picked up both suitcases and marched resolutely to the door leading to the hotel connected to the airport. Once I was in the hotel lobby, I hurried out the front door and into a taxi to another hotel. Hungover, sick, spared, overjoyed.

TWELVE

SEVEN HOURS of orientation for a couple months' worth of new inmates from people who know less about ordinary life and prison life than I do. Most of the brass are from the south—Georgia, Florida, and a lot of them are husband and wife.

Staff member: "Any fuck-ups on these rules, y'all, and y'all will be smellin' diesel fuel and eatin' baloney sandwiches with a rollin' zip code, got it?"

Translation: "You'll be transferred to a high-security joint, and when they do that, they keep you on the road for three or four months, chained in a bus, stopping here and there at various hell holes around the country."

Associate warden: "Boys, my name is Preston. We want to make your stay with us as easy and worthwhile as possible so that when you get out of here, you'll be of benefit to the community. We're spending $27 million refurbishing the place, and we are already well into it. One problem we have here is the asbestos. Every building here is full of asbestos, including the water pipes and walls. We're working on that a little at a time, but it costs a lot of money."

Inmate of several weeks: "Hey, warden, are you gonna

spend any of those big bucks on makin' a bigger an' better visitin' room?"

Associate warden: "We could make a visiting room as big as the football field and you guys would still fill it up. No, we are not going to change it. Now, another thing we have to deal with here, boys, is that we are, uh, downwind from a coal-loading facility, so if you notice constant dust, that's why. Now. A little history for you boys. Terminal Island is a man-made island built from the silt here in the harbor. It was first called Dead Man's Island, then Snake Island, and now Terminal Island. This facility was built in 1938. That's why there is so much asbestos.

"Most of the people who work here are approachable, boys. As it is everywhere, there are some people who think their job is to make everyone's life miserable. When you meet one of those, you have the right to complain through the chain of command. Know that those people also affect their coworkers. We don't want them in the system either. We all have to spend a lot of time together, so let's make it easy. And, boys, if there's a death in the family, Father Bill here will let you know."

A mustachioed man in a white collar steps to the microphone. He smells of cop.

Father Bill: "Yes, boys, I was a mortician before I became a priest, so I know how to deal with death and how to help you deal with it. If you get a furlough to go home should a death occur, and your custody level requires you take an officer with you, the bureau will cover expenses only for one officer for eight hours. You are responsible for the rest of his pay and all of his expenses. It can be burden on the family, so keep it in mind."

Advise your loved ones not to die in your absence.

Mark, the Canadian, stops by my bunk. "Brian, you're not going to take that job cleaning the visiting room, are you?"

"I thought I would, Mark. I was going to work with Harry in the rec yard, but I'd have to get up every day at 6:30 to show up at work to get an outside pass for the day. I thought an hour or so five nights a week would be better."

"Let me tell you something, Brian. Drugs get into this joint through the visiting room. There are guys on that crew who are on it for just that reason. And if someone finds dope in the garbage, they lock you all up until someone confesses, man. Don't take it, Bri. It's the golden triangle, the junk route. And the prick whose job you'd be taking just left on a writ today, gone for the second time to make someone else's life miserable."

"What do you mean, gone on a writ?"

"I mean he's gone to testify against someone like you or me, Brian. Don't take his job, stay away from those guys."

"All right, okay, I get it. I won't."

"Take the job with Harry and I'll get you a job in recreation as soon as I can."

"Thanks, Mark."

Dominoes are echoing off the walls and through the halls—a mindless game to eat nachos with jalapeños by. From every floor, dominoes tinkle and shuffle; dominoes for the Spanish guys, gin rummy for the white boys, blasting rap or TV for the black guys, who stand around jiving loudly with their earphones on and the volume so loud a passerby can feel it. "Say what, homes, fuck, motherfucker, man, shit."

"Hey!"

"A'right!"

"A'right." That's "all right" without the l's. That's how most of these people acknowledge you if they don't know you very well or at all. It's kinda tough, kinda macho, and way cool, way cool. Know what I mean? A'right.

———

"Hey, Brian, wha's up?"

"Nothing, Billy, how are you doing?"

"A'right, man. I never see you, man. You're too busy with the jet set."

"What?"

"Yeah, the jet set, the pot smugglers. I don't think one of you got any tats, man."

"Well, neither do you, Bill."

"Yeah, but that's not because I'm too good for 'em, man, I just don't like 'em."

"Well, surprise, Bill, I don't like them either, homey. I can't imagine getting a tattoo—way too painful for me."

"Yeah, well, see you around."

"A'right, Billy, A'right."

In the cells on the other side of the freeway, I can see them tying each other off, sneaking up behind the first vein to surface, stabbing it with some homemade gimmick loaded with visiting room or cop-muled junk. And all of this just to end up sitting on the benches in the yard, struggling to hold up their heads, a.k.a. sucking dick.

Ricardo is talking. "Oh yeah, 30 percent of these guys are junkies. Think of the crime that would be eliminated if junk was G.I. junk—government issue. Most of these junkies are here because they needed to rob a bank to get the money to keep up with their habit. If the government legalized the shit, the cost would and could be kept down and these people would live relatively normal lives. The problem with junk, as with most other substances, lies in its illegality."

He isn't talking about cocaine, though. Not coke. Coke is something else.

"Counting B Range! Counting! Four o'clock!"

THIRTEEN

I JOIN SOME COUNTRYMEN IN THE TROPICS AND ENCOUNTER A CLERGYMAN OF POOR CHARACTER

I KNEW after I'd brought my first kilo of coke to Canada that I'd found my product—compact and lucrative. But a people pleaser like me, if he wasn't to feel lost, needed to be close to others, needed a team to play with and for.

In the spring of 1974, I dropped in on the bunch of guys from Newfoundland who now had a place in Toronto.

Gary Sexton was a big, bold, tough and—fair to say— miserable bastard who fancied himself the leader of this crew. His father was a teacher at St. Bon's, and I'd known him and all his brothers and sisters from childhood.

His lapdog, Gary Fowler, was wiry and tough, a professor at Memorial University in St. John's, with a master's in psychology, a bit of a sly fox with a major in psychedelic ingestion. Gary loved people to think he was crazy, but he was tougher than a junkyard dog on steroids because he didn't care. His motto: They'll have to kill me first.

Dick Andrews was a gruff guy with balls of steel and a kind heart. He had an extremely rich and successful father who was a cutthroat in business back in Newfoundland.

Will Shears was another burly guy, a university boy with an

honors degree in commerce whose family had wine and food distributorships back home.

Gary O'Brien was an overindulger like the rest of us, but six-foot-five, mouthy, and aggressive.

Without exception, these men, like myself, were the products of middle-class families and were committed potheads and rum drinkers who knew and understood functional inebriation as a way of life. We'd been friendly competitors in the past, though several had a problem with me because I wasn't by nature a follower. I sensed their hostility, but they sincerely wanted into the cocaine business, and I was as close as they'd gotten so far. Gary Sexton suggested I go down to Jamaica, where a couple of the group were moving about freely and a couple were hiding out, having had the misfortune to be involved in a deal that went south. For all the disdain that radiated from some members of this bunch, and for all their physically intimidating presence, I was sure I'd be loved by them all after a few Colombian cocaine trips.

We arrived at an agreement under which we would share the proceeds of the cocaine business and I would supply the contact and the method of transportation as far as Jamaica. They would take care of the rest of the trip to Canada and the sale of the product.

I had stopped communicating with my brothers and sisters and parents. I just couldn't bear the thought of having to answer the "What are you doing?" question. During my occasional visits to Newfoundland, I'd spend considerable energy avoiding them, no small feat in such a small community. Once I was driving down the street and saw my mother and father coming the other way and put my hand to my face.

Toronto to Montego Bay. I stepped off the plane into that tropical air and fell in love. The place was bustling, but I didn't notice the poverty here that was so prevalent in Colombia. At the airport I was met by a familiar, widely wanted face, a face that graced many post offices around the world, a face that the authorities intended to lock up for a boatload of marijuana dropped off in Tors Cove, Newfoundland, a few years back. This was the Bakeman, father figure for this bunch of Newfoundlanders. During the events that were to follow, he and I would remain close.

He was an architect who had designed my father's last brewery in Stephenville, Newfoundland. This was the brewery the premier of Newfoundland stole from my dad and sold to friends for a buck. The Atlantic brewed beer, a mind-altering substance I considered far more dangerous than pot. And this Newfoundland government—the same government that wanted to put him in prison for at least seven years—cheerfully subsidized the building of the brewery.

The Bakeman was a storytelling, wild-haired genius from Bonavista Bay, a Newfoundlander to the very marrow—a real Bayman, as we said in Newfoundland. A group of hippies and cool folk had started moving into the dying downtown of St. John's in the sixties, the Bakeman among them, and helped transform it into the vibrant party town of the East Coast it was to become. As a consequence of his downtown address, however, he had by virtue of sheer proximity become entangled with various smugglers and dealers.

As we pulled out of the airport, I noticed a sign warning unwary drivers of speed bumps in the road, something then unknown at home. "Caution," it read, "Sleeping Policeman." I knew right then that this was where I wanted to be. Any country that had signs telling me where the police were and reassuring me that they were asleep was a country I liked. And the countryside was beautiful. The Bakeman handed me a reefer and we dragged on it as we drove to my new home.

The house was owned by the brother of the leader of the opposition party in Jamaica and was right in the middle of an all-black part of Montego Bay.

The Newfies had the country wired. They were paying off members of the police Criminal Investigation Division (CID), knew in advance if the Canadian authorities were in the vicinity, and were aware of any pending raid on the house by the local authorities. The Bakeman described how fascinating it was to witness a police raid on the house after ample warning by the man who was directing the raid.

For me, this was the first place in my life that really felt like home. Pot, beaches, and golden rum. I have arrived, I thought.

Among their many connections, my new partners had hookups in a town in the mountains called Mandeville, where remarkable Jamaican pot grew in abundance. Through a process of beating and separation, they turned the pot into a hash-like substance that was easier to transport to Canada than the raw weed. Once a week, through a contact at Air Jamaica, they would hustle several pounds through at a time. Each parcel successfully delivered would net them tens of thousands of dollars.

My contribution was the cocaine connection. The cocaine would be secreted in false-bottom suitcases at the factory in Bogotá and muled to Kingston via Lufthansa—usually on Thursday afternoons—by some middle-aged Colombian couple whom no one would think of as the type who would smuggle anything. I would meet the couple in a hotel room in Kingston and pay them enough money to enjoy a nice vacation in Jamaica. I'd then leave with their suitcases, go to a small airline at Kingston Airport, and hire a plane and pilot to fly me to Montego Bay. I'd be met at the airport by one or another of the boys. We'd drive directly to the house and remove the cocaine from behind the secret compartments, then burn the suitcases on a deserted beach. They were mostly fiberglass, and the toxic and inflammable glue burned like crazy; the black smoke plume could be seen for miles. We'd disappear before it drew a crowd. Meanwhile, back at the house, our runners would have arrived from Canada and, having had their vacations at our expense, would be getting strapped up with the product on their thighs and stomachs and backs. Each person would carry between two and four kilos, worth between $100,000 and $200,000.

Will Shears simply didn't trust me, based on our former rivalry in St. John's, or was jealous of my independent leanings and purposely left me out of the decision-making. Meanwhile, not much of the money seemed to be filtering down from Canada to those of us in Jamaica. My bills were paid, I had enough to go to the bars in the evenings, but the rest was being, um, appropriated. Gary Sexton and the others, who had moved operations to Vancouver, claimed higher living expenses than they felt we needed in Jamaica. There was a rumble of disgruntlement among those of us who didn't often venture off the island.

The Bakeman and I had taken up residence in the villa. Funds were scarce, we didn't have a reliable car, and we felt we were living hand to mouth. Some of the crew members were away, setting up a pot deal. Better check on things, we thought. I got some cocaine from my Colombian connection and gave it to one of my Jamaican friends in return for tickets to Vancouver. We got ourselves some false ID. The Bakeman hadn't been back to Canada in quite some time, and we were actually looking forward to getting out of the island paradise.

Gary Sexton picked us up in a beautifully restored antique 1930s gangster Chevy. "Company car," he explained, as we pulled out of the airport. In fact, as it turned out, he and the others in Canada did have extra expenses. He was wearing wonderful clothes and had an amazing place, a fridge full of food, and a beautiful, expensive-looking girl living with him. He took us out to the best restaurants every night, which was awfully gracious, except that his wallet was filled with money that was my money too. My Colombian contacts were making this possible.

I didn't like Gary and didn't like the way he had to be danced around. I wasn't going to last long with him calling the shots in my life. I would have to look out for myself a little better.

Back on the island, the boys and I did what was to be our last cocaine run together. The Newfies had a couple of girls show up to run the product to Canada. These were girls, lovely girls, whom I'd known for years from Newfoundland. One of them was a medical student. I felt terrible about their involvement. I told the group of my fear for them, and, reluctantly, they settled on some other people to run the product.

I would never see anything from this venture, but, meanwhile, I'd made a Jamaican friend whose name was Carrot, a beautiful guy. From time to time I would do something special for him, such as give him money. The boys would warn me not to. "It spoils 'em," they'd say, as if Jamaicans were still the white man's slaves. This coming from a bunch of Newfs.

So when Carrot approached me to see if I wanted to meet the Preacher, the Big Man on the island, I was ready.

Carrot's main job was to keep the Preacher informed about the drug business in Montego Bay in general, and about the boys in particular. He had tried to convince me to meet the Preacher before, but I had refused in deference to the group. It was a great feather in Carrot's cap to be able to bring me to the Preacher, because the Preacher wanted to get into the cocaine trade and was having difficulty establishing a reliable source.

Carrot and I drove up to the sprawling house on the hill overlooking Montego Bay. Servants showed us into the living room and, after a wait of an hour—I was soon to appreciate how brief this was—the Preacher appeared.

The man was huge, his voice a tectonic rumble. He scattered six or seven hangers-on with a sweep of one enormous hand. His patois was such that Carrot had to interpret half of what he said, but nonetheless he made it quite clear that he wanted in to the cocaine trade and that I could have no better contact on the island. He was the main man in Montego Bay, he said, and I believed that. I'd heard the story about his run-in with the Jamaican government.

The Preacher had been the major fundraiser for the opposition party in a Jamaican national election. He had backed the Republican candidate, Eddy Seaga, for prime minister. When Michael Manley's socialist party won, it had a bone to pick with the Preacher. Manley's security forces showed up at the Preacher's house and, after an extensive search, found a bullet shell casing in his yard. In Jamaica at that time, it was illegal to own a gun or any part thereof. Even the possession of a bullet was enough to land you in something called "gun court"—a prison for gun offenses only—under indefinite detention. As long as Manley was in power, few were said to return from gun court.

The Preacher was taken away. Nine months later, such were his contacts, he was back in his bedroom, directing plane- and boatloads of pot to Canada, Europe, and the United States.

This first time was one of the very few times I was to see the Preacher anywhere other than his bedroom, where he spent his days and nights while a couple of dozen members of his entourage loitered about the compound, awaiting his orders. This was typical of many wealthy Jamaican and Colombian people. They had vast retinues of workers cooling their heels between the outside of the house and the outside of the bedroom where the master slept. Those closer to the bedroom door normally enjoyed higher rank. So it was with the Preacher. Some of his servants were children; some were very old. Their wages were food and a very small amount of money from time to time. The youths among them were given drugs to sell. Few outsiders ever saw those retainers closest to and most important to the boss.

Now I was about to join the attendees at the court of the Preacher.

I approached Juan, my Colombian contact, and told him of my plan to get out of the ungrateful clutches of the Newfs. I told him about the new client. He'd become quite fond of the boys, though he knew they'd been unfair with me. But now he stepped back and, not letting sentiment get in the way, looked at the prospect of increased revenue and backed my proposed move. This was not to say that he would abandon my countrymen, but that he would not abandon me.

The next time Will and Dick and Gary and Gary were in from Canada, we had a sit-down and I told them I was out. Dick and Will weren't at all happy but appeared to resign themselves. Gary Fowler was furious.

"Yer a fuckin' traitor, boy," he said.

Gary Sexton stared at me with real malevolence. "You think yer gonna take our fuckin' contacts and just push off, do you?"

"I'm taking my contacts."

"Yer not takin' any contacts."

But I left the house with all my belongings. I'd been able to stand up for myself against these men I'd found so intimidating. Now for the first time, though, I was scared. I was alone again, truly on my own, and I didn't like it.

———

I drove by prearrangement to the hotel district of Montego Bay. There, on a hillside overlooking the sea, the Preacher owned the Lookout Hill. This hotel was sited at the end of a long, winding driveway that led up from the beach through a garden surrounded by tree-shaded cabanas. Everything was sunshine yellow, white and spotless, the rooms bright and cheery, well furnished, with fine linens to swathe the body at night and original artwork to amuse the eye by day. The dining area was outdoors but could be covered if the weather required. An indoor dining area skirted an immaculately maintained pool, vast and empty. There was an ever-obsequious waiter, a bartender eternally shining the glassware with a spotless towel, a maid waiting for me to exit my room so that, the moment I was out, she could tidy it. In sum, it was as though it was a real hotel, where tourists paid real big bucks to stay. Instead, I was the only guest.

One or two other people did show up sometimes— bent-nosed mobsters, Yanks who looked like they might be drug enforcement agents, other dubious sorts—each involved in deals with the Preacher, all illegal at best. On the rare occasions when I was not alone, I did not acknowledge the other guests, and they likewise ignored me. From time to time, a tourist would drive up looking for a room and would be turned away by the servants, with the brusque explanation that the place was full. I would watch from my chair beside the deserted pool while the staff lurked at a discreet distance. Once in a while, girlfriends came down from Kingston to visit me and were favorably impressed by my circumstances, which was seldom a disadvantage.

During these halcyon days as a guest in the Lookout Hill, I was witness to one of the bravest smuggles in the history of the trade in Jamaica.

Just past the Holiday Inn near Montego Bay, in a section of the island called Rose Hall, there is a long, straight stretch along the highway that goes from one end of the island to the other. One Sunday, when the traffic was densest, a group of the Preacher's men, armed and in the uniform of the Jamaica Defense Force (JDF), set up roadblocks at the curves at either end of this straight stretch. Roadblocks were common in Jamaica, and long lines of drivers, who couldn't see the straight stretch, waited patiently in their cars. A twin-engine plane came in over the horizon and landed on the empty highway. The Preacher's men carefully loaded it with pot. The pilot turned the plane around and took off for the United States. The ersatz JDF men were gone as quickly as they had arrived, and the flow of traffic resumed.

Juan was anxious to meet the Preacher. Here was the man, Juan felt, who could make him rich. The Newfie boys and I had a continuing interest in pursuing the big boatload of herb, but Juan wanted to move quantities of coke because coke meant the greatest profit and the least trouble. Pot was too bulky for Juan: $40,000 worth of cocaine took up the same amount of space as a couple of hundred dollars' worth of pot.

Even though the Preacher wanted Juan's product in a bad way, he was not one to let go of power and control. He kept us waiting at the hotel for days. Finally, word came: the Big Man was ready to receive us.

Carrot came to the hotel and picked up Juan and me. We rode to the Preacher's house and were kept waiting for three hours. Juan was unused to this type of treatment. He shifted from chair to chair and paced up and down the garish carpet in the Preacher's living room. His eyes were angry. Carrot and I sipped mango juice. I tried to explain that this was the Big Man's way of telling Juan that this was his island and we were here at his discretion. Indeed, while we were in the living room, the big fella was no doubt lounging in his bedroom, eating jerk chicken and watching the clock before he made his entrance. Before he did, he sent someone out to inform us that he would be with us soon. He wanted us to get used to the idea that it was a big deal to even lay eyes on him. Half an hour went by. Suddenly, his booming voice echoed through the bedroom hallway, calling for a Red Stripe, Jamaica's favorite beer.

Then he walked into the room in his silk bathrobe. I could tell that even Juan sensed the power this man held in this territory—that here was a man not to be taken lightly. The beer was silently delivered to his waiting hand, and the deliverer slipped away just as silently. The Preacher poured a huge gulp down his throat. After a sustained belch, he informed Juan without further introduction that the only person Juan should consider doing business with on this island was him. This was not lost on Juan, who pointed out, however, that his business with the Newfoundlanders was strictly for export and would in no way interfere with any business he might do with the Preacher. Until they had completed some successful transactions, Juan would not be giving up his business with the Newfies on the Preacher's word. The two men eyed one another, and I felt uneasy. How would this be resolved in my favor?

The Preacher stood up. "I want to see a kilo soon," he said. He left the room. Was he being deliberately rude or just folksily blunt?

Juan was insulted, as Colombians can often be. "No," he said in the car as we rode away. "No. I do no business with that pig. That . . . unintelligent pig!"

I knew this was all about saving face; eventually, he would do business with the rude giant. Twenty-four hours later, Juan gave me a kilo to take for approval.

I now had access to the inner circle, the only white man, it seemed. The bedroom was an enormous dark cave with a mirrored ceiling. In the middle was a giant, fat bed, and on the bed was the giant, fat Preacher, eating some invisible thing. I brought the bag to the Preacher's side. He reached in with his paw and grabbed a large rock, crushed it between his thumb and forefinger and shoved it in the direction of his nose. Whoosh! It disappeared—a line big enough to drop an elephant to its knees.

"Not bad," he said. "Come back tomorrow. Leave this with me."

It seemed I had no choice but to do the Preacher's bidding. Juan had told me to return with either the goods or the money, but when I returned to the hotel, though he made a fuss, I could tell it was simply a show for my benefit. He had known what would happen.

I sat alone in the Preacher's living room for days before I got paid for that first kilo. I was never quite certain why that was always the way with the Preacher, but it was.

After I had left the boys, I learned that they had used the Newfoundland girls on the very next trip. The girls had been busted by customs in Puerto Rico and sentenced to ten years in prison. I got word to my former partners that I knew people who could probably help get the girls out of jail. But jealousy and distrust prevented them from calling me for almost three years, and I could do nothing without the cooperation of their lawyers. They finally called on Christmas Eve, 1978. As it turned out, my contacts were able to get the girls released from Terminal Island prison. I picked them up from LA airport. We drove through Beverly Hills together, all of us crying.

The medical student never really recovered from the experience. Once released from prison, she disappeared into Mexico, where she apparently lived the life of a peasant woman, married a peasant man and had four children, then left him and wandered aimlessly, picking fruit in Canada in season and receiving welfare in the off-season. The last time I heard about her, the welfare authorities had taken her children from her for good. The other girl was doing well, living in the sun and happily married.

FOURTEEN

I CAN'T SEEM to get the microwave to work. A *Cubano* is mopping the floor nearby.

"Hey, mang, I'm tryna clean dis lobby," he says.

"Oh yeah. What do you want me to do?"

"Well, das why I unplug dat machine, mang. Don' want none of dat radiation on me, mang."

"Right. Don't want to burn holes in your genes, right?"

"Hey, homes, never mine my fuckin' jeans. You lookin for trouble, mang?"

"No, kid, I ain't looking for trouble, I'm looking for a cup of hot soup. So don't give me any trouble, and we won't have any."

I'm sitting at Harry's side in the law library as he taps out my letter to Mark Bartlett, part of my campaign for transfer to the Canadian system. There are sixteen whirring typewriters punctuating pages and eardrums. You can literally feel the energy pouring into hopeful plans in this room. Prisoners struggle with points of law. They disregard the fact that only one case in a thousand appeals wins on a point of law in today's punitive environment. The police can do wrong, sure, but don't expect it to have any effect on the outcome. Just bring the case in, and nine times out of ten they get a conviction.

"The Jews in Berlin in the thirties had a better shot at life than we do. At least the Nazis'd let them leave. They'd take everything, but they let them leave. Shit, man, they took all my businesses that I had for years—nothing to do with the pot—indicted my wife, and threatened to indict my fifteen-year-old son."

"Yeah, that's fucked," I said, "but that's what they use for pressure, indict the whole family so they get you to plead the way they want. I watched them completely rip my partner Tony's family apart in our case—threatening his nephews with fifty years if they didn't rat out their uncle. I've heard about this stuff lots of times. Look at Danny. They couldn't extradite him from where he was, so they drugged him and put him on a flight to where they could get him. Whatever they need to do, they get what they want."

"Motherfuckers, man. Brian, you get the fuck outta here, man. Go back to Canada. You'll be better off there, at least for a while. Eventually, they'll end up with the same rules and regulations as here."

George and Bob Bitchin' are discoursing on the subject of obligation when the hack Garcia interrupts to provide a new perspective, after which the disputants resume. Bob makes the initial point.

"Listen to me, you motherfuckin' old man, you owe me fifty bucks, motherfucker."

"Fuck you, you fuckin' punk. I got three bags, paid you a hundred. The guy I got 'em for ended up in the fuckin' hole. I ain't payin' you another motherfuckin' cent, motherfucker."

"Oh fuckin' yeah, you old fuckin' prick? Jus' look over your motherfuckin' old fuckin' shoulder plenty, motherfucker, 'cause I'm gonna fuckin' be befuckinhind you, motherfucker."

"Fuck you, punk."

"Hey, you two, break it fuckin' up, or you'll both find SHU in a fuckin' hurry. C'mon, get the fuck outta here, or I'll get some fuckin' help and chain you motherfuckers up. C'mon, move out!"

"I'll see you fuckin' later, old man."

"Yeah, fuck you, you dope fuckin' punk. I killed more fuckers than you ever fuckin' hit."

Sipping joe, sliding the pen across the paper, listening to Bonnie Raitt on 94.7, hack's keys jangling down the corridor, *Cubanos* shouting at each other in their singsong way, Unicor slave laborers lined up at the showers, TVs screaming to no one in particular, dominoes slapping tables.

"Stand down! Four o'clock! Stand down! Count! *Cuenta! Cuenta!* Stand down!"

"Hey, O'Dea, don't blame me if I don't get your visiting shit done, man. I got my own guys to take care of, and I just don't know if I'm gonna have time to get to you."

"Yes, Jenkins, but Weishart said the paperwork would get done and I'd know by three today when Susannah could visit. Edwards said it would be done last week, and now he's gone for two weeks. What the fuck does anyone's word mean around here, man?"

"Hey, O'Dea, Edwards is your counselor, all right, not me. He was supposed to do this shit, not me."

"Counselor? Counselor of what, man? Liar is what it is, Jenkins. Nobody who works here does what they say. The buck gets passed, and you shrug your shoulders. Prisoners after all, right? One thing is sure, Jenkins, you and that other fucking counselor will be here a long time after I'm fucking gone, man, and that's just the way it should be."

I thought people were kidding when they noticed me asking to get things done and laughed.

"Brian, he won't do that. He'll say yes to get rid of you, but forget it, man."

"Turn that radio off during count!"

"Lick my nuts, motherfucker!

"Lick your own nuts. Turn that fuckin' radio off! It's a count!"

"Count! Settle down. Counting B Range."

Cool wind blows over our counted bodies, a sliver of a yellow moon dangles in a deep blue sky. I'm not so blue. I expect to see my family someday soon.

"Here, O'Dea, I got a few of them visits approved."

"Hey, Jenkins, thanks, man. I appreciate the extra effort."

"Yeah, well, I'm gonna give Edwards shit when he gets back, laying all his shit off on me like that."

"Recounting! Recounting! Get where you belong or we'll do this all night until we get the number we need. Counting!"

Something's happening. Five hacks are on the unit doing recount; there are usually only two. One of them glares at a *chulo*. "Hey, Flores, come here."

"Wha's up?"

"I said here, Flores."

"Wha's it, homes?"

"Don't fuckin' 'homes' me. You think we aren't doing this right for you, punk?"

"Hey, motherfucker, wha's yer problem, mang?"

"One more 'motherfucker' outta you, Flores, SHU! You understand? It's 'officer.' We understand each other and who is what around here?"

"Yeah."

"Recount! Stand up count! Stand up and shut up!"
"O'Dea! Down off that bunk! You deaf?"

Mark is talking. "See, Bri, there're different level infractions in
here. When I had a dirty piss last year, I got a level-100 beef.
That's as bad as it gets. A level-100 increases your custody
level one point. Any more problems with me and pot, and
they'll put me in Lompoc—that's the Walls, man—bad fuckin'
joint. Murder is a 100-level offense too."

"Are you telling me if you murder someone or you smoke
pot your custody level increase is the same? It's the same-level
offense inside the system?"

"That's right, man. Hard to believe, but that's the way they
see it."

Shit. Big problems with the count. They're back again. This
time the duty officer is here.

"Open these motherfuckin' doors, motherfuckers. Yer
fuckin' with my phone time. Got people I wanna talk to. Hey!
Open fuckin' up!"

Two guards at one end of the hall, two guards at the other
end, another checking names and numbers. Now they're
standing in front of me.

"Name."

"O'Dea."

"Number."

I reel it off: 20293–086. I feel like I'm in a pressure cooker.

"Hey, motherfuckers! You're fuckin' with my program!"

"Punk, you ever been to the hole before? Shut the fuck up
or you'll have no fuckin' program."

Every level, keys jangle, guards slip around, dozens of them
now.

"Someone's gone, Louie."

It mounts and mounts, thick and soupy, hot like heartburn.

"Stand up count, gentlemen!"

"Name?"

"O'Dea."

"Common spelling?"

"Not really."

"No? Lemme see that ID. O-'-D-E-A. Ha ha. D-E-A, huh? That's a good one. Better be careful around here."

He moves on.

"Name?"

"Cortes."

"Cortes . . . T-E-S?"

"Yes."

"Okay, name?"

"Castillo, Captain."

"Ah yes, Castillo. How are you doin'?"

"Fine, sir, jus' fine."

"Name?"

The tedium of it.

"Name?"

It's suffocating.

"Name?"

Still no resolution. Waiting, whispering, fear, anxiety. Part of the body missing. Who? Where to? How? I could cut the pressure with a knife.

The cops here now are the heavies, plainclothes and mean-looking, traveling in packs of four or more.

"Stand by your bunks and no movement!"

Counting for one hour and twenty minutes. Too many people packed too close together, and they say they're going to put more people in here. They'll be counting around the clock. Whoever is missing this time is hiding, some dark hole, heart pounding, pounding, almost out of control, hands, palms sweating, freezing, shivering, but boiling, metal band around the head, fear, fear, adrenaline surging through the veins, fast breathing, no breathing, holding breath, listening, hearing things, just rats and jailhouse cats, mounting, mounting, the pressure mounting.

"Get in your cells up there! Freeway! By your bunks! Shut up! No movement!"

From down here on the freeway, we can look up to the tiers above, to cops counting, getting names and numbers. I'm starting to get it now: it's some sort of computer error. My heart is slowing and I'm feeling less troubled. Clerical error. Nothing left but to await the outcome. Count. Count. Count. Count tonight.

"Paperwork."

"Jus' paperwork."

FIFTEEN

I THRILL TO BEAUTY AND THE ROAR
OF THE CROWD

I WAS STANDING on the beach at Montego Bay in the spring of
1974 when a young woman passed me. Her every movement
communicated a self-possession as astonishing as her physical
beauty. She passed, then looked at me with uncommon bold-
ness and said hello. I stood in awe for a moment, then gave
pursuit.

"Hi there! How're ya doing?" I had no time to work up
something more suave. She responded with a wide, warm
smile. I was blown away.

I asked her name, and when she answered I stood for a
moment with what was certainly an uncertain smile.

Wendelmoet Schalkweijck had been born in Surinam just
sixteen years before, while her father was bringing Christ to
the heathen in the jungles. He was a Moravian missionary
from Holland who was now teaching theology at the University of the West Indies, Kingston. She was five foot five and
still growing, with long black curly hair, full—almost swollen
—lips and a flawless body. Wendelmoet was remarkably free
of the conventional restraints I might have associated with the
daughter of a missionary, and her self-assurance made her
seem much older than she was.

I followed her to Kingston, where she was living with her parents, and took up residency there. I continued to carry on my business with the Preacher. Since the products entered through Kingston anyway, I was closer to where I needed to be. But Kingston was nothing like Montego Bay. It was a heavy city and home to the famous gun court. The police were relentless in their pursuit of the duppy gunmen. There was constant political violence.

Wendelmoet and I fell in love and were inseparable. I would go to her high school and pick her up and we would go to the beach. When Juan was in town, he would come to the school and wait with me. Two older guys, one wearing an impeccable sharkskin suit, picking up a teenage girl. I was oblivious to the stares and oblivious to how I appeared to others, regardless of what I was doing. I never had a moral problem with my trade—on the contrary, I always felt I was providing a service to the planet. Occasionally, the planet would help itself a little too freely, as when Keith from Chicago absconded with a key of coke. Embarrassing for Juan and me, but it was the nature of the business.

Wendelmoet and I were in a downtown bar renowned for its reggae and its shortage of tourists. We were the only white people in the place. While we were sitting at the bar talking, I had my back to the door and the crowd and she was facing the other way. She told me that a group of white people had just walked in. I didn't want an encounter with anyone I might know from the business, but when one of these people approached the bar in search of a Red Stripe, I glanced over.

"Hey," I said. "Shel? Is that you?"

"O'Dea. Shit. Is that you?"

The last time we had seen each other was a few years earlier in his native Toronto. Shel was a rock and roll promoter, and I'd heard the promoting hadn't been going so well.

"What are you doing in Kingston, man?"

"Hey, Brian. Haven't you heard? I'm promoting Super Soul 74, man. It's gigantic, it's huge."

"Huge how?"

"Man, it's without a doubt the biggest-ever-seen reggae concert. It's gonna be at the National Stadium, fifty thousand capacity. I got Bob Marley, I got Jimmy Cliff, I got all these big names lined up."

"No shit."

"I'm just waiting to.have certain things signed. The dates are gonna be made public at a public signing. Just rounding up some completion investors."

"Whaddaya mean?"

"Just putting money in place for last-minute stuff. You know, details."

"You're still taking investment?"

"Just a few last-minute things."

He invited us to his house to discuss it over a drink. Wendelmoet needed to go home, so after I dropped her off I went on down to Shel's place. He and his entourage were staying in the old Governor General's house, an untidy place on mansion row, but incredibly opulent housing in a city rife with poverty. Shel's people immediately wanted me to leave my hotel and move into the house with them. They had plenty of room, so why not? It was impossible for a person such as myself not to get involved. They were from California, Toronto, Boston. They just knew this was going to become an annual event. If I were to get in on it right away, it would take care of my future and get me out of the drug business. Sometimes I'd say that was what I wanted.

"Say, by the way, Bri," Jeff from Boston added, "do you have any more of that coke left?"

"Damn, that sure is some great pot," said Al from San Francisco. "Think you can get us some of that stuff?"

I moved in and ponied up several thousand dollars to enlist as a Super Soul 74 investor.

We took trips to see Bob Marley. Bob lived in an enormous house near the prime minister's residence. It was filled with dozens of hangers-on and absolutely no furniture. We walked through to his bedroom and spoke to Bob, but I could sense the hostility of the people hanging around there. I was in a hurry to get out.

We didn't sign Bob Marley. We saw many of the people in the music business in Jamaica, and we didn't sign them either. As it turned out, Shel had failed to approach a Jamaican to be a partner, and now there was a conscious effort to freeze him and his people out.

I thought that perhaps a meeting with the Preacher was in order. We rented a plane and flew to Montego Bay. The Preacher was his fat self, and wanted everything for his fat self, but I left Shel and him alone to work out some kind of deal. They both knew what my percentage was going to be. Shel came out of that meeting feeling that he would be able to pull this thing together.

When we returned to Kingston, a couple of slick coke dealers from California were waiting at the house for Shel and crew. They wanted to know what was going on with their money, and how this concert had gone from being Super Soul 74 to being Super Soul 75. Shel explained that we had just returned from meeting the one man on the island who could help us pull it off and how there had been sabotage from the start, but it was all going to be okay from now on.

Wendelmoet, meanwhile, did not like the vibes around these people and refused to spend much time with them. But I wasn't going to be turned aside by girlish qualms.

The next day an attorney arrived from Los Angeles. This man, Terry Fields, represented some other investment money, and he took no time in getting to the house from the airport.

We became friends immediately. I explained my Johnny-come-lately position, and we went out for a drink to talk about what was happening. In Terry's view, I was like the old ladies in *The Producers*—the tenth person to have been sold 25 percent. Under the circumstances, though, I was pretty much bound to stick it out until the bitter end. Terry suggested that when I was ready to move out of this deadbeat country, I give him a call and he'd find something in LA for me to do. I said I would.

Then came news: we could pull off the concert. Burning Spear, a fantastic Jamaican group, had signed up, and there were others who seemed interested. Apparently, the Preacher's intervention was working, but concert time was almost upon us and no one seemed certain who was going to play. Half the sound and lighting people who had come from the U.S. had already split, leaving us with masses of lighting and sound gear no one knew how to operate. I was chosen to man the Trooper, a large spotlight some thirty feet up on a scaffold.

Very few tickets were pre-sold, but the word from Shel was that we would sell out the night of the show. Shel owed lots of people for work, not the least of whom were the Jamaican laborers who had put together the stage. The plan was to pay them out of the receipts from the gate on the evening of the show. This Shel had balls.

The concert was held in National Stadium, where Jamaicans normally watched their beloved soccer matches. On the day itself, the crowd was middling—under ten thousand—the air hot and heavy. Halfway through an outstandingly lackluster show, a rumbling discontent that had been brewing among the attendees began to shift to an angry growling. From my vantage point at the Trooper light system, perched on scaffolding in the middle of the field, perhaps thirty feet in the air, it appeared that disgruntlement was mutating into thoughts of mayhem.

"What's happening?" I called to the stage manager through my headset.

There was a pause. Below, thoughts of mayhem seemed to abruptly transform into mayhem itself. Faces in the crowd were turned in my direction.

"Dunno." I heard the stage manager's voice over the swelling roar. "Might be a quality thing."

I was the only white man in sight who was part of the promoter's team—not only in sight, but a perfect target. Beer bottles began to break against the platform, which might have been twenty square feet. The stage manager was safely backstage. I shouted through to him that I was getting off the platform.

"Uh, look, Brian," his voice crackled through the earphones. "Why don't you just sorta lie down and decrease the target area?"

Shit. I was trying this when I heard a terrible rumbling and looked down to see the fans streaming across the field toward me. I crawled to the edge of the scaffolding and slipped over the edge to begin my descent. At that moment, cops came onto the field in front of the stage and fired their shotguns into the air as a warning volley to stop the surging mob from wrecking the place. I had just reached the first step when a shotgun pellet struck me in the hand. I fell the remaining twenty-five feet to the ground. The festival crowd, none too festive, trampled me in passing.

I was in an ambulance on the way to Kingston Public Hospital. When it arrived at emergency, the ambulance driver got me a wheelchair and headed back to his cab.

"Where you going?" I croaked.

"I'm not goin' in that place, mon."

"Hey, I'm injured. Wheel me in there. I might be dying, man."

"No, mon. That place is full of people, mon. They been hurt, mon, like you—trampled. But you're a white man and one of them promoters. No way."

He took off. I had badly sprained both ankles and my body was bruised everywhere from the crowd running over me. My thumb was the size of a small balloon. I was scared. I wheeled myself into the waiting area, and the hostile eyes of the crowd fell upon me. A large drunk man lurched forward threateningly.

"Look heer, ras clot bwa! It's a bumba clot white bwa wha work wit that blid clit promoter!"

"What the blid clit, mon?" I demanded. "I too am sufferin' at that man's hands. He's long gone and took all my money! I gave him all I had for dis ting!"

He laughed without humor.

"T'ras bwa, white bwa simply another Yankee what gwain to take our money, make us work an' not pay."

My body was screaming, but this was no time to cave in to hostile sentiment.

"No fuckin' blood clot way, mon!" I actually felt some sort of righteous wrath rise within me. "I'm no damn Yankee, mon! I am a Jamaican, mon! Now get the ras clot away from the door. I am leavin' here right now!"

"Fuckin' blid clit expatriate," he snarled at me as I rolled out through the door in my wheelchair.

In the end, the crowd was sympathetic to my plight. One of them gave me a ride back to the hotel, where a lot of the angry workers were staying. They told me that the last anyone saw of Shel, he'd gone to the ticket booth to collect the receipts. Then he'd disappeared. Ah, familiar tale. I wanted to run, but this was my home for now.

At six in the morning, I awoke in my bed, the whole length of my body throbbing. I opened my eyes. A dozen Jamaicans stood over me. Some of their faces appeared upside down from my perspective. They were nonetheless angry faces.

They demanded their money. I pleaded my case. There was a lot more growling. In the end, the compass of their fury swung around to Shel, who happened not to be there. They left.

I was able to track Shel down at the Preacher's. He'd headed for Montego Bay right after he'd grabbed the money. The Preacher was his usual sympathetic self. He held Shel and his people captive for a couple of weeks, took everything they had, made them get some more money sent from the U.S. and Canada and took that too. Finally he let them leave the island. As for the unpaid Kingston workers, they were left to draw their own conclusions about the white man, any conclusions not already concluded, that is.

I was glad to get back to my affairs. For months the concert had taken my time away from the business that paid for my food and rent. Juan, too, was happy to get me back on track. He had a load of coke bound for Toronto via Jamaica that had gone on to Germany aboard a Lufthansa flight. They'd stopped in Kingston to let off passengers, but forgot to take the luggage off the plane for transfer to a Canadian flight. A few suitcases loaded with cocaine were probably sitting around the luggage room in Frankfurt with no one to claim them.

I went to the airline office to voice my complaint. They told me that the bags had, in fact, been sent back from Germany—unfortunately, not to Jamaica but to Toronto. They were seeing if they could locate them. Damn. The product was destined for Toronto, but not this way. And this was looking more and more like a bust all the time. I was told to return to the airport in a few days. They gave me the flight number of the airplane that would carry the bags back to Jamaica. I told them all of my belongings were in those suitcases: what did they expect me to wear? The airline gave me $500 to buy new clothes. It was fun getting money out of them, but it didn't come near solving the problem of the ten kilos.

The day the flight was to arrive, I got to the airport long before the plane and cased the place. Passengers collected luggage in a spacious room with only a roof and partial walls—typical of the islands. The procedure was to collect one's suitcases and carry them to a customs inspection table to be searched.

The flight arrived and all the bags were unloaded into this room. I skulked at a distance. The place was abuzz with tourists getting their luggage opened. Customs officers pawed through everything. When they'd finished and the passengers dispersed, the agents went for a break in a back room somewhere. In the laid-back style typical of the island people, they left the unclaimed baggage in the open. I walked into the room, picked up the bags, walked out to the car, put them into the trunk and drove away with a huge smile on my face, back in business again.

After I had unloaded the suitcases in my room at the hotel, Wendelmoet and I took off for Port San Antonio for an afternoon at the beach. She got in the car, dressed as usual in her bathing suit, covered by only a T-shirt.

"Brian, I have something to say. Father and Mother want to know more about you."

"I can understand that, Wen."

"They want to interview you. Would that be all right with you?"

"I don't see why not."

"Yes, good. Me too. They also require that you supply references they could contact regarding your, you know . . ."

"Character."

"Yes, character. That's right."

"Let me think about that, Wendelmoet. I want to give them the right ones."

So that was how it had to end. This child was talking about marriage to a man who was living in a hotel room. Still, it killed me to say good-bye right then and there. Instead, I provided her parents with the names of my aunt Margaret—a wonderful woman and a nun—and my uncle Barry, who was my mother's brother and a Jesuit. He didn't care for me one bit.

They brought the matter to a graceful close.

SIXTEEN

THE PANES of the freeway windows are mostly broken out, but the morning sun is streaming through to deny the place its character.

"Good morning, Stud," I said.

"Hey, bud, how ya doin' there, buddy?"

"Okay, Stud, okay, how 'bout you?"

"Okay, buddy, okay, buddy, thanks for askin', bud."

"You gotta change that shirt and take a shower today, Stud."

"I will, buddy, I will."

"All right, Stud. You're okay, man, take it easy."

"Hey, buddy, can I ask you somethin'?"

"Sure, Stud."

"Why do you think they didn't like me at MDC, buddy? Why did they always piss in my shoes, buddy? Why did they always beat me up, buddy? Why was that, buddy?"

"Easy does it, Stud. This is no Metropolitan Detention Center. We don't let that shit happen to you here, man. You were too smart for them there, Stud, and too persistent, asked too many questions. Too smart mostly, kid."

"Hey, thanks, buddy, thanks for the answer. Hey, buddy, can they throw me out of my room if I don't pay my fine?"

"Stud, that's the one hundred and first time you asked me that fucking question. You gotta stop asking me that."

"Well, okay, buddy. But can they?"

"No, Stud."

"Hey, buddy, when I was six, I saw my mom kill my dad, buddy. Shot him three times. In the knee, the shoulder an' the face. All I remember is his face blowin' up. Then my mom's boyfriend kept tryin' to fuck me. You got a girlfriend, buddy?"

"Yes, Stud, I got a great girlfriend."

"Lemme see your pictures, buddy, lemme see them, okay?"

"Sure, Stud, c'mon down to my locker."

"You're all right, buddy, you're okay."

I just want to fucking scream. I just want to fucking cry. I just want to fucking ask some-fucking-one why and how the fuck some fucked-up judge could send that poor boy into this hell. Fucking why, motherfuckers?

"*Cuenta! Cuenta!* Counting B Range! Counting!"

SEVENTEEN

I TAKE CAPABLE PARTNERS BUT FALL AMONG THIEVES IN A FOREIGN PORT

1975. WAITING. Waiting for the Preacher. My life was full of waiting for money and listening to grief from Juan about the slowness of payment. As a matter of principle, Juan refused to see the Preacher after the first meeting. If I wanted to do business with the fat, unintelligent pig, okay, but don't expect Juan to have anything to do with it. Not that he was averse to the profits. No, the profits were acceptable. He would hold his nose.

During a long day's wait at the Preacher's, another white guy showed up—a tall, lanky, geeky-looking fellow. We glanced sideways at each other, but said nothing. That evening, while I sipped my Appleton's Amber Rum with lime beside a pool at the Rose Hall Hotel in Montego Bay, I was approached by this same man. He asked if he could join me for a drink.

This was Jerry from Chicago. He said one of the Preacher's people had suggested that we might be able to do some business together. I told him that the last guy from Chicago I'd done business with on the island had gone back to Chicago with my product, never to be heard from again.

"Oh yeah? Who would that be?"

"Guy named Keith Jenkins."

Jerry made a small, dry, sniffing sort of sound.

"What?" I asked. "He your brother or something?"

"I know him," said Jerry. "If you'd ever like to come to Chicago with me, I'll pick up your money for you."

I looked at the guy. He hadn't cracked the smallest smile in the course of our conversation.

"Why don't you have another rum?" I suggested.

Jerry was a Jewish boy, the son of perfectly respectable Chicago restaurateurs, and had perhaps the worst disposition of any human being of my acquaintance. Charitably, his rages may have been symptomatic of a blood-sugar problem. He was thirty, gaunt, with curly hair and a long nose. He smoked a couple of packs of Kools a day but was careful to throw away any partial pack before going to bed. He liked to start fresh in the morning.

I may not have actually liked Jerry—in retrospect, that would have been a challenge for most people—but as the days passed, we realized that we each had something to offer the other. I had the Colombian contacts, and he had links to capital and the American pot market. Despite the current rage for coke, we both dreamed of giant pot deals. I was starting to dislike the coke business. The stuff itself wasn't too bad for you, I believed, if you paid attention, but people in the pot trade seemed less inclined to stiff you, and you felt less inclined to stiff them. And there may have been a trace of nostalgia for both Jerry and me, since pot was the introduction to drugs for both of us. We decided to form a partnership.

Had we decided to issue a formal prospectus, the introduction might have explained that "synergy has been achieved by the merging of compatible companies, providing a perfect melding of product, financing, and distribution. The new company is presently prepared to accept ground-floor investment." Any business able to provide the kind of instant profits familiar to experienced investors in the basic marijuana business would attract capital, all kinds of capital, endless capital, seeking multiple returns in kind. The diversity of citizens an entrepreneur was able to, or was forced to, or was cajoled into, or was simply obligated to meet in the course of offering a four-to-one return on investment in ninety days without guarantees or SEC filings was staggering. Jerry had lawyers—naturally, usually, eternally, inevitably—investing other people's money. He had doctors, politicians, police officials, accountants, and many businessmen. In short, in that place and time in history, there was more money looking for a brief home in the drug trade than there were places to invest. Try as we might, we could only fly so far and so fast. And, frustratingly, pot is a plant and must be allowed to grow.

Jerry had a partner, Richard, who came and went in the pursuit of their business interests and seemed to be something of an expert in transportation matters. He was a tall, mustachioed veteran, easy in manner and soft-spoken.

"Hey, Brian."

Richard and I were drinking alone one night out on the terrace of the Rose Hall Hotel.

"About Jerry."

"Yeah."

"You're going to find Jerry, uh, goes a bit, uh, wild sometimes."

"No problem, Richard."

"I mean a bit haywire."

"I thought he seemed a bit, sort of, excitable."

"Completely haywire, and for no reason."

"Really?"

"No reason at all."

"I see. Sounds like coke."

"For sure, but more than that, I think. Anyway, he's good at this, what he does. Know what I mean?"

"He sounds like he knows what he's doing."

"He does."

"So how do you handle him, Richard?"

"Uh, he never goes haywire with me, see. So it's easy."

"Huh?"

"I probably killed too many guys."

I nodded at this.

"'Nam and all," he said, without further elaboration.

"Right," I said. We sat there for some time, listening to the waves flop on the sand below.

"What about that gun he carries?" I asked. A lot of guys carry guns, though.

"It's just in case somebody goes for his strongbox. That's all. That's all he cares about."

"So we're safe messing around with his wife," I said.

"I dunno," Richard said. He was a nice man but not really good with sarcasm.

Two weeks after our first meeting, I was on a plane for Chicago with Jerry at my side. We'd forwarded some coke there for Juan and stood to make a little dough. I had a feeling —okay, it wasn't the first time I'd had the feeling—that life was about to take a turn for me. I was finally going to get rich at this business.

We landed in Chicago and went to Jerry's lakeside apartment to crash. The next day, Jerry went to his safe deposit box and got his gun. I don't like guns and told him so.

"Relax," said Jerry, one of the least relaxed men on earth. "It's just to show him we mean business."

We staked out Keith's house for about twelve hours before he finally came out. We followed him to the neighborhood supermarket, where he picked up beer and cigarettes—no food. This was a sure sign that he continued to enjoy cocaine as much as he had when he absconded with mine. Jerry pulled up next to him as he was about to get into his car. I jumped out.

Keith actually flinched when he saw me.

"Hey, hey," he said, and then hung there, his mouth a bit open, clearly trying to remember my name.

"Brian O'Dea," I reminded him.

"Hey, Brian."

"Jerry and I were just in town," I said, although this was self-evident.

Keith looked over at the car with visible alarm. "Hey, Jerry," he said, although Jerry was showing no interest in the encounter.

I was paid two days later. They could say what they liked about Jerry, but he and I had some sort of future together.

Juan, that look of perpetual worry stitched across his face, flew up to Chicago to collect his coke money. I introduced him to Jerry, and Jerry and I explained that it was really pot, not coke, we wanted to trade in. Perhaps Juan feared an introduction to someone worse than the Preacher, but he said he had another man for us, a Colombian who had all the right connections along the pot coast of that country. This man was Santiago, an Indio from a north coast Colombian seaport called Barranquilla. Two weeks later, he was in Chicago.

Santiago was in his late thirties, calm in manner, soft-spoken, yet at our first meeting the combination of his beautiful clothes and his grave, pockmarked, weather-beaten face instilled fear in me.

Our first task for Santiago was to run a few kilos of coke into Chicago to show him we were capable and make him a little money. Our primary interest, however, was in running a load of pot. After a few successful blow trips, we were able to get Santiago's cooperation. He would rather have kept the cocaine business going, but we were adamant, and he agreed to take us to the coast, to Barranquilla, to meet the pot connection and the people who would be running the pot to us off the coast of Colombia.

Jerry, Richard, and I flew out of Chicago to Miami. The plan was for Richard to carry on to Puerto Rico to talk with our potential boat people, while Jerry and I went to Barranquilla. We bid Richard good luck and hopped an Avianca flight south.

Barranquilla was the epitome of a rough, old-fashioned, New World seaport, the kind the pirates never really left because here they'd found a home.

Santiago and Juan picked us up at the airport and took us to the Royal Lebelo Hotel. There we were met by Rosa, a woman who often accompanied Juan. She was married to a Jamaican of British descent, and had her two daughters with her, a four-year-old and a five-year-old. I believe this woman to have been Juan's money courier, the one who would take his dough off to the Cayman Islands to deposit in an account right next to that of some international weapons broker or another of the world's covert agencies.

Over the next few weeks, we had meeting after meeting with various Colombians whose job it was to get a boatload of Colombian Gold to our boat somewhere off Colombia. We studied charts of the Caribbean Sea in search of the right time and place.

On a Sunday afternoon in April 1975, we met at the hotel and agreed to rendezvous on June 11 near a craggy protrusion called Savan Rock, off Savan Island in the Grenadines, south of St. Vincent.

When the meeting was concluded, I didn't feel like socializing with the group. I took Rosa's two little girls and headed out into the city for a Sunday afternoon stroll and some window shopping in downtown Barranquilla. This was only a little cheaper than actual shopping in Colombia, then a shopper's paradise. Paramilitary police toting machine guns were on almost every corner, and their fingers were on the triggers of their weapons. I had been cautioned about these strolls, but I believed I had a way of looking through these cops and avoiding trouble.

As I walked out of the hotel, the little guy who sold me cigarettes approached me and, as usual, tried to get me to buy some pot from him. Of course, I had no interest whatsoever, but I thanked him for his concern for the well-being of my head and bought a pack of Luckies. The girls and I headed downtown. I was feeling good: out for a stroll with two of the sweetest little girls in Colombia, my deal set, my wealth assured.

We were about two blocks from the hotel. I was holding the hand of each of the little girls. I noticed my cigarette salesman running across the street toward me. As I smiled and said hello, he reached his hand toward my shirt pocket and stuffed what looked like a small brown paper bag into it. I pulled the little girls around to the front of me and held my pocket open with one hand while I reached into it with the other. The guy disappeared into the crowd. As I looked down, fumbling for the bag, an open hand displaying a police badge showed up at the base of my pocket.

"I get it," was all I could say. A plainclothes cop made me stand against a window of a shop as he fingered what looked to be some beautiful gold bud in the bag.

"Bery, bery bad, señor gringo, bery bad. Ju comin' weeth me, señor."

As he spoke, he motioned with his head in the direction of two young paramilitaries, machine gunners. They looked at him nervously as they fingered their guns. The sting was on. Money was the name of this game. This was going to cost me a few hundred dollars before it was over. I gestured toward the little girls, who had no idea anything was amiss.

"*Pero, señor,*" I asked, "*las niñas?*"

"They come too, señor."

I was pissed off. I said this was a goddamned setup and I wanted to see someone in authority. He told me I could either straighten it out with him or see a judge. Fuck that rotten little prick with the Lucky Strikes was my only cogent thought. This was certainly not lucky. All the time I was buying that guy's cigarettes and thinking I was helping him out, he was working to set me up with these clowns.

"So, señor," I tried to sound cooperative. "It's money, is it? What? Five hundred? A thousand, maybe, and we can all go home?"

He laughed. "Ju eensult me, señor. Perhaps we should go to the judge."

That was all the money I had on me, and I told him so. He suggested we go to the hotel, where he was sure I could find more money in my room. My room. Shit. I had my last $8,000 there, and he was the last person in the world I wanted to give it to. On the other hand, if I didn't cooperate, I might be accidentally shot while trying to escape custody. I agreed to go to the hotel and used the walking time to try to figure out a way around this. The two nervous machine gunners walked close behind us and stood outside the hotel on the street corner. They had their shaky little fingers on their triggers.

We walked through the lobby, and the clerk said hello to me as though there was nothing wrong. As far as she was concerned, I had a friend with me. My friend, of course, looked like something out of a B movie, with his hand secreted inside his gun pocket as conspicuously as possible for his own reassurance and my information. How the hell was I going to get out of this one? We ascended the stairway to my floor, and I sent the two little girls off to their mother's room. I waited until I saw them enter. As we walked past the room where the boys were drinking and talking, I experienced a terrible temptation to lead the thief in there. Santiago would see that I got out of this. There was, however, a slim chance that he would not be able to help, and I might blow our deal in the process. No, I was on my own here.

We reached my room. Something about this entire fiasco didn't ring true. This guy seemed more nervous that I felt, almost as though if I were to call his bluff, he would crumble. But I wasn't willing or prepared to take that chance. I had heard too many stories about North Americans and Europeans languishing in Colombian prisons for years under just the same sort of setup. They were invariably held until they could raise tens of thousands of dollars in payoffs; only then could they secure their releases, complete with horror stories of the treatment and the conditions.

I slipped the key into the lock and popped the door open. The housekeeper was in my room, cleaning, and the cop ushered her out in his best authoritarian Colombian manner. I crossed the room to my suitcase, unlocked it and pulled out $2,000. This cop and the two outside combined didn't make that much money in a year. He laughed at me and motioned toward the door with a shrug of his shoulders. He pulled the gun from his pocket. I threw up my hands in exasperation.

"C'mon, man, what the fuck do you want?"

"Mooch, mooch more than thees, señor. We are too many for so leetul."

I reached into the suitcase and handed him another $2,000. He knew he had me for everything. He became relentless. "Señor, plees, $10,000 may be enough, but thees is too leetul."

"Look man, I don't have $10,000, you fucking thief, and if I did, you wouldn't fucking get it."

"Okay, señor, then I have thees moneys now, and ju com weeth me."

"All right, look, man, I have $4,000 more, and that's all I have, not a single fucking peso more."

Just what he wanted. He knew he had everything now, and he was a different man. He explained that this was simply business, he needed a leetul money for his beeg family. He became apologetic, almost friendly. The Colombians have a great fondness for their weaponry, and he proudly showed his .38-caliber revolver for my admiration. As I looked at the pistol in my hand, the thought went through my mind to hold this guy up at gunpoint, call hotel security and make the little shit squirm, but as those brave thoughts were coursing through my mind, I noticed the two machine gunners standing on the street corner, looking up at my window. I returned the gun to his waiting hand and got a sense that he felt what had happened inside of me. He thanked me profusely and left. I had just built a new house for his family.

I rushed next door to where the boys were partying and banged on the door. Santiago opened it, and he could see that something was amiss. I poured out my story. When I was done, there was a moment of silence.

"He got all your money?" Santiago asked.

"That's right. Every fucking penny."

The Colombians cracked up. They laughed for the rest of the day. For years afterward, every time they had the opportunity to tell that story to someone who had not heard it, they laughed just as hard. I was amazed and upset. I had expected them to go after this guy. Instead, they called it "the Colombian IRS system." I stormed out of the room. That was all the money I had in the world. Sometime later that day, Santiago came into my room and put $2,000 on my bed. I felt better. I smoked a couple of golden reefers with Jerry.

I needed to get drunk, so I wandered into the Barranquilla night in search of trouble. I found myself in a bar—typical of the Colombian night scene—where every customer had his own waitress. This woman's job was to hustle drinks for the establishment, and she was not compensated by the bar but received her compensation from her customer. Between drinks she would sit at the table with the customer and fetch whatever he needed: cigarettes, food, more drinks. This arrangement more often than not resulted in the customer accompanying the lady to her living quarters. My waitress was understandably certain that she had scored heavily, gringo and all, something rare for this part of town. She was the envy of the rest of the girls at this little establishment, and she got my drinks for me and I got drunk. Before I got too drunk, however, she got me out of there and into a taxi, and off to her house we sped. While in the cab, I got the uneasy feeling that she and the cab driver were planning something that would be a repetition of earlier events. But in my drunken state, I figured this was simply residual paranoia, and I settled into the ride. She and the driver babbled on in a coastal Colombian Spanish that I was going to require some time to understand. We jarred and bounced over potholed, darkened streets, and the two of them prattled on as he drove. I looked blearily from the window. We were quite a distance from the hotel.

We pulled up in front of a small white stucco one-story house in a neighborhood filled with the same and got out of the cab. She paid and walked to the front door. This was some door. It was iron, with a deadbolt that required a key to enter and leave. All the windows were barred, presumably to prevent unwanted intruders. I felt another twinge of paranoia as she locked the door behind us and pocketed the key

I settled down with a glass of *aguardiente*, a joint, and a small line of cocaine. I was too fucked up to be of any use to this woman, and finally, in a huff, she gave up and fell asleep.

As she slept, I investigated the house and found no way out. I looked through the barred window in the living room and saw the taxi parked just fifty yards away. For sure I was in danger. I looked everywhere but could not find the key. I was beginning to panic.

"Hey, baby! Wake up! I gotta go. Gotta lotta stuff to do. Wake up!"

She wouldn't stir. Dawn was upon us. Finally I dragged her out of bed to the door and pointed at the lock. "Open this fucking door."

She seemed to have another plan. She tried to convince me to forget about leaving and come to bed. I made it very clear that if she did not open the door, she would have more trouble than she could handle. This she understood, and she found the key. I sprang from the house like a wild animal released from a cage and ducked into an alley behind the house. The taxi was still parked up the street, and the driver appeared to be asleep. I darted across the street and kept running.

I had absolutely no idea where I was or how to find my way, but I knew that if I kept walking a taxi would eventually appear. The sun was coming up when I slipped back into my hotel room. A day later, we were on the Avianca flight for Miami.

Adiós, Barranquilla.

EIGHTEEN

"**HEY, BRIAN,** you wanna read the paper?"

"No thanks, Ric. I don't read them."

"Whaddaya mean, you don't read? I see you read all the time."

"No, man, not newspapers. Don't read them, don't like them, don't believe them."

One guy puts thirty-five cents in a newspaper machine here, and everyone in sight takes a paper on the same thirty-five cents. Not much changes for most people here. No reason, no help, no love.

Eight-forty a.m.

"All right, from now on, everything goes inside your locker except for your shoes and one picture. Anything that doesn't fit there has to go."

An old rule is suddenly, arbitrarily, enforced. The Cubans complain the loudest. They have more stuff than anyone else. The curse of stuff, even in prison.

"*Hijo de puta! Nunca jamás. Nunca jamás.*"

They don't really shake us down on the freeway. They don't even look over here, because we have no place to keep any contraband. We don't even have room for what is permitted.

José comes by to return my earphones. "Whatcha doin', mang?"

"Working, just working. Got eleven letters done today. Copied a lot of shit that needed copying. Been a great day. How's by you?"

"Jus' doin' it, mang. Time, homes, time. They want all of it, mang, every motherfuckin' second, homes."

"That's okay, man. Listen, man, you can call me Brian, but not homes, all right?"

"Okay, homes. Here's your earphones, homes."

I walk by SHU tonight and see through the rarely opened door that they're letting a physician's assistant enter so he can administer to an injured occupant. Monitoring equipment blinking red and orange lights. Hell's antechamber. The vibration is visible, tangible. Sounds from the hole, sounds without vision, sounds from an Edgar Allan Poe story: the shuffling of chains across a concrete floor. Arch pain, otherworldly, compassion-free. I feel myself to be inside a Hieronymus Bosch painting, pieces of my body stuck to the jagged teeth of a gnawing beast—only my body, though. The core of me—my integrity, my humor, my loyalty—is inaccessible to it. The feminine part of me cannot be touched by the machismo of it all. Weep, bleed, die for them, these men in SHU.

There's a small exercise yard in the hole, fifty feet long and fifty feet wide. One of its walls is connected to the walkway that leads to the back stairs to the library. I walk by and look out into the yard through a barred window. I can see three holers running around the yard in their boxer shorts. Their faces are stiff, blank, as though they're too angry to break. One of the punk secretaries walks out into the hallway beside me.

"Hey, you. What do you think you're doing there? Move on now!"

Homemade haircuts on the third tier, ironing service on the second, chatter and TV everywhere. Everybody's got a hustle.

"Hey, Brian, they gave me two shampoos by mistake today. You wanna buy one?"

"Sure, James. Whaddaya need, bra?"

"Buck and a half, homes."

"James, I can't be buying anything if you're going to call me homes. I don't want anyone calling me homes."

"Aright, homes. Jus' kiddin'."

Who the fuck is Homes, and what did he ever do?

"Attention in the yard. Attention in all areas. Brian O'-Dee-a report to the visiting room. Inmate O'-Dee-a to the visiting room. To the visiting room. You have a visit."

"Over here! Name!"

"O'Dea."

"Number!"

"Two oh two nine three dash oh eight six."

"Spread 'em. All right, listen up, brief hug and kiss only on saying hello and good-bye. Anything else, SHU, got it?"

We hold hands and look for relief in each other's faces.

We wave good-bye through concertina wire. She shows her entry stamp to leave, I show my testicles and anus.

Harry, the lawyer who knew the Shaffers, comes by.

"Hey, Bri, come on to the movie with us."

"No thanks, guy. I'm just going to walk. I've got some writing to do later."

"C'mon, Bri. You okay, man?"

"Yeah, I'm all right, just a little sad."

"First few visits'll do that. Once you get a little more settled and have a routine, it'll be easier. Get outta here, man, get to Canada. They have trailer visits, conjugals. See ya."

"Yeah, see you at breakfast. Hey, Harry, going to Attitudinal Healing in the morning?"

"No, Brian, my wife and son are coming, and I haven't seen him in almost two years. Frightening for me. I'll see you at dinner tomorrow, or in the yard."

"G'night, guys."

Susannah feels the time we spent waiting for my sentence to begin was the hardest part. Certainly that's over. "I'm sticking around for the best part of this," she says.

Before this, I took us for granted. Now I am a coward, but I will grow, learn, and let go of everything.

"Stand up count! *Cuenta!*"

"Hey, Brian, got a minute?"

"Phil. What's up?"

"We're gonna have a vacancy on three soon, and we'd like to make sure of who moves up there. Boys thought you'd be right for our neighborhood. You interested?"

"Sure, Phil, but I can't be in with a smoker or any of the Aryan shit, man."

"We ain't that. We just have a white neighborhood. It's not that we don't like black people, man. We just don't like niggers—black ones, white ones, Cuban ones, Mexican ones. You dig?"

"Yeah, I dig. You just keep in touch with me about it, Phil. Thanks for asking me."

Another day falling down. The freeway is more packed than usual as we wait for the 9 p.m. count.

"Whaddaya mean, you Mexican motherfucker? This is the best motherfuckin' country in the world. Tell me one that's better, man."

Guy is black, from Watts, and he still believes those words. Most of these people do. In this country, even the victims of the regime don't get it. What a thorough job our rulers have done. Now he's arguing with one of the Cuban victims, one of those Castro put on a boat and shipped out. He's been in jail since he hit our shore. He doesn't understand the significance of the Statue of Liberty or the Liberty Bell or the Bill of Rights and the Constitution. All he knows of this country is concertina wire, high fences, guard towers, and hand jobs. Fuck this country for what it's done to him.

The hole got busy tonight engulfing the hungry ones who were stealing food from the kitchen. They were walked through the yard with their hands cuffed behind their backs and the cops holding on to the cuffs like there was somewhere for them to run away to.

"Hey, Orabuena, you talk any more when I'm doin' count, I'm gonna find a new bed for you."

"Fuck you, Silva. I didn't say a word man. You're hearin' things."

"One more word, Orabuena, one more!"

Sam the Inkster is back, and I'm walking past his cell.

"Hey, homey," he says.

If I'd had another second to think, I would have kept walking.

"Yeah?"

"Whatcha readin'?"

"Book."

"I know. I know. I see ya readin' all the time."

He clambers out of his web and flashes across the cell to the door. His face is flushed, as the faces of junkies often are.

"But what are you readin' now?"

I show him *Nine Faces of Christ*. He takes it from my hand and studies the cover.

"A book of the spirit," he says.

"Yeah."

"Y'ever read *The Way of a Yogi?*"

"Yeah."

"That's a wonderful book, homey."

"Yeah, it's a great book."

I stand there looking at his wicked face, and I finally see his eyes—he has the gentlest eyes.

"What do you do, Sam?"

"Me, homey? I'm the greatest livin' tattoo artist in the world."

"They sort of frown on that here, don't they, Sam?"

"They put you in the hole, man, when they find your gun. But they can't stop an artist, man. Come in here, homey, come in here an' see my portfolio."

"I tole ju so, mang, I tole ju so. Jur sneakers are nex', mang."

"Shut the fuck up, José. I didn't ask you for a lesson, I asked you if you saw my radio. Son of a bitch."

Top bunk, on my locker, higher than me, middle of the night, a junkie's hand slips past my face, appropriates my radio.

Big-eyed Hermano comes over. "Hey, mang, das fucked up, mang. I gonna find it for ju, mang. Is dose fuckin' *Cubanos*, mang, fuck demn. Wan tine, mang, my phone's missin'. I tell dat fuckin' *Cubano*, dat wan deer, mang, dat skeeny wan, mang, I poot a fuckin' shank in his fuckin' reebs, mang. I tell heem, 'Fuck ju, mang, my phone before jard close or else, motherfucker, ju dead.' Seex o'clock I got my sheet, mang. I find jur radio today, mang, don' ju worry, I find it for ju."

"*Gracias*, Hermano."

"Hey, Brian, that crazy black queen, that tall one, Smitty, he was looking for a set of phones last night, man. Check him."

"Right. Thanks, Joey."

"It's this fuckin' freeway, man. We keep those fuckin' junkies goin'. Everythin' from here ends up in A unit, man, with the fuckin' junkies."

"You're right, Joey."

"Hey, Brian, they took your radio, man, don't give 'em your joy. You're just forty-five bucks from that radio, man. You can't buy your joy at the commissary, man. It's just a radio."

Rivas is the black hack (guard), one of the few decent hacks in this place. He comes over too.

"Lock it all up, man. Lots of motherfuckin' thieves here, man, steal the eyes outta yer head an' come back for the fuckin' holes, man."

"Hey, Rivas, O'Dea don't belong down on that fuckin' freeway, man." That's Dudley, heroin, twenty years, on the third tier. "He's the only one who speaks English there, man. You gotta get him up with us. Fuck, they're stealin' his shit now."

"Yeah, I know, man. I told the old man George he was first. Then I'll put O'Dea up there, right after George. Okay, Dudley?"

"Okay, Rivas. Soon, okay?"

"Sure thing, Dud."

"*Cuenta! Cuenta!* Counting B Range! Counting!"

"Hey, Brian, c'mere. This guy here's sellin' a digital radio. I told him you might be interested in buyin' it."

"Sure am, Ricardo, thanks. Let's have a look. Not bad. Hot, huh?"

"No way, man. I'm sellin' it for a friend, man."

"Looks in good shape. Is that your buddy's number engraved here?"

"Yeah, man, wha's yer problem, man?"

"No problem, man. Get your friend's card and show me his number, and if it matches the radio number, I'll think about it."

"Forget it, man. You a fuckin' cop or somethin'?"

This afternoon I visualized waking up and giving the thief the radio. I gave it away. It's gone now. I'm getting a new one on Tuesday.

"Thanks for the effort, Ricardo. You're a good man."

Derek Mendez, in a nearby cell, has a problem with a big black queen who's stopped by for a look.

"Get away from the fuckin' door, you big black queen, lookin' at me fuckin' piss."

"You must be outta your mind. Don't even put me on that caliber."

"Yeah? Get the fuck away from the door."

"Fuck you, you big white bitch. Don't you ever talk to me that way again or I'll slap the shit out of you."

"Oh yeah?"

"Oh yeah, motherfucker. I'm right here any time you think I won't, honey."

"Fuck you."

"I'd love that, sugar. But I'd need someone with a dick."

Dan was a pot smuggler living in Costa Rica. There was no extradition treaty with Costa Rica, so the DEA kidnapped him, drugged him, and put him on a plane for Mexico, where they could get him extradited. Sixty-year sentence. He's painting a satirical mural for the pool room. One part of it depicts a white guy with a swastika tattoo on his neck and "Mother" inscribed next to the swastika. The white guy is handing off a joint to a black guy as they watch a pool game in progress.

A professional convict, Jimmy Johnson, a mustachioed *chulo* with a hundred tattoos, comes up to the doorway and peers into the room, watching Dan work. "Hey, man, what's that tattoo on that guy next to the toad?"

"It's a swastika. Lot of the guys here have that. Don't you have one?"

"Yeah, I have one. Don't you know what that means, man? That means white power. What you're doin there is a fuckin' insult to us white boys, man. He's handin' a joint to a fuckin' toad, man. Toads got nothin' coming, motherfucker, nothin'. Don't you see how we sit in the chow hall? White on white. Don't sit with no fuckin' toads, man. That goes up anywhere, man, I'll tear the fucking thing off the wall."

"Oh yeah, you don't like it?"

"It's a fuckin' insult to the white race, man. You dig? A fuckin' insult."

We're four pot smugglers in the visiting room at the same time: Dan, me, Ben, BD. Ben sees danger.

"Shit, Dan. He wanted you to take that off right then, man. He's not kidding. In his world, there is no satire or sarcasm. Not when it comes to race, anyway. This is his home, his politics, his government. We don't belong here, Dan. This is not our place, so save your life and take it off."

"You think so?"

"Are you fucking crazy, Dan? Where's the white paint? I'll do it for you."

"All right, all right."

"Fuck that motherfucking Aryan prick, man."

"Hey, Ben, easy."

"No! Fuck him, Brian! We get that fucking Jimmy to cut our hair, do a lotta shit with him, give him a lotta money. No fucking more, man, we cut that white punk off."

Sam shows me how he makes a tattoo gun. When no one's watching, he liberates an electric motor from an adding machine or from a cassette player in one of the offices on the yard. He makes the needle from the inside of a guitar string, and he runs it between two toothbrushes or two plastic spoons whose handles he's warmed and flattened. He carves a groove in them and tapes them together. The mechanical ingenuity comes in when he attaches the motor to the wire by making this little jigger that converts the rotary motion of the motor shaft to an up-and-down motion. I don't quite get it. He gets regular ink from ordinary ballpoint pens. Anyway, the wire pushes the ink under the skin just like a needle in a commercial tattoo gun. Give Sam five minutes in any place with anything electric, he says, and he'll have a tattoo gun made. The rest is art.

"Hey, Sam. Why don't you kick the junk? That's no way of the spirit, man. That's a dead end, man. I know that."

He shakes his head. "I want to, homey, I do want to. But they come up to me with that horse an' they say, 'Inkster, you're the best, man. I'm gonna have this tattoo for the rest of my life, man. I only want you to do it, man, an' all I got's this little bit of horse, man. Will you do it?' An' I try to say no, homey, but after I while I gotta say yes."

Ricardo is reading the newspaper. José is drinking in every word of a letter from his wife, Maria. Santo is counting change. Tony's reading the Bible and listening to The Wave, a new-age FM station. Freddie's drinking coffee, saying, "Fuckin' right, motherfucker." James is coughing. Patricio is wandering the corridors. The *Cubanos* are screaming at one another.

The secret police show up here today. The word is horse and gimmicks—heroin and needles.

"Hey, RJ. *¿Qué pasa, amigo?*"

"Like this: Cowboy went down. Seems some Mexican gang hooked up his mother and was making her smuggle the horse at visits. 'Hey ma'am, ju want jur Cowboy to leev, mang, ju take thees eento the veesiting room to the garbage can by the desk or ju both fuckin' die.' You gotta be so careful, Bri. Mind your own business and don' mess with any of these slime buckets—no deals, no foolin' around at all. Before you know it, they're knockin' on Susannah's door, saying, 'Ju want jur man to leev, well, ju gotta pay us.' Fuck that, man, you don't need any problems. Just stay close. Ever since the feds started lockin' up crack punks, these joints haven't been safe for us white boys. They think we're weak and stupid, especially if they think you have any dough. You kinda got a bit of an upper hand 'cause you speak to them in Spanish and they respect that. Just be careful, Bri. Gotta go, meet me at Spago later, babe. Ciao!"

Ricardo—thirty years, first offense, coke conspiracy—walks by in his boxers.

"Here, Brian, you might need this paper the way you write. Let me know if I can do anythin' else for you. I love you, man. You're good people. We'll be fine, we are fine, we're gettin' out of here."

One of the gentle people in this world. We're here to help each other make it through this time, this trial of faith, faith hardened and quickened in this smithy, this firepit. I am strong. I grow stronger with love, love that comes to me through the telephone and through daily letters, love that it is my privilege to receive but that is not given to so many others here.

Officer Lee.
    "What do you want?"
    "I'd like a pass to the library, please."
    "Come back in ten minutes."
    Ten minutes later.
    "What do you want?"
    "I'd like a pass to the law library, please."
    "Where do you want to go?"
    "The law library, please."

Officer Lee is one of the miserable ones the assistant warden mentioned in his orientation speech. Tell us if you run into someone like that, boys. We want to get rid of them too. Translation of the assistant warden's statement: Any complaints about anything or anyone in this system will result in you doing hard time, cited for the slightest infraction and "eatin' baloney sandwiches, smellin' diesel fuel, with a rollin' zip code."

Resist not.

Law library. Hot and sticky. Springfield, our seeming escapee from the prison's psychiatric institute, is sitting next to me. He's studying coin and rare manuscript trade magazines.

"They said I stole valuable paintings and manuscripts, then I'd mail them to myself—balk, balk, balk, balk, balk, woof, woof, woof, grrrh, grrrh, bow-wow, bow-wow, bow-wow. What was that again? What's your name? Ah yes, D-E-A. Ha ha! Where was I? Rhetorical question. And I would never open—woof woof, grrrh, balk balk balk—them. I'd just put them in storage and never look at them again. That's what they said I did. Woof woof."

Possible case of Tourette's syndrome.

Harry, the lawyer, fifteen years, on my left reading Rumi. Mark, the Canuck, fifty plus forty years, on my right reading a *Toronto Globe and Mail* editorial my dad sent me entitled "Jails: Any Alternative Is Better." Ricardo, sitting across from me working on paperwork for Families Against Mandatory Minimums. BD, fifteen years, behind me reading "California's Suppressed Drug Report" from the most recent Robert Anton Wilson newsletter. Typewriters humming, clicking, whirring out the latest discoveries in appeal-land, a land of no response, a land where the only sound is an echoing No-o-o-o.

———

In groups, differences are exaggerated, become caricatures. One on one, differences seem to melt away, and somehow, briefly, tentatively, I am in union with black or white, yellow, brown, beige. The toughest to find union with are the white Aryan Brotherhood types. Their sole purpose in life is to put everyone else down. That is the sum total of their conversations with me to date. I do a lot of listening, little talking.

"Shit, man, I can't get a response from anyone."

"What's happening, Phil?"

"I'm out in November, but they've got me in this halfway house in Hollywood, and I'm from Orange County. They say they can't send me to Orange County because of bed space. I won't make it in Hollywood, man. Hookers out the front door, queer hookers out back, and dope everywhere. A buddy of mine got released to there, and he was in a room with this Mexican gang member. They were selling dope out of the fucking bedroom window. He said he was going to ask for a room change, but his roommate said if he did that it would be the same as snitching him off. He told the guy he couldn't stay anyway. That night, a dozen of them paid him a visit and told him if he wanted to leave he could go in a body bag; otherwise, he was staying. That night he left the house and now he's serving sixteen months on an escape charge. Shit, man, I've even had blacks and Mexicans tell me that place is fucked. I tried talking to anyone who could help, but they don't give a fuck. I don't know how I'm gonna make it there, man, I just don't fucking know."

Everyone in here is on a seesaw. Even the seemingly clearest among us go up and down several times a week, no feelings hidden. Down is visible, up is equally visible.

"*Cuenta! Cuenta!*"

NINETEEN

I GO TO SEA, WHERE I EXPERIENCE HAPPINESS AND MANY DELAYS

WITH THE COLOMBIAN pot deal lined up, Jerry and I returned to Chicago to hang out. A week later, Richard flew in from Puerto Rico. We met him at the airport. He was smiling.

"I got a beauty," he said.

During the ride from the airport, I sat in the back and Richard rode in front with Jerry. He turned to look at me, his usually somber face transformed. "Okay, this is so good, you won't believe it. She's a hundred-foot Baltic trader, built in 1899 in Denmark."

"Wow. Shit. An antique."

"Man, this is a truly beautiful boat. Seventy-four years in the North Atlantic. And you're going to love this: she was christened the *Fremad* in 1899, and that's still her name."

"My God, the *Fremad*?"

"The original name."

"Far out. Free mad. That's us, that's us."

"I know, I know."

"So what's the catch?" said Jerry, who hadn't said anything until now.

Richard looked a little hurt. "What do you mean?"

"Nothing's perfect," Jerry said. "What's the bad part?"

"Well, uh, nothing, really."

We rode along in silence for a half a minute. "Okay," Richard said. "The only little problem might be that the boat's owned by two guys."

"So what?"

"And their girlfriends."

"We're fucked," said Jerry.

"Shit," I said.

Every time this particular configuration—romance and business—had come to my attention, it was a horror story. They seldom mix.

"Hey," said Richard, who understandably didn't want his parade drenched before we got back from the airport, "they own this damn boat and they say they can damn well do it."

Jerry was silent and so was I. We were so hungry for this deal to happen.

We got our charts together and Richard returned to the Caribbean with the information the *Fremad* crew would need to make the rendezvous at Savan Rock. Everyone was excited. We called the Colombians, and they were ready to load up and head out.

Meanwhile, down in Puerto Rico, the *Fremad* set out for the southern Caribbean with the charts and dates and two couples on board. We sat back in Chicago and waited for word of the rendezvous. It would take about seven days. Seven days passed. Eleven days passed. Two weeks passed.

"The bitches have murdered one another," Jerry said.

This was not the case. Soon, the *Fremad* crew radioed in a report. They'd been buzzing around Savan Rock for days and reckoned they'd drawn quite enough attention to themselves. Fishermen from Bequia were summering on otherwise deserted Savan Island, very close to Savan Rock, and these fishermen had to be wondering. Savan Rock just wasn't that interesting. Also, it seemed, tensions were running high and the two women had had some sort of falling out.

"So what's new?" asked Jerry.

We discussed the situation. Should we have them wait there longer?

A frantic call came in from Rick, one of the owners. They couldn't continue. It took more than two to crew the *Fremad*, and the girls were threatening to kill each other.

"No kidding," said Jerry.

We had the guys stand by in Bequia while we arranged for a friend of ours from Virginia to join them there. This wasn't good enough, though. We needed to do something to hold this together while we sorted out the bigger problem: no product.

We started calling Bogotá, and each time, a friendly voice told us to hang in there, the boat was on its way to meet us. It would be just a matter of time, just a little time. Santiago would look after it.

We waited two more weeks. We spoke directly to Santiago, and he finally wrapped it up.

"Hey, they sunk and all dead," he announced. "Or maybe worse: they say, 'Hey, wow,' and sail to U.S. with our shit."

We all agreed it was a tragedy. Either the Colombians were dead or, as was so often the case, they felt they had to deceive us several times before they could come through. No one really knew why Colombian dealers did this. It was just some exotic cultural quirk.

Another load had to be organized, and it was a joint decision that at least one of us had to be on the *Fremad* to assure Rick and his partner that this was real. Jerry and Richard were invaluable in the United States because they could set up the off-load situation and organize the trucks and warehousing. I was the logical choice. I felt sympathy for the *Fremad*'s owners, wandering in the Caribbean, and I felt confident we'd bring this off pretty soon. Besides, my strong suit always was assuring people that everything was headed in the right direction, even if it wasn't.

Jerry took me to O'Hare Airport. In St. Lucia I was to get on a mail boat that left every two days for the nearby islands, then meet our boat in St. Vincent. The problem was that I'd lost my small money stash to that cop in Barranquilla and had blown through the two thousand. What money we were making on the cocaine was going into this pot off-load. I'd traveled enough to know that a one-way ticket into a foreign country was unacceptable. I reckoned Jerry would pony up a little extra.

"For chrissakes," he said on the way to the airport, "you're meeting a boat there. You're just passing through their crummy island. That's all the Immigration guys in St. Lucia want to know."

"You think so?"

Jerry was holding the purse strings, and he was . . . well . . . a difficult person, and I liked to think of myself as the type of person who would lay down his life before getting into an argument.

"You think so?" I asked again.

"I know so. Good-bye."

I boarded the plane for St. Lucia with a one-way ticket and $200.

We landed and I went into Immigration. The officer asked for my passport and return ticket. Oops. Seemed I had only a one-way ticket. Money? Hmm, not too much. How much? This much. Not good, not good at all. Immigration in St. Lucia was run according to the book. I would not be permitted to enter this island paradise.

I sat in the Immigration room and watched it empty of the happy tourists who only minutes before had been my fellow passengers. They all had a good look at me. They spoke openly of my folly. I was quite embarrassed and shocked that no one offered to help. Worse, I could see no way out of this. All of my buts, all of my you-don't-understands went unheard by this officer. When he broke for lunch, he told his junior that when he returned he wanted a resolution to this matter. He went out without another word.

The subordinate cast a sullen look in my direction. The wind stirred his papers, the room being open to the outdoors, just a tin roof and walls with large breaks in them. Fucking cheapskate Jerry. I'd given up too much of my power to him, and I was beginning to seriously regret it. While I was here on the front lines, he was back in Chicago, probably telling Richard there was no way I was going to get anything like an equal share of the profits from this trip, that he was going to give me $30,000, or something like that. In fact, as it turned out, that was exactly what Jerry was doing. Jerry was one of the greediest people I had ever encountered in this business, and I was beginning to notice that a lot of the people in the trade got pretty hung up on the dough. For these guys, when it came to deals for hundreds of thousands, there just didn't seem to be enough to go around. My problem, on the other hand, was just the opposite: I'd exhibited a lifetime pattern of giving away whatever I could get my hands on. A dollar bill or a bag of them, I'd see it somehow got spread around.

I shifted my butt on the wooden bench. A freshening breeze wafted through the hall and rustled the trees that stood around it.

"I'm in a bit of a jam here," I said, my voice sounding a little forlorn. The junior officer shrugged, as if to say he understood my predicament and wanted to help me but there was nothing he could do. He had his orders, and that was that. A few minutes later he glanced up at me again. I thought I saw some anxiety in his expression. What exactly were his orders?

A half-hour passed. The junior officer got up from his table and crossed over to me. "Mon, I gotta have my lunch now. Within just one hour, I will be back here."

He put a lot of authoritative emphasis on the "here." He turned and left. The breeze rustled the trees and made something rattle on the tin roof. I got up and looked around the room. I looked into the vacant offices. I peeked outside into the street. There was no one in sight.

My heart began to race. I picked up my suitcase and hurried out. I just could not understand what had happened. A bus was barreling down the road toward me. I put my hand out and it stopped. I jumped on and asked the driver if he knew where the mail boat dock was.

"Hang on!" he called.

The bus was filled with people and goats and chickens. I had a strong sense it had not been headed for any pier. The passengers smiled broadly and studied my costly Hartman luggage. They seemed to like having me aboard on their way to . . . wherever they were going.

Fifteen minutes later, we wound down to the shore and pulled in at the entrance to a wooden pier. No one moved but me.

"Um, thanks," I said. "How much will that be?"

"Nothin' at all, sir, nothin' at all."

He smiled. All the women and kids smiled. Even the damn goats seemed to smile.

"God bless you," I said, although apparently He already had done that. I jumped out. The driver let out the clutch and lurched back inland from where we'd come. In the back window, two kids waved at me. That was the Caribbean, then.

Something like a scow was moored at the end of a wooden dock, but that something was the mail boat, and it looked like a yacht to me. I hopped on, and a small, dark-skinned grouchy-looking island man approached me. This was the captain.

"Where you going?" he asked without preamble.

"St. Vincent."

"Twenty dollars."

I paid him and he put the money in his pocket. On the deck with me were a dozen or so other passengers—big women with big parcels, a couple of children peering from behind their mothers' skirts, an elderly gentleman with a cane who might have been blind, a man with a goat—all bound for the small islands where the mail boat stopped. Each of us found a crate to settle on. The smell of fried food wafted up from the hatch. There must have been a galley below decks, but that was apparently out of bounds to all but the crew. The skipper was a tough old salt, a no-nonsense guy who ordered his men around as though their jobs depended on it. They responded in a way that suggested this was true. They hustled and bustled and managed to reshuffle almost everything on the deck. Down below, the engine boomed and sputtered, and the prop kicked up a slow surge at the stern. I settled back against my packing crate and shut my eyes to reflect on my good fortune.

A sudden commotion. I opened my eyes. Everyone on deck was looking toward the entrance to the pier. I looked too, and there, to my horror, were four Immigration officers, including the two who had pulled me out of line. Even as I gaped, they rushed the mail boat. I sat paralyzed, an escaped violator who would now sweat the night away—perhaps many nights—in their island prison. A moment later they were on the deck. The chief officer called to the captain, who snarled a response. They shouted something indistinguishable at one another, and the cops began the search. I looked longingly at the blue stretch of sea that lay between this sordid scene and St. Vincent. The officers approached me. I found myself staring at the cracked decking. They passed me. I looked up to meet my fate, but no one's gaze met mine. They did not, in fact, appear to see me, despite the openly dumbfounded expression I must have worn. Finally, one did look at me.

"'Scuse, mon, but we got to look in that crate there. Could you stand a moment?"

I stood. They looked inside the crate. While they were doing this, a cry of triumph went up, and another officer struggled briefly with one of the shoeless crew. All joined in. When they'd gotten this hapless individual well in hand, the senior officer turned to us paying passengers.

"We're sorry to have disrupted your journey. Thank you. Have a good day."

They departed.

We motored across a short stretch of gentle sea to St. Vincent. The sun was bright but not oppressively hot. The sea was every agreeable shade of green and blue. As we neared the harbor, I spotted the *Fremad*. She was anchored just offshore in the lee of the bay, and looked as though she were posing for an oil painting.

Rick, one of the owners, was waiting for me on the dock. We climbed into a small boat and rode over to the ship. I knew as I climbed the rope ladder onto the deck that I was going to love this assignment. This was the pirate vessel of my childhood fantasies. Every time I'd worn a bandana, with a patch over one eye and my rubber knife in my mouth, I'd imagined climbing aboard a boat just like this one.

"Aahaarrr!" I cried. "Avast, ye hearties!"

All hands were on deck. Instead of rolling their eyes, they actually laughed. They'd been worried prior to my arrival, understandably concerned about shifting around on these waters in such a vessel, looking altogether too much like smugglers. Now they had someone they could share their anxieties with. For Rick, especially, it was a relief to have one of the principals of the load aboard. I assured them that, from now on, things were going to be different, things were going to be okay. I was the only one who had never sailed before, but I was ready to learn. If any of them had any problem whatsoever, they should talk to me and together we'd find a way to overcome it.

We were four: Rick, Amnon, Marty, and me. The girls were apparently on permanent shore leave. We men were comfortable with each other from the start. Amnon showed me to my berth, small and cozy and below the front-deck hatch. I immediately put my suitcase up, slipped into my shorts, climbed back on deck and jumped over the side of the boat into the warm turquoise water, which had been waiting for my arrival.

As I swam, small fish darted around my feet and I experienced happiness such as I'd never known. There had been Chicago and Jerry and waiting and waiting, and then the Immigration cops, and now here I was, free and alive, and I was prepared to spend the rest of my life doing just what I was doing at that moment. I'd finally found what I'd been looking for in every drop of whiskey, every toke of every joint, every line of coke, everything I'd ever sniffed, gulped, or inhaled. I climbed back onto the deck and stepped into a new terrycloth robe. It had been laid out for me next to a tall fresh fruit drink poured over ice with a slice of lime dripping over the side of the glass.

Before anything further, I needed to go ashore, find the nearest telephone and call Jerry for an update. The plan had been that, after I left for the islands, he would call Bogotá to settle times and dates and places. Our Israeli crewman, Amnon, and I took the small boat to shore, and in five minutes I had Jerry on the line.

Mañana, tomorrow. That was the news. The Colombians needed time to gather another load of pot. Santiago and Juan claimed to have incurred great expenses in the loss of the first load, and it was going to take them considerable time to get another together. In the meantime, they thought Jerry might like to move a bunch of coke to help defray their loss. Coke was okay with Jerry; his feeling was that, as long as we had to wait, we might as well make some money to help defray our expenses as well. I complained that the Colombians were simply using us to move their shit, but my complaints fell on deaf ears. We settled on a time and place for our next attempt at rendezvous: six weeks later at the same location, Savan Rock. Jerry, meanwhile, would transfer five grand to a bank in Martinique. Okay. I hung up.

Amnon and I shopped for a few goodies for the trip to Martinique and slipped back to the anxiously waiting Rick and Marty. Everyone was disappointed at the delay, but they all felt more secure in the knowledge that I was aboard for the duration. We now had a six-week, all-expenses-paid holiday sailing the Caribbean. What could be better?

The weighing of the *Fremad*'s anchor was accomplished by slipping a heavy iron bar into a geared pulley system and moving it up and down hundreds of times, as you would a water pump, until the anchor held fast to the side of the boat. This mechanism was part of the original 1899 equipment, and it worked as well as the day the boat first nosed out into the chilly North Atlantic. As the recent landlubber, I was assigned the anchor while Marty and Amnon, who understood the language of sailing and could follow Rick's directions, set the sails. Within a few minutes we were underway, sailing out of the protection of the bay into a sleek and azure sea.

Cruising speed was six knots, and the breeze was blowing over me like a cleansing shower. Surely I had died and arrived in heaven. I stepped back to the wheel with Rick, who began my nautical education with a glossary of terms: a rope was no longer a rope, but a halyard; left became port, right became starboard. I remembered this by remembering that "port wine is left on the table," although, in my case, few intoxicants were ever left on the table. In what was then my accustomed fashion, I learned just what I needed to get by. When I thought I had enough knowledge to make it, I shut down and learned no more. I may have been running around the world alone, but I loved a comfortable groove, however uncomfortable it might be.

We set up watch rotation. Steering was as simple as chasing the point on the floating compass in front of me, which indicated our heading in degrees. It took a little getting used to, as the tendency was to oversteer. I gradually got over that, and steering became my favorite job. I had to be pried out of the seat at watch change.

These were my happiest days—free from drugs, with the exception of a little pot from time to time, and free from the burdens and responsibilities of life on land. Out here, the phone never rang and my only assignment was to be where I was, completely content with my surroundings.

Midnight, my first night at sea, and I was on watch, alone. I sat at the ship's huge wooden wheel and felt like Ahab himself. I looked into our receding wake as we slid over the water and saw that the sea sliding from under the *Fremad* was aglow with phosphorescence. I gaped in astonishment, then went below and woke the lads to show them something they had seen a hundred times before. They slipped good-humoredly back to bed, chuckling about the crazy they'd left in charge in the dark. I went back to the wheel.

Often, in Newfoundland, I had stood on shore, looking out to sea, and a sense of terror would rush me like one of the oncoming waves. Invariably, I'd be forced to avert my eyes. Yet here I was at sea in the darkest night, and there was nothing, not one thing about what I was beholding that I found the least bit frightening. I tried to conjure up sea demons and serpents in my mind's eye, to imagine them rising in the darkness behind the boat. Nothing frightened me.

I stared with deepening intensity beyond the bow to the horizon. I was enveloped then by a rich and unfathomable blackness pierced above by constellations I didn't know and below by their shattered and dancing reflections. I knew myself to be free, for a moment at least, from the demons that had plagued me for most of my life, demons that had lurked everywhere in the dark corners of my childhood, savage Catholic demons placed there by the fearsome God whose love I had never felt. I had been in constant flight from that frightening deity—or his representatives. I looked to the stern. This calm and inky sea, streaked with the glittering radiation of countless organisms, now set me free from all of those lurkers. I was home, filled with the excitement of the beginner.

At some point in the night, I looked at the compass. The *Fremad* had done a one-eighty and was headed back to St. Vincent.

At dawn, Rick came on deck and did some navigating. "Jeez," he said, "I'm amazed we didn't make better progress last night. We've got a good enough breeze."

The others joined us and looked with puzzlement at the readings.

"I think I can explain," I said, and then did, more or less honestly. A moment of silence was followed by a merciless howl of laughter. I remained the brunt of the day's jokes and nautical wit, but none of my new mates were to know how rare such a confession was from a man who had taught himself to erase every trace of responsibility.

As the morning wore on, I could see what appeared to be waves breaking in the distance, off toward the horizon. Minutes later these would be at the front of the boat, then crisscrossing, racing ahead, curious smiles on their playful dolphin faces.

We were snorkeling just off Bequia when the dorsal fin of a shark, bigger than I had imagined such things, appeared fifty feet off the stern. We swam frantically for the boat, but Amnon found himself cut off by the fish. As the rest of us clambered on board, it rushed to him and brushed against him. Amnon called out in terror. We stood frozen, helpless. Then, seemingly out of nowhere, another large, dark shape streaked through the water like a torpedo, just below the surface. The shape struck the shark dead center, and the shark stopped in the water. Amnon performed a desperate breaststroke to the safety of the boat. The dolphin bounced from the water, once, twice, then sped away.

"Hey!" Rick called. "Hey! Thanks!"

"Hey, yeah!" the rest of us called. "Thanks!"

"Thanks!" called Amnon, and no one was more sincere.

The ocean looked as empty again as it had before the shark's appearance.

I haven't seen any of my fellow crew members since the end of that voyage, but no doubt each tells this story as often as I do. It was among the most touching moments of my life.

Fort-de-France, the capital of Martinique, was quaint and pretty. The funds were waiting at the bank for me, and we hung out for a few days before heading back toward Savan Rock. I wanted to be familiar with the area before anything came down. Meanwhile, I was content, the admiral of this fleet of one.

Savan Rock is a craggy outcropping in the Grenadines with little to distinguish it other than its being there. It was, however, close to Savan Island, a larger piece of real estate lush with vegetation. Savan Island was to become my favorite place in the Caribbean. The descendants of New England whalers and African slaves had processed their fish there and used it as a safe haven when storms prevented their return to their home port on Bequia. But Savan Island offered one spectacle that almost erased its charm: a huge, reef-bound hulk, a French cruise ship that had suffered a humiliating end when it ran aground some decades earlier. It perched ominously on the reef, huge holes cut in its side through which the engines had been extracted. It was said that everyone with access to a boat for miles around had come to strip the gigantic ship. The homes of even the poorest fisherman soon had brass- and gold-plated fixtures in their kitchens and bathrooms. Their otherwise simple living rooms were lit by chandeliers, and oak doors led to their bedrooms. Someone even got the immense ballroom organ. When a professional salvage team finally arrived on the scene, they found only the engines intact. It was said that the wreck had become a magnet for the crews of other vessels, and that some had strayed too close, been battered against the hulk and gone to their graves.

As far as I was concerned, the farther we stayed from the wreck the better. When I was growing up in St. John's, we would occasionally attend Mass at the Roman. Catholic basilica. Others might find this type of architecture awe-inspiring, but I found it frightening. The nave was the largest interior space of my childhood. Every niche and recess hid statues of the bloodied and beaten Jesus, who loomed down on me from gigantic crucifixes. No matter how often I came upon them, I would be frightened out of my breath. The altar had a huge and bloodied Christ just removed from the cross, with his head in the lap of a defeated and broken-looking Mary. On the wall just inside the entry was the largest crucifix with the bloodiest and most disfigured Jesus I have ever seen. Every time I entered the building, I would, without fail, be overcome by anxiety, and I could hardly raise my eyes once inside. My breath would come in short gasps only, and my chest would fill with an aching, burning, anxious heart.

If I peered at the corpse of the cruise ship through my Minolta binoculars for a moment too long, its ghost elicited all of these unintegrated feelings of my childhood. She was the only sea serpent I was to encounter in these otherwise peaceful waters, and like all the demons of my life, she was man-made.

We finished our reconnoitering of Savan Rock and departed.

The island of Bequia was a favorite stopover for us. Its bay harbored the only settlement, and we could drop anchor in that bay no more than a hundred yards from shore. On the right, there were openings in the cliff face. They looked like windows and in fact were windows: this was Moon Hole, named for the hole that pierced a towering outcropping in the cliff. If you were standing in the right place at the right time of year, the moon would appear in the hole. Developers from Chicago had built houses into the cliff for those who truly wanted to get away from it all and had the millions to afford it. When the deal was done, I decided that one of these houses would be mine.

The ancestors of the people of Bequia were New England whalers who had come during the height of the whaling industry, when whales were harpooned by hand from small rowboats. These whalers stayed and, like the fishermen of Savan, married the descendants of African slaves who had been brought to the island by British slave traders years before. The legacy was a tawny-skinned and gentle people. Whenever we would sail into Bequia, even before the anchor hit the water, I was over the side and swimming to shore.

None of this could prevent my importing my own inclinations into this idyllic setting. On the far side of the island, there was a pasture dotted with elegant palms and grazed by cows. Where there are cows, there are mushrooms, and after an evening's rain we would head for the field, where hundreds of psilocybin mushrooms were growing from the patties. I would wander from pile to pile, eating dozens and dozens of the mushrooms. On one memorable occasion, when I should have known I was eating too many, I had great difficulty figuring out whether I was alive or dead. Every now and again, I'd nudge Rick and ask his opinion on the matter. I have not had the pleasure of eating mushrooms since.

On other occasions, we'd sail into Club Med in Martinique. Locals were not permitted access to these resorts, which were strictly for tourists. But these tourists loved to see us, with our great boat and diverting companionship that cost them nothing but a few meals and a few drinks. Thus, six weeks passed almost unnoticed.

I called Colombia and Chicago. All was in order; the trip was a go. We would be loaded with the very best Colombian Gold available anywhere. Then on to the United States and financial freedom.

Before pulling out of Bequia for the final time, we had a going-away party for our island friends and the other boaters we had come to know over the weeks of sun and fun. The evening was a beautiful one, but we could not do it justice: we were on a mission, our mission, and now all we wanted was to get this trip underway. We were as ready as any crew could have been.

The next morning, butterflies in our stomachs, we pulled out of the safety of Bequia harbor and, with a perfect breeze behind us, sailed to Savan Rock.

We were first to arrive, and we settled down to circle the bleak profile of the rock. One day lengthened into two days, two lengthened into three, three into seven. It seemed we needed to make contact with Chicago and Barranquilla again. The catch was that, when we'd left Bequia, we'd said we were going home. Best not to go back there now, blow our story, and bring suspicion down on ourselves.

We headed for Mustique, a small scrub-covered island inhabited only by such fauna as Mick Jagger, Paul McCartney, and members of the royal family. We could expect to find the place agreeably empty in summer.

There was one small, quite expensive hotel with a couple of housekeepers in attendance. The radio phone system was powered by automobile batteries and protected by a combination lock. It took me a couple of days and a number of dollars before the custodians could be persuaded to reveal the combination. We called Santiago in Colombia. He could not understand what was going on. He'd had a call from his boat's captain the day after we were supposed to meet them at the rock. The captain had complained we were a no-show. Santiago directed them to rendezvous again one week from the day of our call.

We spent the next six days exploring every uninhabited rock in that part of the Caribbean. We had fun, certainly, but we were getting edgy, and it was getting hard for any of us to hide it. At the end of that week, we headed back to find no Colombians. For three long days we cruised the empty waters around Savan Rock. I finally pulled the plug and directed the boat back to Mustique. There was no difficulty gaining access to the phone now that I knew the combination. This time Santiago had heard nothing from his people. He said his next step would be to get in touch with the families of the boat crew, which would take him a few days. We should hang out in the area and call again in three days. I hung up and could feel Rick's gaze from behind me.

Everyone had so much time invested already, I was able to persuade them to hang in just a little while longer. It was becoming harder and harder to keep the respect I needed. Mutiny was imminent. We kept going, circling the rock for another three days before finally returning to Mustique. This time Santiago had to agree with us that the load had been lost. No one had heard from the crew, and they had no idea how to go about looking for them. The only option was to put together another load and make plans for a pickup at the same coordinates six weeks hence.

The guys were practically breathing down my neck as I spoke to Santiago, but they couldn't understand the Spanish. I had a few minutes to formulate how I would ask them to hang in for another attempt. In the end, I played on the time investment already made and the vast amount of money lost so far by the principals. I assured them that I would get some money for each of them to enjoy while we waited. They agreed. I called Jerry.

Jerry went crazy, as was his way. Eventually, he calmed down enough to understand that I had the crew for another six weeks and we needed money in the bank in Martinique, fast.

"Shit. How much?"

"Ten thousand."

"Are you out of your fucking mind? Ten thou—"

"You don't like it, Jerry? Pisses you off? That's good. Forget it then. I'm not hanging out one day longer in the empty ocean with guys we're cheating. I'm done."

"Fucking hold on! Fucking hold on! Did I say no? Did I?"

He promised that the money would be waiting for us when we arrived in Fort-de-France. It was.

Another six weeks: island hopping, playing with the tourists and natives, forgetting what we were about. We got along as though we were a new crew on a brand new venture, and time flew by as though in a dream.

We headed back and circled Savan Rock for two days. At the end of the second day, the crew decided they were not going to waste another second on this trip and they would return me to where they found me and wash their hands of us. They headed for St. Vincent. En route, I was able to persuade them to pull in to Mustique once more so that I could call Jerry and make arrangements for my ticket out of St. Lucia.

No one came ashore with me. As a matter of fact, no one was speaking to me except on an as-need-to basis. I got Jerry on the line and told him of the mutiny.

"What the hell?"

"Jerry, man, if you have any hope for this trip, you better get Santiago on the line and meet the boat when it arrives in St. Vincent; otherwise, it's a lost cause."

"Shit."

"That's how it is."

The next day Jerry and Santiago walked onto the deck of the *Fremad* for the first time. They faced a hostile crew, but a crew that still wanted to be convinced that this could happen. Santiago pulled a Polaroid photo out of his breast pocket. It showed a boat pulling out of the port. It was laden to the gunwales with pot, Santiago said, the day it left for the rendezvous with us. He'd taken the picture himself. The boys passed the photo back and forth in silence. Finally, Rick spoke.

"We're not going back there without you."

"I'm coming," said Santiago.

Rick looked at Jerry.

"Yeah, shit, sure," Jerry said.

Our spirits lifted. If Santiago was willing to be an active participant, this thing was happening.

Later that afternoon, Jerry explained that he was needed more in the U.S. than on a boatload of pot. He was a good talker, Jerry, and a better screamer, but his best feature was his ability to sell the product once it hit shore. I could make no objection to that, and I was realizing I didn't much like being around him, anyway. Without further ado, he flew back to Chicago.

With Santiago aboard, we set sail for Savan Rock. The man was a natural on the water and entertained us with tales of his years as a youth in the Colombian merchant marine.

No one was waiting for our arrival. We sailed around the rock for another two days. I had every nook and cranny of its every face memorized. Santiago had us head for Mustique.

The innkeepers were beginning to wonder about us. We were the only visitors they'd had since last season, and now we had a Colombian aboard who was doing all the talking, a Colombian who looked like a gangster sent over from central casting.

The Colombians on the other end of the telephone assured Santiago that the boat had not returned and had not been heard from. We agreed to one more pass around the rock.

We sailed back, circled the barren hump, the hulk of the wrecked French liner looming in the distance. At the end of the second day, we called the deal off. Santiago was willing to return to Colombia and set the whole affair in motion for another boat and another load, but the guys were burned out. They were not actually in this business as a rule and were not used to the disappointments and endless waiting that we smugglers knew to be part of every deal. They wanted to forget all about us and get on with their lives, and in that respect, we probably did them all a favor. They would have left us on Mustique if they had not been afraid of Santiago, who had that way about him. With reluctance and resentment, they sailed Santiago and me on to St. Vincent and dropped us off. I never saw that wonderful boat or its crew again.

Not for the first time, I was between deals. Santiago and I hopped the mail boat to St. Lucia, and from there we bought tickets to Chicago. It was a longish flight, long enough that we began to plan our next adventure. By the time the plane was circling O'Hare, we knew what we wanted to do. Now we had to convince Jerry.

TWENTY

THE SAME PEOPLE are in the library every day, banging out briefs and appeals for themselves or other inmates. It is an unending process of pointing out to the judiciary that they may have fucked up in their sentencing. Judges do not actually appreciate an inmate of a federal prison pointing out to them how one of their colleagues may have fucked up. Yet hope persists. Once there is no hope, when these poor, seeking, typing sonsabitches no longer care, when they realize this is all they have to look forward to for the rest of their lives, they will deal with it in a dark, dark way. Can you feel their pain and desperation? No? No one can. No one hears the cries or sees the tears or understands the fear.

"Count time! Stand up count, gentlemen! *Cuenta! Cuenta! Cuenta!*"

Harry shares with me his experience of thirty-eight days in the hole. "Yeah, it's a 100-series shot if you don't piss for them, Brian. That's the most serious offense there is. If for any reason you cannot pee—shy bladder, prostate trouble, any reason—it is considered to be an unwillingness to piss, and you are charged as though the urine sample was returned to them dirty. And that's the same as murder."

"What, Harry? You can't give them blood? You can't let them lock you in a room with all your clothes off, alone, then produce it for them? No way out?"

"The Bureau of Prisons' policy states that you must be observed pissing for them. A guard is seated approximately one foot from your penis while you stand there in front of him with your pants at your ankles. He looks directly at your penis as the urine is passing out through the hole into the cup."

"Jesus fucking Christ, Harry. I'll never be able to piss for them. I can't even piss in a public restroom. Hell, I have a difficult enough time pissing if I know someone is waiting at the door to get in after me. It's fucking fucked, Harry. These bastards drink and smoke, and we are caged even deeper if pot shows up in our piss."

"Plenty of them do dope too, Brian. Don't let them fool you. The only difference is that when they get piss-tested, they have plenty of warning so they can clean up their act, and they are not observed pissing. But, Brian, time to use what you've learned spiritually—your Sufi shtick and all that. Time to use that stuff you're always sharing with others. You've got to get through this thing, man. Don't let it or any part of this experience defeat you, Brian. You have too much to give."

"Hey, homey, how're ya doin'?"

"Okay, Jimmy, okay. How 'bout you?"

"Aright, Brian, aright. Hey, I need to talk some business with you, man."

"Okay, Jimmy, fire away."

"I need to get some money moved."

"Whaddaya mean, Jim?"

"Money moved, from one place to another, and I need someone I can trust."

"Thanks for thinking of me, Jimmy, but I can't help you."

"Well, that's clear. Thanks for not fuckin' me around. I like straight."

Yeah, I'm sure he does. He's trying to set me up for something. In prison, you're always doing some sort of business— negotiating phone time, buying cash or clean underwear. But I wouldn't do business with him if it was my last opportunity ever.

Bad Billy makes a ring from a Canadian quarter in his metal shop today, then gives it to me. When it comes to metal work, there are few better than Billy. On the street in 1978, he came to my house in Chatsworth one day with a submachine gun he'd made. He'd made the silencer too. He fired the thing off in my driveway. It sounded like someone spitting.

Head cold. I can't drag myself out of bed. As I lie here, I notice something strange. We're all locked down on the unit, in our own ranges. Normally the place is open at 6 a.m.

"Hey, Rivas, open the fuck up, man, you fuckin' cop."

"I'll open you up, motherfucker. Now shut the fuck up an' go lie down and lick yo' nuts."

There's a continual chatter in here about goings-on in other prisons. There has been a riot in Talladega Prison, Alabama. They're holding a lot of *Cubanos* there, and the *Cubanos* are getting pissed off about being held in prison for years with no charges, no trial, no sign of release. For them, there is no end in sight. They are living Kafka's *The Trial*. The word is, they have taken a dozen hostages. And here come the cops.

"Gomez! Alvarez! Delgado! Stand in your cells!"

One by one, they begin rounding up the *Cubanos*, and they disappear through the unit exits to who knows where. The authorities are afraid of a sympathy strike. The last time the Cubans went off, it took only a couple of days for the rioting to spread nationwide. So now the Bureau of Prisons is carrying out some preventive injustice as they take the Cubans out of here in handcuffs, in their boxer shorts and T-shirts. Frightened looks on their faces, muttering incomprehensible words, they shuffle out to a mysterious destiny. I can hear the diesel engines of the waiting buses, the mobile prisons, and it's rolling zip codes for the Cubans. My heart bleeds for them, caught by birthplace in a web, their meager property left behind in their little eight-by-eight-foot cells to be ripped off by the waiting vultures. I wonder, if the Canadians in one of their prisons lost it, would they track us all down and ship us too? I think so.

Now all the freeway dwellers are fighting over the emptied cells, but I can hear them talking, making sure I get the first choice. I've been on the freeway the longest.

"Ask Brian if he wants it, and if he doesn't, then it's mine."

"Thanks, fellas," I call, "but they're keeping a cell open for me on the third tier, so go ahead."

"Hey, O'Dea, c'mere." It's Rivas, the best cop we have here. "Listen, O'Dea, don't get caught up in that third-floor bullshit, man. They are racist pigs there, an' you don't wanna have any part of their shit, man. You aren't that type of guy. You're a good man, O'Dea. Don't get involved in their bullshit."

"Y'know, you're right, Rivas. I don't need that shit. And besides, I kind of like it right here on the freeway. I think I'll stay right here."

"Hey, Brian! Up here!"

I look up and see Marty's head craning out over the railing. "What's up, Marty?"

"Are you comin' up?"

"Come on down a minute."

A minute later, he's at my bunk. Marty's on the third with the Aryans.

"Marty, I can't. I wouldn't mind bunking with you, man, but I'm into doing my own time. Those guys up there are all over your time, Marty. You got to toe that philosophical line. I can't do my time like that. I just want to do my own time and stay away from all that shit. You understand, Marty?"

"Yeah, but it doesn't have to be like that."

"Marty, you're a good guy, a nonsmoker even, and we both know that's hard to find here, but I've thought it over. I'm not going to live on the third floor, man. Find a cell on another floor and I'm there, but for now the freeway is great. Thanks, though."

Fuck white power.

The hole is emptied to handle any of the Cubans they didn't take to an Immigration holding facility. The prisoners from the hole stream into the freeway—black eyes and tattoos, junkies and thieves. The place is buzzing. I move four bunks north, under a light and away from the common john, closer to the screaming TV and slapping dominoes, but still an improvement. These new faces on the freeway are not happy faces, and the whole place feels angrier. Out of sixty guys in my direct vicinity, two are white and the remainder are olive-skinned Mexicans and American blacks. Trading, bartering, and bickering is happening over the spoils from the departing Cubans. The guys from the hole are the vultures in the pecking order, ripping and tearing at the socks and boxers.

"I had that firs', motherfucker! Git yer han's off, man, less you wanna lose 'em."

Night. Night is Sam's time.

"Hey, homey."

"Sam. Hi."

"Look at this, homey. Look at this one."

"Sam, that's beautiful, man."

"You like it?"

"It's great."

He takes the sheet of paper back from me and stares at the demon-faced bat he's drawn. "Yeah," he says, approving his own work.

"Sam, how'd you get into this? I mean, who taught you?"

"Had to, homey, had to."

"Like, had to be an artist?"

"No. Had to cover the tracks on my arms. That's where I started, on my arms. Started with this here big dragon."

"Wow."

"That's what I've been doin' all these years, chasin' the dragon an' chasin' him hard. These here tattoos are my guardians. They protect me. Them and being crazy."

"You're not crazy, Sam."

"Shh, homey. Keep your voice down. Nobody knows that."

True. His bizarre collection of cast-off eyewear, his ink-stained clothes. The man takes a keen interest in having the authorities, and everybody else, think of him as a little—no, a lot—crazy. He actually pours ink on any new clothes he comes by.

"When you're out, Sam, you could make a living as an artist."

"They're lined up outside my cell, homey."

"I know they are."

"It's a shot to get caught tattooin' or havin' a tattoo gun."

"I know it is."

"It's the hole."

"I know it is."

"I'm willin' to pay the price."

"I know you are."

"It's my thing now."

"Right. You could do it outside."

"I don't know about that, homey. I don't know. Not now."

"Sure you could."

"Joy used to say that."

I knew Joy had been his wife. We sat in silence a minute.

"What happened to Joy?" I finally asked.

"Joy? Oh . . ." He stopped. "Joy?" he asked again. "Oh, me an' Joy were just shootin' up at home one day an' she just sorta lay down an' she said, 'Oh, baby, I think that was too much' an' she died."

I couldn't think of anything to say.

"That was a lotta years ago."

"I'm sorry."

"Lotta times, I'd lie down where she died an' call out to her, to her spirit, like. 'Joy, baby!' I'd call. 'Can you hear me callin' you, baby? Where are you? Why don't you talk to me, mama? I miss you too much. Come back, Joy!' Stuff like that."

He'd turned his face from me in the dark cell.

"Sometimes I'd fill the syringe with enough horse to kill anybody. I'd lie down on that spot where she died, I'd slam, I'd start cryin', I'd say, 'I can't wait any longer, baby, I'm comin' to you.'"

But he never died. He just went back to prison, over and over and over.

"Before I got to stayin' in prisons pretty much all the time, I'd go up to her grave in Rose Hills Cemetery, in Whittier. I'd lie down on this plot next to where she's lyin', an' I'd talk with her, cryin'. I'd plead with her to help me. I'd go there sometimes in the evenin' with a bottle of wine and a couple of joints, an' I'd talk with Joy for hours. I'd fall asleep on her grave an' wake up when the sun rose. Then security would come along an' find me there an' throw me out. They didn't want no sick junkies in their cemetery."

"It's all going to be so different than ever before, Sam. When we're out, it's all going to be different."

"Maybe, homey. Maybe I'm changin'. Maybe I am."

———

In the visiting room, if you want to take a piss, you have to have a cop in there with you. With my problem, if I want to go, the visit has to be cut short so I can go back to my cell.

"Hey, Brian, ju back so soon, mang. Bad veesit?"

"No, I had to piss."

"Ha ha ha, ju had to pees. What the fuck ju mean, ju had to pees?"

"I had to piss, José. I have a hard time pissing with some cop looking at my dick."

"Ha ha ha, ju what, mang?"

"Shy bladder, José. They called my friend Harry in for a piss test, and he couldn't piss for them. He got thirty-eight days in the hole and a 100-series shot for dirty urine. He offered to take all his clothes off, get locked in a dry cell, the whole bit, man, let them take blood, anything, but they still gave him a shot, all because he couldn't piss. They wrote on his report that he was unwilling to produce a urine sample for them."

"Tha's fucked up, mang, real fucked up."

"It sure is, José."

TWENTY-ONE

I FOOLISHLY VOLUNTEER FOR A DANGEROUS ASSIGNMENT

SANTIAGO SAID he wasn't happy.

We were waiting for Jerry in a quiet corner of the family restaurant. Santiago had taken off his immaculate suit coat and draped it carefully on the back of the chair. He'd shot the cuffs of his perfect shirt. He'd looked at me from under his dark Indian brows. "So. Three loads, no? Vanish." His always raspy voice had a tiny edge to it, and for a moment, despite myself, I thought of the pistol he carried. He took out a cigarette and looked at it with huge seriousness. He wanted me to understand that he was worried about where this pot had gone. "Vanish," he said again. "*Mucho dinero, amigo, mucho dinero.*"

Not that it was my fault, dammit. I wasn't really sure if he'd done all he said he'd done. Something about the whole boat fiasco failed to ring true, but what the hell? It was history. We were still working together.

It was like he shared my thoughts. "*Sí,*" he said—he pronounced it as the lisping Castilian "thi"—"*Sí.* Thees is a very good idea we have. Very excellent plan. But, Brian, you must do something, maybe something hard. You must find the airplane, right? A big one. You find it, and I load it in Riohacha, right?"

Then he smiled. I always knew Santiago liked me. I always liked him. I nodded. "That's right. That's right. And who's paying?"

He smiled again. "You pay for thees airplane and all theese people. I front you the pot—fifteen, twenty thousand pound."

"That's right," I said.

"*Sí*," said Santiago.

Jerry reacted without enthusiasm, but he did not actually scream or swear, and before long it was clear that he liked the plan in principle. We agreed that he would head to Riohacha with Santiago while Richard and I flew to Atlanta to meet Richard's old friend, Dick—Dick the Courier.

Dick claimed to have logged some two thousand hours in medium and large twins, including DC-3s, on overnight runs for Purolator. He was now ready, anxious even, to join the world of dope smuggling in a major way. According to Richard, Dick had great flying instincts, truly loved airplanes, and knew a lot of kindred spirits in the South.

We met him at the Holiday Inn in Atlanta, and I liked the man immediately. He was young, a genuine Southerner, gangly, with short brown hair and lightly freckled skin. He spoke with a trace of a drawl until his third bourbon, when his true ancestry surfaced as a full-blown whole-hog drawl.

Dick felt the best plane for the job was the DC-6, a real airliner and a military workhorse for years. Richard and I nodded.

"Uh, I haven't actually flown a four-engine plane before," Dick said, somehow managing to nod as he said it.

There was a brief silence. Richard and I looked at him steadily.

"Wouldn't be, like, that much more complicated than a twin." He nodded again, and we nodded too. "You give me a shot at it, and I'll buy you a plane and read the manual and all. Just gotta get the, you know, the theory, like."

In that moment, I was somehow overpowered by a thrilling sense of the man's intrepidity. "I'll copilot for you," I said. We were both nodding now, and I could feel Richard looking at me from the side. A moment after I spoke these words, I was wondering why, precisely, I had. In retrospect, it was probably my flying experience that prompted me to volunteer. That experience was zero.

We gave Dick a couple thousand dollars. He would investigate the DC-6 market and meet us back in Chicago in a week.

Richard had another friend, Bob, in Gainesville, a large university town in the gently rolling hills of north-central Florida, home of Gatorade and one of the best pot markets in the new South. We wanted a look at the territory, so we rented a car and drove from Atlanta to Gainesville. We met at President Ed's, widely regarded as the South's ultimate rib house.

Bob was a gentle and idealistic capitalist, a laissez-faire pot broker who stayed away from everything else. He was well liked, honorable, and had cultivated a great many close and trusting relationships in the upper levels of the pot smuggling and distribution business in the deep South. He was known to be well connected to larger loads. Besides his reputation, he had a good sense of humor, believed in fair play and was possessed of genuine human decency. His network reached into most large Southern universities and could absorb ten thousand pounds of pot in a week. He could have the money back in your hands in two or three weeks. He was a good guy to do business with and, as I was to discover later, a good guy to have as a friend.

I had little hesitation about giving Bob some notion of what we planned. He listened with attention and, when I was done, looked at me carefully.

"All right, my friend," he said, "I have some acquaintances —I'm talking about good old boys in the very best sense— men who've served our country with honor. These men are now making their living as . . ." and here he paused for just a moment ". . . as aircraft mechanics."

"Uh-huh," I said.

"They've recently leased an old airstrip in southern Georgia to carry out repairs on all types of planes, including some Air Force planes."

"Uh-huh."

"Now, Brian, this small town in Georgia is a very poor town. It's never enjoyed its share of the goodies, American style. As you can imagine, the people of this town view my friends as heroes of a sort, and their work is expected to bring great benefit. Howzabout, if you have an airplane and need somewhere to, say, keep it, or possibly land it, putting it there? I'm confident my friends would be more than happy to talk it all over with you."

We invited Bob to join us in Chicago, and he graciously assented. When we left, I could feel it again: that surge, that excitement, the adrenaline of the deal. No amount of prior frustration could extinguish that rush.

A week later, Jerry was back from Colombia, and he, Richard, and I met Dick and Bob in Chicago. We hung out at the family restaurant. No question, the service was good.

Dick made his report. He'd located a DC-6 in Alabama. One never knows, when hiring expertise, whether the hiring cart may precede the expertise horse, but in this case things worked out to our advantage. Dick had uncovered a gentleman broker whose office was at a large Alabama airstrip, an aviation graveyard full of tired old radial-engined work planes. This tried-and-true son of the South was willing to allow a plane he represented to go missing for a few days. His paltry fee would be $100,000, with just $50,000 up front.

Dick explained that a DC-6 is a large aircraft. It has an overall length of 106 feet and a wingspan of 117 feet. It's tough, it's possessed of a great undercarriage for landing on rough strips, and it's powered by four R-2800 Pratt and Whitney engines, each putting out 2,500 horsepower and very reliable if maintained at all properly. In the hands of a good pilot, a DC-6 will cruise at 265 miles per hour, with a maximum payload of over twenty-four thousand pounds, for at least three thousand miles.

Our particular warhorse was a beauty, according to Dick, retired from her duties as a military troop transport and shuffled from one small cargo operation to the next. Now her next campaign would be the transport of eight tons of Colombian Gold. Dick was busy reading the flight manuals and was confident he could handle the old girl.

The plane was probably worth only $150,000, but this present offer allowed us to use it for a few days without the tiresome complications of having to buy it and set up an off-shore company (complete with paid directors, corporate charter, and fees) to operate it. The broker was known only to Dick, but if Dick was making an end for himself, we were not offended. The price was right. We were all pleased not to be exposed in any way. When I say "all," I mean all except Jerry, who sniffed and bitched through every event, however exciting. Now he ranted and raved his way through half a gram of coke, then settled down with the concept and agreed to pay.

If you mark a certain small town in the Guajira Peninsula of Colombia as the center and draw a three-thousand-mile radius on a map of the Americas, you'll find that all of the southern and mid-Atlantic United States falls within the limits of our range. But if you allow for low-altitude radar-evasive maneuvering, a high-altitude takeoff in Colombia and navigational deviations based on the location of U.S. radar coverage and commercial aviation zones, and you allow another half-hour for emergencies, our effective range was two thousand miles. This included only the southernmost strip of the continental United States.

That's why we were so happy to hear from Bob that his aircraft-repair boys in the poor south Georgia town of Moultrie would welcome us and were perfectly willing to look the other way while we went about our business. Moultrie was only a hundred and fifty miles from Gainesville, which, as Bob's home, would be our distribution center. Best of all, these gallant grease monkeys would share their facilities in return for the (apparently popular) round sum of $100,000. Jerry went nuts, as I had now come to expect and as he would have done if Bob had told us that the price was $5,000. We had no choice, though. It was a bargain at twice the price.

The runway itself was five thousand feet long and would easily accommodate anything we might want to bring in, including commercial jets. A large hangar guaranteed cover for the off-load and would serve as a place to keep the tractor trailer trucks out of sight while they awaited the load from Colombia. All these considerations are crucial to the success of any airborne smuggling operation. The greatest vulnerability is on the ground, where one's movements are both limited and predetermined by the available roads and facilities. You are rarely seen in the air, and if you are, it is very difficult to throw up a roadblock, given the additional dimensions and freedom of movement. Danger is on the ground, and it is here that the greatest attention must be given to your choice and mode of operation. Moultrie was made to order.

When the meeting was over, Bob and Dick headed out into the Chicago night. Jerry, Richard, and I went next door to a bar to hear about Jerry's trip to Riohacha. Jerry disappeared into the washroom without a word. I was familiar with his pattern by this time. He'd be gone just long enough to crouch down in a booth, trickle some from the nosebag, form one line, two, snort, snort again, stand up, piss, look at himself in the mirror, come out.

"What the fuck?" he asked Richard and me when he emerged.

"Hey, Jerry," Richard said, sort of wearily.

"What's the fucking matter with you?" Jerry wanted to know.

"What are you drinking?" Richard asked.

"We've just ordered bourbon," I chimed in.

Jerry looked at us suspiciously.

"Tell us about Riohacha," I suggested. "How'd it go?"

"Fuck," said Jerry, but quieter. He sat down.

Thus are otherwise sound minds devoured.

Santiago had introduced Jerry to Billy G., the self-proclaimed chief of the Guajiros. Jerry was impressed with the man, who'd shown him a large warehouse filled with Santa Marta Gold, one of the world's most favored pots, and told him they were shipping out loads every day. Billy seemed to be in control in this part of the world, and he impressed Jerry greatly. While they were at the warehouse, the local military chief, a Major Fernandes, showed up to meet with the new gringo and discuss the price for military protection of the load from the area's many *bandidos*. He was a generous man, as he repeatedly reminded Jerry, and his fee for the hour required for the transfer from the trucks to the plane was a laughable $25,000, payable in advance. Then the manager of the salt mine where the shipment was to be stashed showed up as well. According to

Jerry, he was a very "Western" man, seemingly more American than Colombian. It turned out that he, too, wanted just $25,000 when the plane hit his little dirt strip.

Modest as these demands were, the money we needed to pull this off was beginning to add up. Jerry was talking with, well, certainly not excitement, but with a sort of positive energy. I felt the time was ripe to discuss with him the money he had made on cocaine transactions while I was waiting in the Caribbean for the load that never made it. Half of that was my money.

"Jerry," I said, when he stopped to open a fresh pack of Kools, "how are we doing at the bank?"

He fidgeted with the pack, trying to get it open. You'd think a guy who smoked that much could open a pack in his sleep. He didn't look up.

I glanced at Richard. "We're going to need a lot of our money," I said. "That's what I'm seeing."

Jerry got the pack open and pulled out a cigarette, lit it. He looked up. "What money?" he said.

"The money, man, from the business. While I was at sea."

"What about it?"

"We're going to need it."

"How else you think we're going to do this?" asked Jerry. "Fucking beg for quarters? Sell our fucking butts in the Port Authority washrooms?"

"It's starting to add up," I said.

"There's enough," he said.

"How much?" I wondered.

"Enough," said Jerry. He leaned his head back and looked at me through slitted eyes.

Dick left the next morning for Alabama to finalize the arrangements for the plane. Jerry, Richard, Bob, and I flew to Atlanta for our inspection of the airstrip. I sat with Bob during the flight. At one point, he leaned in close to me.

"Hey. Been watching your friend, Jerry," he said. "Your colleague, right? I think the guy shows tendencies to volatility. I mean, like, erratic."

"Yes," I said. "I've noticed that."

"Know what I think?" Bob said softly. "This guy's ruled by the bag. Know what I mean?"

I nodded. "Cocaine, you mean?"

"I mean cocaine. That's something I never—I mean never—touch. In any sense."

"You're right, you're right. But Jerry's been like that since the day I met him. He couldn't be doing coke every hour."

"Hm." Bob was a little too close for me to turn toward him, but I could feel his mild, worried gaze. "No. Perhaps not. Worries me, though."

"Don't let it. The guy has some sort of personality disorder. We can handle him. I'm not worried—he's hypoglycemic, that's all."

"That's good." Bob sat back in his seat. "Good to hear."

From Atlanta we drove south to Moultrie. It was a beautiful day, and I felt very glad indeed to be alive. I glanced over at Jerry a few times. He was staring balefully out the window. What was going on inside that angry head, I wondered. What did he want? Money? Or did he secretly enjoy the whole lifestyle? Secretly, of course, because he gave no indication that he enjoyed anything whatsoever.

The airstrip was six or seven miles from town, and after we left the paved road we drove two miles on gravel before we saw the hangar and the windsock. The place was wonderfully secluded, surrounded by tobacco and cotton fields. The nearest neighbor was at least half a mile and a country road away.

The repair guys were waiting. They'd rented a trailer and were sitting in the shade, sipping from tumblers. There were two bottles of Jack Daniel's on the table.

The younger of the two waved a lazy arm in our direction. "IIey, lookit, Bill," hc drawled. "Here come some folks look like they need an airplane fixed."

"Well, you're right, Don," said Bill. "And they've come to the right place too."

Bill and Don were recent veterans of Vietnam but still touchingly young and fresh, with grins from ear to ear such as any men might wear who'd just been offered a hundred grand to pick their noses. I stopped for a moment to take in the scene. The sun was hot in a blue sky studded with a few lazy cumulus clouds. The cicadas were singing from a stand of beech off to our left. The soil I'd noticed from the car was sandy and ruddy. Now I took my shoes off and let it squish between my toes. I loved the South.

We did a tour of the facilities, then drove into Moultrie, saw the sixteen streets, the five restaurants, the roadhouse, the undersized Piggly Wiggly. The boys were treated like VIPs by locals desperate for a breath of new life, or new money, anyway. These folks just knew the moment those rich Yankees heard what exceptional repair work they could get done down here, they'd be flocking in and showering good money everywhere. Were we not evidence of this?

The next morning we headed south to Gainesville. We needed about $400,000, and in view of the risks involved, we didn't want to use all our own money. I stayed in Gainesville with Bob while Jerry and Richard headed back to Chicago to collect the needed funds, including fresh investment. Bob showed me the local scene over the next few days, and his business associates offered me storage facilities and transportation in the event that I might like to move some of our product to Canada for my friends there. This was exceptionally thoughtful. We Canadians so seldom saw this quality of herb at reasonable prices.

Meanwhile, Dick was in Alabama with the DC-6, bent over flight and engineering manuals, trying to determine at what point he was prepared to solo without instruction in a four-engine airliner. Finally, he contacted Jerry, and Jerry called me to say that Dick would fly into Moultrie at ten in the morning on Wednesday.

We were all there—Jerry, Richard, Bob, the airfield boys, and myself—standing on the tarmac at 9:35 a.m.

The strip at Moultrie faced the direction of the prevailing winds and on an aviation map would be labeled as 24, meaning 240 compass degrees from north, or almost due west. We were in the shade of the big hangar, already sweating in the humidity and stuck to empty wooden engine crates and broken-down chairs. We'd gotten into a little ice-chest-cold Budweiser and were nervously shooting the shit, the Allman Brothers pounding out dimly audible rockabilly from Bill's truck.

"Y'all sure this courier guy can really fly?" Bill asked. He then made a kind of humorless chuckle. "Hell, a 6 is an engineer's plane, ain't it? Even real pilots need an engineer on a 6, don' they?"

The portable VHF radio crackled occasionally in the background.

"Don't worry, man." I shook my head to dissipate any concern he might have about his hundred grand, and any fears I might have about my own mortality. I was the one, after all, who'd volunteered for a ten-hour flight, twenty hours return, mostly over open sea, at low attitudes, in an aircraft built, as it turned out, in 1949, the year Newfoundland joined Canada. "He knows what he's doing," I added. "Purolator doesn't hire guys unless they're good, do they?"

Who knew what Purolator did or didn't do? I was again living impulsively, trusting what I called my instincts. Perhaps in my heart of hearts I felt that no one should take those kinds of risks alone for a fistful of dollars. Certainly I understood that having somebody along for the ride can mean something when you're in the shit.

The radio crackled and a tinny drawl said, "One, two, three, four, five. Uh . . . you read?"

"Good fucking thing," Jerry mumbled, though nobody heard him but me.

Bill picked up the mike. "Read you, over."

"Yessir, 'bout fifty miles out, over." It was Dick, though his voice was carefully modulated an octave lower, and noticeably crisper than usual. I tried to imagine him alone in the cockpit of a thundering airliner.

"Read you and see you soon. Over."

We all jumped up and ran out onto the broiling concrete taxiway.

"Eight minutes," said the voice from the speaker behind us.

There was a trifling breeze from the west. We stood together, with our left hands shielding our eyes from the sun. The air was heavy, steaming. After a few minutes, Jerry started fidgeting with his pack of Kools, trying to get a last cigarette out.

The sound started as a low, almost soothing hum in the west, beyond the beeches. Within a minute or two it turned into a low-pitched drone that gradually built to a dull roar and then suddenly exploded into an overwhelming, earth-shaking tympanum, a threatening fury of sound and vibration as an immense silver monster, alive, vibrant, appeared from behind the trees and ate the sky over our heads and rattled the teeth in my gaping jaws. My God, this was beautiful, powerful—a Stygian sky-riding thunderwagon. I fell in love.

"Fuck!" screamed Jerry, which may have been his equivalent.

She swept east for a mile, banked left, leveled, and then turned right for the final approach. The prop pitch changed to a deep air-cleaving roar as the underwing landing gear bit into the concrete and the nose gradually and lightly fell forward. She rushed toward where we were standing, abruptly slowed, and finally stopped, props feathered, then still.

Complete silence, save for the ticking of heated metal in the heated air. We were silent too. The front hatch opened, and there was Dick, grinning and scratching his sandy hair. We—all of us—hollered and stomped. He could fly, the sonofabitch.

Dick clambered down. "Y'all hold that for the real thing," he said.

Together we walked around the beast, marveling at her size, her strength, her potential.

We drove into Moultrie and got drunk.

TWENTY-TWO

"HEY BRIAN, how're ya doin'?"

"Mike. C'mon, share this ice cream with me, man. Don't see much of you since they moved you to E unit. How's it there?"

"Beats J unit, Brian, especially that freeway of yours. What a decrepit dump. Hey, looks like you're losin' weight."

"Thanks, man. Not quite yet, but that's the plan."

"Good for you, man. Hey, I gotta go for count—you too. See ya later."

Mike was offered ten years under the old law to plead guilty to a pot conspiracy charge. They did not get a single joint in his case. He turned them down, wanted to fight it, was found guilty, and was sentenced to thirty years under the new law. The way they work it, either you accept their offer or you will be killed in court. If you are indicted, you will be found guilty. If you will not plead guilty, if you make them work for a guilty plea, they will wipe you out. They don't lose any cases. The judges, the prosecutors, the DEA, they're all in it together. There is no getting around it anymore. They have the ultimate weapon: conspiracy.

———

I look back on my first few days here and remember how afraid I was of being friendly with Billy, afraid of what it would cost me. But now I see he was a little boy wanting to share his knowledge, wanting to show off his jailhouse smarts with me, the fish. He was giving everything he could, and I was a scared person for whom every action held so much power.

"Hey, RJ, how're you doing?"
"Cool, Uptown, cool. You know José?"
"*Con mucho gusto*, José."
"Yeah, José is one of the few *Cubanos* they didn't take. Tell Brian what you were sayin' about the Cubans inside the joints all over, José."
"Hey, Brian. These guys with the hostages in Alabama have nothin' to lose, man. They said they want freedom or they'll kill these people, and they will. They been in prison since '81, man—fucking 1981—no trial, no charges, nothin'. When Castro let them go, he emptied the prisons, the mental institutions, and then he sent their jackets—their official prison files—to the U.S. government. The Americans have kept these guys in prison since then. The fifty-six guys here in SHU are in the same boat. They have nothing to lose either, so the bosses are afraid. And who's to say that the paperwork Castro sent here is real? These poor guys may simply have been his enemies. It's very fucked up, man."

The scene outside of SHU looks like a garbage strike. The mountain of plastic bags is the salvaged belongings of a few of the Cubans. All that's left of their material world awaits disposal. The noise level has dropped several decibels since their departure.

"Counting B Range! Counting! *Cuenta! Cuenta! Cuenta!*"

Morning cartoons on the television—loud, the way my children used to like them. My children. If only Suzi would bring them once. A dozen men watching Scooby-Doo in Spanish. Childhood missed, they search for it in prison. Weep for these children not allowed to be, abused children doing time.

"Shit, O'Dea, you gonna stay in there all motherfuckin' day?"

"I think I've had enough shower time now, Rivas."

"Yeah, O'Dea, you missed Attitude Group this mornin'."

"That's okay, Rivas. My attitude's getting better just knowing you're working."

"You're some kinda bullshitter, O'Dea. Good, though."

There are tables for cards and dominoes, but nothing to write on other than your bunk. I stand next to mine and use it as my table to maintain one of the few journals on the planet written entirely in the standing position. But it could be worse for me. I could be someone else.

Walking the yard, alone, at 8 p.m. Clusters of beards and muscles and, incongruously, the stacks of a giant cruise ship through the window.

"Hey, Kenny, how are ya?"

Brick walkways punctuated with drug smugglers, bank robbers, the Crips and the Bloods, Aryans and goofs, blacks playing basketball in the north yard, Mexicans playing handball, Colombians playing soccer, flamenco guitar dancing in the air under a blossoming magnolia tree, and I am lonely for you, you my friends, you who heard me when I spoke, you who didn't wander to another world when I had something to say, you who stayed.

Here's poor young Stud.

"Hey, Stud, walk with me."

"Gotta clean the auditorium, buddy."

"Okay, see ya later."

———

Walking the yard. Greenest of lawns, blackest of iron keeping us here, silverest of razor wire to shred the skin of the nonbeliever, plenty of wheelchairs—one leg missing or both. How did they get here? I'm alone on a Saturday night and it's okay, I'm okay. Hit the candy bar machines. No Fifth Avenue bars. Shit. Something else now, anything—sugar and chocolate pressed together, blended, homogenized, crispy, smooth, anyway, anyhow, anything chocolate. Hey, there he/she is, Kim, the well-breasted. Where does he/she get those clothes, those tight black slacks and sky blue tank top off the shoulder, with his/her little titties just hanging out, and why do none of these bad boys bother her or any of the he/shes in the neighborhood?

"Attention in the yard! Attention in the yard! Attention in all areas! Clear the yard! Clear the yard! Clear the yard in preparation for the 9 p.m. count! The yard is closed! Clear the yard!"

The moon sheds its light on me as I leave the yard.

TWENTY-THREE

I ACQUAINT MYSELF WITH THE HYDRAULIC SYSTEM OF A LARGE AIRLINER

JERRY AND I made a call to Santiago's house in Colombia from a pay phone at a gas station on Route 75, thirty miles out of Moultrie. I advised Santiago that Jerry would be arriving in Barranquilla from Miami the following evening. Santiago understood that things were on track and said he'd pick Jerry up at the airport.

"*No hay problema. Hasta mañana, amigo. Ten cuidado.*"

That was that. Jerry was on his way to Colombia; Richard was headed back to Chicago to take care of some other business. Back at the airfield, Bill and Don had already begun their inspection of the aircraft. They'd found a few glitches and needed to order parts from Atlanta. It would be at least a week before we could take off.

I decided to go back to Gainesville with Bob to pursue a recent acquaintance with a young Greek-American named Yvonne. Surely every impulsive fool deserves to spend his last hours in the company of a sincere and voluptuous companion. Yvonne was a waitress at the bar in the Gainesville Hilton, a favorite hangout for college kids. This is where I'd met her, and it was Jimmy the bartender who had introduced us. He didn't like Yvonne's boyfriend, who mostly ignored her, and he thought she and I would make a good team. In fact, we almost hit it off right away. Almost, because she was wary of what she thought was too much mystery surrounding me. But this mystery attracted her too, and the attraction triumphed over the wariness.

Between Yvonne and the gentle and good-hearted people of the South met through Bob, I was able to pass an idle week without difficulty. Between dirt-bike racing, motorcycle touring, swimming, making love, and eating, it was hard to choose.

In Bob's car on the way back to Moultrie, the fear started to settle in, nestled in my gut like a sleeping rodent that might at any time awake and chew its way out. At the airfield, we found Bill and Don sitting in the shade, drinking. They told us they'd need another day to have the DC-6 ready. Parts were coming in from Atlanta in the morning.

"How does it look?" I asked.

Bill regarded me with a merry twinkle. "Seems like it might make it," he said. He swirled his drink, making the ice tinkle, and wiggled his eyebrows. Maybe he was trying to be funny.

Dick and I settled into a motel room with a TV and our own bottle of Jack Daniel's. We talked about the flight plan, fuel arrangements, the on-load, the strip in Colombia, the return flight, radar positions, and my duties as copilot. I realized I knew nothing about large, noisy, powerful aircraft—or any sort of aircraft—and I knew in my heart that I was way out of my depth and had followed the wrong impulse by volunteering in the first place. We fell asleep with the TV on and our glasses full.

About 3 a.m., I flipped straight up in the bed, drenched in sweat. This was my second plane crash dream. We'd just taken off, from where I did not know, when the plane suddenly, absurdly, began to fill with water. When the water rose above my head and I was drowning, I woke up. I lay in the dark in my motel bed, frightened and sick from alcohol. Instead of sleeping, I passed the hours until dawn by going into the bathroom from time to time to vomit in the toilet. At sunup I woke Dick, and we headed for the strip.

Bill and Don were aboard, working on the problem. We could expect to leave around five or so that afternoon, they said. Dick stayed to help them, and I returned to the motel alone. Sleep came in fitful snatches, but if I was to be of any use on this flight, I needed whatever rest I could get.

Around three in the afternoon, Dick came buzzing into the room and headed for the shower.

"C'mon, ya Newfie drunk, no time for that now. We got a plane to fly."

I opened one eye and watched him get ready. This pale, slight frame and these freckled hands would carry me across twenty hours of midnight ocean all on their own. These hands and no others, because, as long as we were in the air, mine were useless. I felt a wave of weakness and shut my eye again.

"There's something there on the night stand that'll help," said Dick. He was rubbing his hair with a towel.

"No, thanks," I said.

"Nah, not bourbon. It's a little present from Bill and Don. They saw how sick you were."

I opened an eye again. On the night table he'd set a little packet of shimmering powder.

At the field, at about five o'clock, Bill and Don were just taping over the matriculation numbers on the side and tail, numbers we wouldn't be wanting anyone to run if they should happen to grow curious.

"Y'all ready now?" asked Don.

"Sure we are," I said, speaking for my pilot but almost meaning it after the line of coke. "How's she look?"

"Looks okay," said Bill, climbing down from the ladder.

"Too bad we ran outta that there duct tape," said Don.

"Yessir, that was useful," said Bill.

"And baler twine," said Don.

"Never do seem to have enough baler twine," said Bill.

Dick and I had each brought a small bag, just food and drinks for the trip since we'd be back by the following night. Dick climbed up into the big hatch behind the cockpit and pulled me up behind him.

Bill drew away the ladder, and as he did, he laughed. "She-it," he said. "You don't look like no pilot."

"Fuck you," I said. "Good-bye."

I peered into the yawning cavity of the interior, then followed Dick into the cockpit. I could feel my heart pounding when I sat down. Dick had written out a checklist and sat quietly going through it and flipping switches. I counted almost forty gauges on the control panel and another twenty overhead. We were surrounded by gauges. I set my hands on the steering yoke.

"You won't be needing that," Dick cautioned. He turned to me. "But, like I said, I'm going to be busy at a certain point, and I'll want you to withdraw the flaps. Take ahold of the flap lever—that's it—and work it."

I moved the lever back and forth. It required quite a bit of force.

"Okay, it'll be like this while we're climbing. Then, when I tell you, you'll slowly push it like this."

With that, he put on his headphones. While I was pulling my seat belt tight for dear life, he started flipping on the engine ignitions. I saw Don standing in front of us on the tarmac. The engines were loud, very loud indeed. The plane began to shake. I could hear something bouncing around, way back in the fuselage. Don waved and ran off to the side. I put on the headphones. My hands were vibrating, my jaw was vibrating, everything in the cockpit was vibrating. Dick placed his right hand on the linked throttles in the middle of the console and advanced them. We began to roll forward. This is the stupidest thing I've ever done, I thought.

We taxied out onto the main runway and trundled off to the east, then swung around. A mile of pavement stretched before us. The sun was just above the cockpit windshield. Oh my God, I thought, this is nothing—nothing—like Pan Am. There was just this freckled boy beside me. Then Dick looked over and shot me a quick smile. I didn't smile back. He advanced the throttles to full. The din was deafening, even through the headphones. We rolled forward. The sky was clear. Within seconds we were rolling faster than a man could run. There were a few clouds, after all, I noticed. A moment later, we were rolling as fast as a speeding car, then faster than any car. The empty fuselage behind us boomed with every bump on the runway. The runway—there was the end of the runway, there were the trees in the field beyond the runway. Then, abruptly, there was only sky. The vibration stopped. I held my breath. Sky and more sky. Dick reached up and retracted the landing gear. Time passed: thirty seconds? He put the yoke forward, and there was the green and red landscape of Georgia spread out before us.

"Retract the flaps," Dick called.

"What?"

"Retract the flaps."

I retracted the flaps. The engines grew quieter. We were on our way. Like a boat wants to float, this old girl wanted to fly.

About six o'clock we flew out over the Florida coast and into the Gulf of Mexico. Toward sunset, Dick climbed to five thousand feet. The sky was an aching blue, and the running lights of the fishing boats below began to twinkle on the darkening sea. I lost all sense of fear: Dick seemed more than competent. He seemed invincible.

I got up and toured the ship to warm up a little. I opened the green door and entered the cavernous cargo bay. No fake wall coverings there. The bare skeleton of the thing yawned around me, her rugged bulk stretching into the dim recess of the tail.

I came back to the cockpit. Dick stretched and looked at me. "Ready to fly?"

"I won't get readier in the next few hours."

"Okay, take the stick. Move it forward a little."

The stick was a wheel on top of the control column. I moved it gently forward. The horizon crept up.

"Right. Now draw it back."

The horizon fell as we began to climb.

"Now level it off."

I was able to keep the horizon steady. Dick unbuckled his safety harness.

"See that? You're flying, buddy."

I clutched the wheel and looked ahead.

"Okay, see the compass here? The bearing's one-eight-oh. Keep her there."

"What if it changes?" I remembered the *Fremad*.

"Well, it won't, but if you wander off, just gently turn her back, sorta like a car, then turn her back again to stop turning. That's not like a car. Don't mess with the rudder pedals."

"Uh, I don't know if I got that."

"Never mind. Just keep her steady. I gotta piss." He got up, stopped. "Sure you're okay?"

"Get outta here, will you?"

He went aft. After a minute or so, I relaxed my grip on the stick. She was steady as a rock. I breathed out a deep sigh. My God, it was beautiful. Now the sky was inky, and there were more stars out that night than I'd ever seen. I moved the stick gently forward and back again to assure myself of control. The stars dipped and rose, dipped, rose. At this altitude, I could make out their different colors without difficulty. These stars, I knew, were actually suns burning at different temperatures, that one white, that one blue, that one red. The light that reached me now had left them centuries ago. The universe was humming with a tracery of light, light of all ages.

"Christ!" Dick staggered back in through the door. "Christ! What's happening?" I looked at him in shock. His pants were undone, his belt hanging loose. "Let go of the stick!" he shouted.

"What? What's wrong?"

"Let go of the fucking stick!"

"What? Everything's fine!"

I didn't let go of the stick, but I didn't hold it too tight, either. Dick seemed to have trouble getting into his seat. He seized the stick in his hands and drew it back. I felt a funny elevatory feeling in my stomach.

"Shit," he said, and then he didn't say anything for a minute.

"What's wrong?" I asked, a little weakly, maybe.

"You were flying into the ocean," said Dick, and his voice was very calm. "You got vertigo, I guess. You were heading down."

"Down?"

"You couldn't tell?"

"I was steering by the stars."

"You were steering by the lights of fishing boats."

"Oh."

For a few moments, we both sat in silence. Dick leaned forward and flipped a few switches on and off. He tapped a gauge. Finally, he spoke. "Uh, Brian, don't worry about that. I should have let you practice more."

"Sorry."

"Don't worry. Look, we've got a problem."

"What do you mean?"

"I noticed it a little while ago. Thought it was an instrument error, but no, no it's not."

"What's happening?" I could feel the squeaky overtone in my voice. I looked out the windows, but the stars above and the boats below were all where they should be. "What's the matter?"

"I thought the hydraulic gauges were just giving false readings, but I can see now they're not. I think we've lost the hydraulics."

"What are you talking about, man? What does that mean?"

Dick kept his eyes ahead. "It means, do you want to crash in Colombia or the U.S.?"

My heart rose to my mouth. "Don't fuck with me, man." I didn't intend a threatening tone, but I didn't intend a joke, either. Nonetheless, I made a laugh, small, hollow.

Dick shook his head. "Nobody's fucking with you. There's a leak in the system. Looks like we've lost our hydraulic fluid. If we can't do something about it, we won't be able to drop and lock the gear. That's what's called a crash, man."

I could say nothing whatsoever.

"You're the boss," said Dick. "You've got to make a decision right now. In a few minutes we'll be beyond the point of no return. We'll be over halfway, and over half out of fuel."

Very softly, I said, "Holy fuck," and then I sat in silence. I hadn't intended to make decisions of this sort, but it was certainly my responsibility to make one now. Not that there was much to decide. If we were going to crash an airliner, the United States was the better place to do it. "Turn it around, man, and start talking to me."

"'Round we go!" called Dick.

I clutched at the seat as he banked steeply right. The lights of a fishing boat wheeled by below my side window. We leveled out, and the compass stood abruptly at north.

"Glad you suggested we turn around," Dick said. "I didn't want to die in fucking Colombia."

I felt a prickly sensation along the back of my neck. "Die? What do you mean, die? Don't say die, man. There's no dying fucking happening here. We're going to figure this thing out. You hear me? That's all there is to it."

"If we can get . . ."

"Listen, Dick. No die, no if—nothing like that. Only live and when. That clear?"

"When we get this thing on the ground in Moultrie, we'll get it fixed for sure. But if we had to put down in Riohacha, hell, who knows what it might take? Whatever it is, they wouldn't have it."

"Exactly."

"Look, we get enough hydraulic oil flowing through this thing, we drop the gear and it locks in place before the pressure drops again, we might be okay."

"Will be okay."

"You're going to have to go back there, Brian. You're going to have to go back to the hydraulic entry just behind there, where you're sitting. When we go for it, at Moultrie, wherever, you're going to have to pour oil like your life depends on it."

"I'll do it like my life depends on it," I said, and then I started to laugh.

"Yes, you will," Dick said, and he started laughing too. "You damn well will."

We both fell silent.

"Okay," he said. "Go through the door and look on the floor directly behind your seat. You'll see a bolt on the floor. Unscrew it and lift off the cover plate."

I was already out of my chair.

"You'll see the entry port for hydraulic fluid under there. Then, back by the head, there's a case of fluid. Make sure you don't take the wrong stuff—there's engine oil there too. Drag the case of fluid up to the tank entry. Go do that and come back when you've got it done."

I found the entrance to the system easily enough. Back at the rear of the aircraft, I found the case marked "hydraulic fluid." I couldn't get that wrong. I dragged it forward. The adrenaline was surging up and down my body, but I wasn't afraid. I came back to the cockpit and sat down. Dick didn't say anything, and neither did I.

For the next four or five hours we sat in silence next to each other, each lost in his own thoughts. The heater seemed to have stopped working, and gradually the cold seeped in. At some point, I came to grips with the fact that I might shortly die. I felt ready.

About two in the morning we spotted the lights on the coast. Vero Beach, Florida, according to the chart. A long line of high-rises stretched the length of the town, parallel to the beach ahead. Something was wrong.

"Hey," I said. "They're too high."

"What?"

"Those buildings. They're high."

"How do you mean?" asked Dick, his voice calm.

"They're too high! We're too damn low!"

We were heading straight for them.

"How low are we?" I called. I could hear my own voice, thin above the roar of the engines.

"Just low enough," said Dick. A moment later we were flashing between the towers, thundering between the bedrooms of the sleeping people of Vero Beach. I clung to my seat, riveted by the sudden thrill of speed. We roared over the town and out into the Florida countryside—very, very low. I'd read about this radar-evasion stuff in other people's pot-smuggling stories, but that made no difference whatsoever. My heart was in my mouth.

We flew up through the middle of Florida, gradually gaining altitude while the lights of the towns and highways skidded by below us. The thrill gave way to an unease that, due to our mechanical peril, began to work up again to fear. How would we find that little airfield in Moultrie, Georgia? How, for that matter, would we find Moultrie, Georgia?

"Okay," said Dick, still calm, silent. "We're crossing the Georgia state line." I didn't ask him how he knew. I wanted so much to believe in his infallibility. He descended to what seemed like a few hundred feet off the ground and began to circle. I was beyond comment now. I watched the dark landscape of lights spin by below my side window. Suddenly, the bank grew steeper.

"There it is."

"What? Where?"

"There. Moultrie."

"How can you tell? How can you be sure?"

He looked over at me. For once there was no flicker of a smile. "All of a sudden you're questioning me?" he said. "Just get back there and open up every one of those cans of fluid. I'll call to you, and you start pouring. You pour, you understand?"

"I understand."

"You pour like there's no damned tomorrow."

"Roger."

I climbed out of my seat and scrambled back to the hydraulic intake. I took the cans out of the case and opened them methodically, one at a time. My hands were trembling a little, and fluid—not much—splashed out, making the cans slippery. I lined them up on the floor, where they started to shift as Dick banked more steeply. I gathered my precious clutch of cans in a group, and I could feel our circle getting smaller. I looked up to where a God I once knew lived, a God with whom I'd had little recent communication, a God I hadn't much liked.

"Okay," I whispered. "Whatever you want, okay? But no pain, all right?"

I had not spoken with this entity for years, but now I felt free to bargain with it.

The engines faded from the great howling drone that had been the backdrop for ten hours. They were relaxed now, a loud hum, a burr. The air was a little unsteady, and the great, lean frame of the aircraft bounced and shuffled. I patted my cans together, straining to hear every sound. The engines faded to a fluttering whisper.

"Brian!"

"Now?"

"Pour!"

"I'm pouring!"

"Pour! Pour!"

I put both hands around the first can and tipped its contents into the open valve, where it disappeared immediately. I tipped in the second. I felt the rumble below the deck that must have been the landing gear beginning to drop. How would I know if it had locked into position? I partly spilled the third can of fluid, and the fourth overflowed the valve. Now hydraulic fluid was everywhere. I was pouring frantically. There was a bump beneath my feet. Had the gear given way? I was pouring the fluid from the fifth can, but it was no use: the system would take no more. I shut my eyes. The plane was trembling, trembling as we—yes!—as we ran along the ground. We were on the ground. We were slowing. We were stopping.

They may have heard our hoots and hollers in Alabama. Dick taxied up to the hangar and shut the engines down. He came out of the cockpit and stood looking at me, sitting in a pool of hydraulic fluid, unsure whether I was laughing or crying.

"Hey, Brian," he said. "Stop pouring."

We jumped from the plane. Oh God, to be on the ground. For a few moments my legs were rubbery, like a sailor just staggering ashore. Great to be alive. Thank you, God, who-ever, whatever you are.

TWENTY-FOUR

THERE HAS BEEN this silent scream inside of me since I arrived. If I allow it to continue, I will get nothing but anger and hatred from this experience. What a waste of time that would be. Enough time has been wasted. Enough life sacrificed to the bitch goddess of drugs.

"Hey, man, I'm thirty-five." Sam sits across from me at supper. "I spent most of the past fifteen years down. If heroin was legal, I wouldn't've spent one day down. I only stole to get the shit, homes. If heroin was legal, I wouldn't've had to steal nothin', homes. I could always function on the stuff, just couldn't do without it. They could empty the prisons by doin' that, man, makin' it all legal. How come they don't, man? What about all them people hooked on Valium, man? Make that illegal. You'd see plenty of housewives doin' strange shit to get that stuff, homey. How come, man? How fucking come?"

"Recount! Recount!"

Dan's mural is done. It went up today, and the boss of recreation, Simmonds, a black man, loves it. Some of his black brothers do not.

"Motherfucker funnin' us, bro, motherfucker. I'll fuckin' kill the motherfucker, man."

"Why, bra, wha's wrong with it, mang?"

"Look at the size of our motherfuckin' lips, man! What the fuck, man? He's gotta make 'em fuckin' smaller, motherfucker, or this motherfuckin' paintin' goes an' so does the mother-fuckin' painter."

Mark, the Canadian, and I are painting walls in the rec room in the south yard.

Young Stud comes in. He's looking sheepish. "Hey, Mark, hey, buddy, was that jacket yours?".

"Whaddaya mean, was that jacket mine, Stud? It is mine, and where the fuck is it? I give you somethin' to watch while I'm paintin', and it disappears. Where is it?"

"Listen, Mark. You know Vito, right? He comes up to me an' says, 'Hey, where'd you get that jacket?' I says, 'It's Mark McFarlane's.' He says, 'It looks like mine. Lemme see it!' An' he takes it from me."

"Fuck me, Stud."

"There was a glasses case in the pocket, Mark, with the initials J.S. on it."

"Yeah, there was. They're my glasses, Stud."

"Well, he said his last name is Stallone an' that the jacket was his an' if you want it you gotta go talk to him."

"Fuckin' Vito. Two-bit washed-up Mafia hood. He must be fuckin' kiddin'. I'll fuckin' talk to him, all right, Stud, right after I get done here."

"Sorry, Mark, sorry, buddy. I didn't wanna cause any trouble, buddy. Didn't wanna end up in the SHU box, buddy. I let him have the jacket, buddy, an' came right here to see you, buddy. Sorry, buddy."

"Hey, Stud, it's okay. You did the right thing; don't worry about it, kid. We'll get it back."

"Okay, buddy. We'll get it back, buddy. Okay." He goes off.

We continued painting, Mark and I. And Barry, a big, gentle Jewish boy from California, stopped to help. Barry was kidnapped in Costa Rica by the feds. Now he's slapping pale green paint on the walls of a federal prison.

"So they charged me with fraudulent interstate transactions and money laundering, sixty-two counts. I was looking at a total of 508 years."

"What's that mean you gotta serve?"

"Six and a half years," Barry said. "I wasn't guilty, but they'd charged my wife as well, because she was an officer of my company. I agreed to plead guilty if they gave me six and a half and cut my wife loose. She'd been in eight months already, held without bail, and they said they would give her time served. She got two years. She wanted to take it to court, but I just wanted to get her home with the kids. That's why I made the deal."

"They charge everyone's wife and kids now so you'll plead guilty to get them cut loose. But, shit, they didn't even keep their word with you. Did you have it in writing from them?"

"Brian, this was my first time ever being in trouble. I was a voting Republican, a good taxpaying Jewish businessman. I believed them. I could have beat it, I'm sure, but I just wanted to get my wife loose. I should have listened to her and fought it. I'd been with her eighteen years, and I didn't listen. Oh well, she'll be out two weeks from today."

"All right, Barry, that's great."

"Hey, Mark, how come you're painting this room?" Chuck had stopped to watch us.

"That fucking lop Vic's supposed to do this, man, I don't know why we're doing it. If Simmonds didn't put me in charge of this job, I wouldn't do it for Vic, that prick."

"What's wrong with Vic?" I asked.

"Tried to hijack a planeload of Canadians. Said he was going to blow them up. My mother could have been on that plane, man. Hey, blow up a Canadian plane over some Turkish/Armenian thing in 1917? I mean, I got sympathy for those Armenians, but what the fuck does a planeload of Canadians have to do with anything? Right, Chuck?"

Chuck, fifteen years, pot pilot.

"Yeah, Vic the Prick," says Chuck. "That's not the best of it. He got seven fuckin' years. I get fifteen years for a lousy little planeload of reefer, and he gets seven for a planeload of human beings."

"Four o'clock! Stand up count! Stand up! Counting B Range! Stand up!"

"Hey, Jimmy."

"Brian, whatcha doin'? Answerin' all that mail? You're the only guy here goes to mail call and comes back with half a dozen letters."

"I know."

"Who's writin' you?"

"Friends and loved ones, Jimmy."

"Don't worry, Brian. Give it eighteen months. They'll drop like flies. You'll be lucky to get one a month then."

"I hope you're wrong, Jimmy."

If you're right, it'll be because my miracle occurred and I've been cut loose.

"Hey, buddy, let's do a *Cool Hand Luke* thing, buddy. I'll eat fifty candy bars in half an hour, an' you an' Mark bet on me."

"Fifty candy bars, huh? That's 12,500 calories in half an hour, man. You may be a 250-pound stud, Stud, but you could get insulin shock or something like that. You don't want to do that. You want to do something you do well, and be recognized for it, is that it?"

"Yeah, I guess that's it, buddy. That's it, buddy. Whaddaya have in mind?"

"Maybe a fifty-yard race. You're fast in short sprints, aren't you, Stud?"

"Yeah, bud, I sure am. Can't be beat."

"Okay, Stud. I'll talk to Mark, and we'll organize a Labor Day race. We'll talk about it tomorrow, Stud."

"Okay, buddy, good night, bud. You're doin' a great job, buddy."

"Good night, Stud."

Kid wants love. Like me, like all of us. We just want to love and be loved, no matter how many tattoos, no matter how many gangs, no matter how many drugs, no matter how many bank robberies, no matter how many murders, no matter how many child molestations, no matter what. Love.

Sam slinks into view. His eyes, eyes that seemed so shifty to me when I first got here, are lit up bright.

"Homey?"

"Sam."

"Homey, these books, man. These are the greatest books ever written."

"Did you like them?"

"This is the way, man. This here's the way!"

I'd given him Reshad Feild's *The Last Barrier* and *The Invisible Way*. These are Sufi stories or, rather, stories about the making of a Sufi. In *The Invisible Way*, a woman, Nur, carries a ball of blue wool with her wherever she goes. The wool is a sort of Ariadne's thread that represents life.

"Know what, homes? We're all motherfuckin' Sufis in here. Everybody's tryna get over themselves in one way or another here, an' stay outta each other's way."

"You're right, Sam."

"Pretty fuckin' good, too, homey, 'cept those fuckin' toad motherfuckers."

"What?"

"Ha ha. Jus' kiddin', man. You jump too quick, homey. Hey, them toads're no different from us, homeboy—enemies of the state."

"We're in it together."

"This time, homey, I've got a feelin' I never took outta here before, an' maybe that feelin' means never comin' back. An ink-slingin' Sufi in the world. Yeah, that sounds good—an ink-slingin' Sufi. Motherfucker, homes, an ink-slingin' Sufi. Next thing they'll be writin' poems about me. Come, come, whoever you are, prisoner, junkie, bank robber, it don't matter, the ink-slingin' Sufi tattoos y'all."

"That wouldn't surprise me, Sam."

"We're here, homes, to better the lives of the other poor mothers."

"You're right, Sam.

"As a tribute to God, man."

"Yes."

"That's right. Okay. Gotta go, homes, backs to paint."

Huge depth and a tremendous shallowness. The most intelligent man in the prison.

"Thank you, homey," he says, and he scrambles off into the night.

"*Cuenta!* Counting B Range!"

TWENTY-FIVE

I ESCAPE BY VIRTUE OF SEVERAL EXAGGERATED REPORTS OF MY DEATH

WE WALKED to the trailer park in Moultrie. It was about three in the morning. To my surprise, the town was quiet. Surely the roar of the airliner had awakened everyone for four parishes around. We got out of the car and crept through the streets. A dog barked in the distance. A couple of tomcats snarled at one another as we passed.

The trailer was unlocked. There was no reason to lock your doors in this part of the world. Inside was what looked like remains of a night of partying. Half-full glasses of bourbon on the dining-room table and bourbon on the coffee table, next to an open bag of cocaine. Lying on the couch was Homer from Virginia, the newest recruit to our venture. He had been brought in to handle the details of the off-load.

We walked into one of the bedrooms. Bill was on his back, sprawled fully clothed on the bed. Dick gave him a shake.

"Wha? Wha?"

"Time to wake up, Bill."

Bill opened an eye, then sat up suddenly, confused. "Hey, hey, now there, Dickie. Y'all ain't s'pposed to be back till tomorrow night."

"Yeah. That's what we thought too."

I looked at Dick. He didn't seem like a scrawny kid any-more. I felt his wrath seeping up, even from where I stood.

"But you know what? We were five hours out, middle of the Caribbean Sea, black as pitch, and guess what? Guess what?"

Bill's eyes flicked over to me. "What?" he asked.

"There was a leak in the hydraulic lines and we lost all pressure."

Bill rubbed the back of his neck. He wanted to get off the bed, but that would have put him too close to Dick. "Aw, shit," he said. "That's bad."

"We decided it would be better to crash in the United States than in Colombia."

"Oh shit, no! Y'all crashed?"

"You know what, Bill?" Dick said.

"Come on, Dick," I said. "We're okay. Nobody's fault."

"You know what, Bill?"

Bill looked at me again, trying to judge where he stood. "What?" he said, not at all in a lazy, drunken way. "What?"

There was a long pause while Dick looked at him.

"Be real good if you found that leak," Dick said.

By now it was four in the morning, but Dick and I were strangely alert. We walked over to a pay phone. I had my trusty rolls of quarters with me, and within minutes I had Riohacha on the phone. Somebody ran and woke up Jerry.

"Who is it?" he snarled.

"Jerry. It's Brian. And Dick."

"What? Where are you?"

"In Moultrie."

"What the fuck? What the fuck are you doing there? What the fuck is going on?"

For a moment, I couldn't reply.

"What the fuck?" Jerry screamed across the Caribbean.

I took a breath. "Uh, Jerry, we've had some mechanical difficulties. We're getting them fixed, maybe today."

"Look, you assholes, I'm hanging out here, looking after everything. You think I like this shit? I need action, man! You understand me? I need people to do what they say they're going to do."

"Jerry, I know it's been hard."

"I'm fucking fed up, man! Fed up!"

"I know. I know. If you can just hang in, everything's going to be okay."

"Fuck me."

"The important thing is, Jerry, are you safe and well?"

"What the fuck does that mean?"

"Are you okay?"

"Why the fuck wouldn't I be?"

"Exactly. We'll call you as soon as we have the problems rectified. Just relax and enjoy yourself."

By the time we got back to the trailer and showered and had a bite to eat, it was time to go to work. Something about driving out to the airfield was energizing and uplifting for both of us. Bill and Don were already there and on the job, clean and sober. Dick didn't say anything more about the nightmare we'd experienced, and I got the impression he even felt a bit bad about the way he'd spoken to Bill. But Dick was a man who'd turned his blood to ice water when things went bad. He was entitled to blow off a little. I was ready to fly to the moon with him.

Within a couple of hours they located a crack in the nose gear hydraulic line. It was going to take a few days to work out. We needed more parts from Atlanta. I decided to run back to Gainesville to see Yvonne. Dick stayed in Moultrie. On the way to Florida, I found a pay phone and called Colombia again. This time I spoke with Santiago. He got the picture.

Allowing for further complications, we set the arrival time for the same hour, five days hence. Santiago said there was no problem with the delay, other than having to relocate the merchandise from the salt mine strip back to the warehouse. There would be a little added expense in paying the police and military to protect the load during this transportation, but no big deal. I felt better, and the next few days in Florida were precisely what a man requires at times like these.

I arrived back in Moultrie the day before our rescheduled departure and found our boys putting the finishing touches on the plane. As far as they were concerned, it was ready.

"Shee-it," said Don. "There ain't nothin' wrong with this little girl I can find. Tell y'all what. Y'all don't feel good, I'll jus' ride along in the back with ya. Jus' gimme a crate a beer, is all."

"Hey, no, Donnie, you don't want to go down there. Those Indians are dangerous, man."

"Shee-it. Can't be worse than Nam."

"We'll be okay, Donnie."

"I dunno. Y'all might jus' be glad to have a good ole boy 'long with a decent set of wrenches."

"We'll be okay. You just sit tight and look after the Jack Daniel's."

"Yep, an' that sparklin' Peruvian."

I laughed, but not too much. "You know what I'm starting to think, Don? Maybe we should all sorta give the sparkly Peru a rest."

"I dunno. Works good for me."

I nodded. "Yeah, yeah. I know what you mean."

About the middle of the afternoon, I was in the cockpit, going over what Dick had shown me about handling the controls. After all, what if something happened to him during the flight? I wanted a shot at survival. I heard a car door close out on the runway, so I peered out the window to see who was there. A hefty man, about fifty, with a white moustache, was getting out of a squad car. I could see his sheriff's badge. I ducked back in the cockpit and sank to the floor, a huge knot in my stomach. I heard Bill and Don behind me in the doorway of the plane.

"Howdy, boys, how're ya'll doin' today?"

"Well, we're real good, sheriff, how 'bout yerself?"

"Tolerable, tolerable. Whatch'all up to here?"

"Jus' fixin', sheriff. Fixin' that first job right here."

"Oh yeah? Doin' what?"

"Uh, well, hydraulics, sorta. Leaks an' shit."

"Leaks."

There was a long silence. I didn't dare look out.

"Sure do hope this here won't be the last job," I heard Bill say. "I was jus' sayin' to Don here, sure hope this ain't the last."

"Well, I hope not, boys. We're sorta countin' on you boys to bring some Yankee money down this way."

"That's what we got in mind too, sheriff."

There was another silence.

"This here is quite an airplane, boys, ain't it?"

"Yep, it is."

"I dunno but this ole girl don't look like one of them marreewanna smugglers you read about."

There was another silence. I felt cold sweat on my face.

"Y'know," said Bill, his drawl real slow and lazy now, "that's jus' what I was sayin' to Don yesterday. This ole girl's jus' the sorta crate them smugglers want."

"Thas right," said the sheriff.

"But we jus' fix 'em, an' she's gonna make us some money, this one. Maybe not smugglin' money, but good money."

"Sure hope so, boys."

There was another silence.

"All righty, gotta push off now. The wife wants me to take her shoppin'."

"Don't you keep the missus waitin', sheriff."

"Hell, no," Don chimed in. "Not if you know what's good fer ya."

"Take it easy, boys."

"Hey, sheriff, you come on by more often, have a drink with us."

"Might do."

"Give us a call ahead, an' we'll have the coffee on."

"Might do."

When he was gone, I came out of the cockpit. I must have looked pale.

"Y'all better go on back to the trailer with Dick," Bill said. "Jus' hang out there till you leave tomorrow night."

I had started down the ladder when my blood froze. There, in full view, was the taped-over registration number on the side of the plane. I looked off in the direction of the road, half expecting to see the sheriff coming back. I decided not to dwell on that possibility.

I found Dick sipping Coca-Cola, watching TV. We talked over the sheriff's visit and agreed that somebody—but neither of us—should spend the night with the plane, just in case we had visitors. Be better to know.

The following evening was a beautiful one, the air dry and cooler, the sky clear. We put an ice chest full of sandwiches and Coca-Cola aboard. The heater had never worked, and a working heater had not been a priority on the repair list, so we'd brought jackets and a couple of blankets instead.

"The cold will keep us awake," Dick said while we were taxiing out to the runway at about seven o'clock.

We passed the halfway mark about midnight, the two of us huddled in our seats, the blankets around us. The defroster kept the window clear, but we could see our breath by the dim lights in the cockpit. Dick passed the time teaching me to fly, and by the wee hours I was able to keep the beast in the air for long stretches without putting our lives at hazard.

Just before sunrise, when the eastern horizon to our left was already bright, we spotted the lofty, forest-darkened coast of South America. I had the chart spread out in front of me and a big arrow pointed to the strip at Riohacha. I gave it one more careful look.

"Okay," I said. "We're here, so we turn right and follow the coast."

Dick banked and we headed toward the still dark western horizon. Below, I could see the occasional town along the north coast of Colombia. We had flown for about ten minutes when Dick said he could see a city in the distance.

"No," I said. "No city."

"Yeah, yeah. Look. At the foot of the mountain. See it? What's that?"

It was clearly visible now. I bent over the chart. The only city was Santa Marta, at the foot of Sierra Nevada. I'd been there once, knew a girl, went surfing.

"Oh shit," I said.

"You haven't made a mistake, have you?"

"I . . . I've got you heading the wrong way, man. We were supposed to turn left when we hit the coast."

"Oh, that's nothing," Dick said. "Left, right—they're pretty much the same thing."

"I'm sorry, man."

"All I have to do is turn 'round, then?"

"Uh, yeah. Sorry, man."

"Well, I know how to do that," he said. I could tell he was fighting to stay cool. "'Round we go, then!" he shouted, and we banked out to sea and turned back up the coast.

"I'm sorry, man," I repeated.

"No problem, turning around. What I can't figure out is how I'm going to get us there without fuel."

"We're low?"

"Well, Brian, with you wanting to turn around and all that, we're on fucking fumes."

I sat motionless, mortified. I looked at the altimeter. Fifteen thousand.

"Can you cut the engines for a while and glide?" I wondered, not too loudly.

"Hey. That's actually a good idea, Brian. I thought you had no flying experience. The only catch is that when you're in a big aircraft like this and you cut the engines you tend to go down."

"Okay, okay."

"No, what we need to do is, we need to get rid of excess weight. I suggest you go back, open the hatch and then, real careful like, step out. I'll meet you at the airfield."

He cut two engines and feathered them to the position of least drag. The altimeter began immediately to spin down.

"This is where we hit the coast before," he said. "Where's that damned strip?"

The sun had risen and was in our eyes. I squinted down the coast and looked at the map. At least I was now sure of where we were. Riohacha was maybe twenty-five miles away.

"Can't be more than a few minutes."

Dick tapped the main tank gauge. "Lotta time," he said, but I wasn't sure what he meant.

We sat in silence, both of us straining for any indication of the dirt strip that served the salt mine of Riohacha. Suddenly, Dick turned to me and flashed his old smile. "Better do up that harness," he said, "case we happen to spot a place to land."

That's when I saw the strip. "That's it!" I shouted.

"Where?"

"There! See that? Look, there's a truck at the end."

"Yessiree. That's a strip. And that's where we're going."

We flew by, parallel to the runway, at about a thousand feet. Dick dipped the wings, and I thought I spotted Santiago and Jerry, standing together. We flew out about a mile and turned in for the final approach. Dick flicked several switches on the panel and throttled back.

"That's it, all right," I said.

"How do you know?" Every fiber of the man was focused on the runway ahead.

"They've all got machine guns," I said.

"Sounds good," he said. "You ready?"

My job was to pull the throttles all the way back the moment we were actually on the runway. Dick would be intent on controlling the beast as she raced along the dirt.

"Yeah, I'm ready."

We passed over a long stretch of green meadow, and we were lined up precisely with the runway. We crossed a line of trees, a road and a fence, and then we were on the ground.

"Throttle back!"

I pulled back, and the sound of the engines disappeared behind the rumble of the airframe as we ran along at 125 miles an hour.

"Shit!" Dick cried.

"What?"

"Shit!"

"What?"

"Something's wrong! I can't control the nose gear!"

I watched in silence, suffused by excitement so great it transcended fear. We bounced and shuddered off the runway and across a strip of grass, then plowed through a heavy barbed-wire fence and into a forest of tall cactus. Absurdly, I thought about how prickly cactus were. We shook to an ignominious stop in the sand. I rushed to the door, pushed it open and jumped to the ground. There, strangely weak, I lay down and shut my eyes. I was still alive.

"What the fuck?"

I opened my eyes and looked at the man who stood over me, his face contorted with anger. "What the fuck?" he repeated.

Dick appeared in the doorway of the plane. "The nose gear steering quit," he said without emotion. "I had no control."

"What the fuck?" Jerry said again, like a thing demented. I shut my eyes.

"Jerry," I said, "in a moment I'm going to stand up. When I do, if you say another word to me, another syllable, I am going to have to kill you. The Guajiro will understand."

By now the Guajiro Indians had surrounded the plane. They all wore revolvers with holsters on their hips and machine guns strung over their shoulders. I stood up. Jerry stepped back, got out a Kool.

Santiago and Billy G. were approaching. In front of them was a small man who introduced himself as the manager of the mine. He shook his head. "No, sir," he said, his English flawless. "No, sir. This cannot be. You must get this plane out of here today. I don't care what it takes, but you must get it out of here."

Jerry went back and sat in the truck. Dick and I climbed onto the wings and started to unravel the barbed wire from around the props and rotors. Some of the Guajiros helped us, and it was about an hour before we were satisfied. Dick climbed into the cockpit and fired up the engines on the starboard side to turn the plane in a small circle and maneuver it back onto the strip. He revved the engines hard. Without warning, the outboard starboard prop sheared off and whizzed through the air, embedding itself with a whack in the desert floor, inches from a group of Guajiros standing by. They backed off as though the thing was radioactive. My heart sank. I saw Jerry get out of the truck. Dick shut the engines down and came out. We stood in silence looking at the disabled engine.

"We can make it on three," Dick said.

And I felt relieved.

Santiago came up, and he and Dick decided to clear a bunch of cactus out of the way and get the beast back on the runway.

Machetes appeared instantly. A dozen of us began hacking away at what must have been ancient cactus. I approached a particularly tall specimen and slashed it with abandon. It collapsed without warning and came down on top of me, catching the left side of my body. I staggered to one side, then stood up grinning, feeling the fool. I went immediately back to work, but within minutes I felt as though I'd somehow broken every bone on that side of my body. Soon I was unable to bend my fingers, my arm or my leg. It didn't occur to me that the growing pain was related to the spines of the cactus. I hadn't felt them penetrate my skin. I thought the impact had somehow broken my bones. Billy G. came over and looked at me. His face was grave. He spoke quickly in Spanish to one of his workers, who began to cut slabs from the cactus. By this point I had sunk to my knees and begun to lose focus. I felt the strong grip of the men who picked me up and loaded me into the back of a pickup truck.

We bounced and jolted over broken roads. I remember a sweet-faced Indian woman. Later I would learn she was Billy G.'s wife, Maria. She was waiting for us in front of a small, stucco house roofed in red tiles. A couple of Billy's sons carried me into the house and laid me in the front room on the floor. With their help, Maria took off my jeans and shirt. I looked down: my body was horribly swollen. Maria swore to herself in Spanish. She hurried into another room and returned with the filets of cactus the size of large sirloin steaks. She covered me with these from head to toe.

"No move!" she said sternly, as though I could. They brought me a small jar "for pee" and told me to hold off on anything else. The poultices would draw out the thousands of cactus spines. What were once an integral part of the cactus's skin, and then a part of my skin, would return to their natural home.

I lay on the floor for the next three days. My fever reached a terrible pitch. There were moments when Billy and Maria thought they were losing me. Then the fever disappeared and the pain receded. I lay still, but awake. I saw Dick come and go. Apparently he was staying at Billy's too.

During the next day or so, it seemed as though every inhabitant of Riohacha came calling on the family. Though they undoubtedly wanted to see the broken gringo lying on the front-room floor, these people appeared to consider Billy their true leader. They brought all their problems and disputes to him for arbitration and settlement. Rarely did anyone leave dissatisfied.

Meanwhile, my guys had remained at the airfield to negotiate with the airplane and the military. As it turned out, the military was easier to deal with. The officer in command simply wanted $10,000 for each day we stayed. The plane, on the other hand, required a good deal of coaxing before it agreed to take up a position at one end of the runway. The men covered it with tarps, and it was guarded day and night by a detachment of the Colombian army under the command of a certain Major Fernandes.

The day before I was up and around, Santiago had a friend, Juancho, a first-class mechanic at Aero Condor, come from Bogotá to Riohacha to check out the DC-6. By the time we arrived at the strip, Juancho had figured out what was needed to repair the nose gear. There was no hope for the departed engine, but Dick was certain we could make it on three. Juancho needed a couple of days to go to Bogotá and retrieve the part necessary to complete his job. Major Fernandes had his man drive Juancho to a regional airfield to catch a commuter flight to Bogotá.

This major conducted himself like clockwork. Every day you could set your watch by his arrival to pick up his ten grand, and as long as he was being paid, he helped out wherever and whenever he could. We adjusted to a uniformed officer being part of the team—it gave us a sense of security.

"Thees ees so good for our people," he often assured me. "You, señor, do what you do for money. But what you do for our people, you cannot know."

"I'm glad you see it that way, Major."

"That ees why I help so much. Because it ees so good for our people."

He was a jovial—even enjoyable—little hypocrite. But it was too easy to imagine this mustachioed, pudgy-fingered South American officer applying the electric prod to those who displeased him, and I was not excluded. Were we ever to run out of funds, as he explained, he would be forced to arrest us. "That, señor, that would be a great displeasure to me."

For now, he was the most congenial of hosts.

We had a couple of idle days in front of us, and Billy wanted me to see his world, his true sphere of influence. For the next two days, we went by truck from sight to sight, from one friend's house to another's, beginning with his parents' home, a small cottage on the outskirts of Riohacha. Chickens pecked in the dirt outside, and a few savage geese honked defiantly as we approached. We walked through the gate leading into the compound at the back of the house. Billy's mother was sitting at a loom, weaving a ruana. She didn't look up to greet us but spoke to Billy in a Spanish unintelligible to me. His father came from the house, carrying a plate of fried bananas. We ate together in benign silence and drank fiery *aguardiente* from small cups.

Everywhere we drove on the peninsula, the people knew Billy and wanted me to understand that I was in the company of royalty. All the men wore handguns in holsters and relished showing their scars and flaunting their bravado. According to Billy, for example, he had once hopped into the hammock in his kitchen and, as he did, the .38-caliber revolver tucked into his waistband had discharged, blowing away one testicle. He assured us that the remaining testicle was more than up to the job.

Only one road links the Guajira to Venezuela. As we drove along it, Billy mentioned that his truck came from this road. As far as I could see, the road was uninhabited, and I said the last thing I could imagine along here was a car dealer. He laughed. All of his boys' cars came from that road, he said. Whenever one of his friends in Bogotá or Barranquilla heard about an accident involving a late-model car or truck, that friend would buy the wreck for nothing, then send its papers to Billy. Billy or his cronies would watch this single, lonely road from Venezuela for a similar make and model to pass. They'd stop the vehicle, force the unlucky occupants out into the desert, wish them well, give them a canteen of water and be gone with the new car. They'd then change all the numbers on the victim's car to match the numbers on the demolished one and—voila!—a new and untraceable vehicle.

Everywhere we went, I was a novelty, a blond gringo pot smuggler. To these people, smugglers were heroes and smuggling a legitimate business, an honorable trade that helped the economy as nothing before. As a Newfoundlander, I had some insight into this. As we drove through the streets, folks smiled and waved, and in the rural districts they invariably wanted to touch my hair and skin. Sadly, I was not particularly inquisitive about the culture and history of these gentle people. I was there on business.

The beast was as ready as it would ever be, the nose-gear steering in good repair. If we were going to make our move north, now was the time. Our bill for the military alone was $70,000, and the manager of the salt mine needed another $30,000 for taking care of the local police chief and, needless to say, himself. We also had to come up with a bunch of cash for Juancho, our mechanic.

Dick had to approve of the repairs, or the trip wasn't going to happen. He had been over the whole plane himself. "Yep," he said. "Reckon we can still make it with twelve thousand pounds aboard."

"Make it . . . ?"

"Off the ground and into the air."

"And then?"

"Moultrie."

"I'm in there with you," I said, as though there was somewhere else to go.

Once again the trucks were loaded at the warehouse and, our military escort before and behind, we made the short journey to the strip. The people we passed along the way knew exactly what was happening, what was aboard these stake-bodied trucks. They could see the bales wrapped in sacking, the army escort. What else could it be? I drove in the jeep with Major Fernandes.

"*Sí, Señor Zorro,*" he said several times along the way. "It is so good to know you and meet you. So good. It is such *buen negocio,* with you and your friends. We look for you many more."

No doubt.

The loading took about two hours. By the time everything was ready, it was deep twilight. Santiago and Billy clapped us on the back and wished us well. Many of the other Guajiro boys came up to shake hands and say good-bye, no one more sincerely than the major, who was bidding adieu to $10,000 a day. Jerry walked unsteadily around the plane, smoking and scowling. He'd been drinking gin and tonics all afternoon. He was to leave immediately for Barranquilla and the States. Finally, there was nothing to do but climb aboard.

The cockpit was starting to seem a familiar place. Dick had already run through his checklist. I spread out the chart and tightened my harness while he started the engines. The old girl felt a little different, I thought. From my side window, I could see the silent outboard engine. Dick throttled forward, and I waved a last time out the window. Santiago and Billy waved back.

We taxied to the end of the runway.

"We can get off, right?" I asked. I hadn't until that moment allowed myself to consider the alternative.

"Gonna find out," said Dick.

He advanced the throttles and we began to roll. I could feel the difference, I was sure, although whether it was because we had three engines or because we had six tons of weed in the back, I couldn't tell. We rumbled along the strip, gathering speed, but without the powerful sense of acceleration I'd experienced at Moultrie. Dick's eyes were flicking from the airspeed indicator to the runway and back again as the needle crawled up toward the 140-knot mark. I could see the marker at the end of the strip.

"We gonna make it?" I called over the roar of engines, but Dick didn't answer.

Then we were off the ground and climbing slowly. He held his bearing for several minutes as we gained fifteen hundred feet, then banked out over the coastline, the engines straining. There was the distinct sound of a misfire.

"What was that?" I yelled. Dick didn't answer, and I didn't hear the sound again. We were at two thousand feet. The sun was set now, and the tropical sky already inky. Twenty-five hundred feet.

It was a sharp bang, more like a backfire than an explosion. I experienced a spurt of terror like an electric shock.

"Uh-oh," Dick said. The aircraft shuddered and banked to starboard, then immediately corrected. I looked out my window. The inboard engine was trailing smoke, the prop rotating lazily.

"The engine's stopped!" I shouted.

For a few terrifying moments, Dick said nothing. The nose dropped and the horizon rose.

"That's it!" he yelled.

"What?"

"That's it."

"Can we get back?"

"No! We're going to go down! Buckle up!"

"We're going to hit the water?"

"Shut up! We're going to ditch. Shut up and let me fly!"

"Oh shit, oh shit!"

He banked the plane sharply, and I clung to my seat, speechless. He leveled off. The angle of descent did not steepen further. The port engines were running at low revs. He strained against the rudder and stick. We yawed twice and straightened. The wings dipped and leveled.

"Boats!" Dick shouted after he had shot a glance out the port window.

"Do we have any life gear, Dick?"

The nose dipped again.

"Dick? Life gear?"

"No! Hang on!"

God, I thought, you remember me? We were just talking the other day, God. Remember? I was the one pouring the hydraulic fluid.

The dark surface of the sea was just visible as it slid toward us. When it seemed like we were about to plunge in, Dick applied the flaps and killed the remaining engines. There was an awful quiet. The nose rose, and he pressed the stick forward. The nose dipped steeply. The water glinted below us.

"Oh shit!" I yelled.

The nose rose up and then leveled. We hung suspended.

A giant padded hammer struck the aircraft in the belly, once, twice. In that instant, the eight tons of weed broke loose and crashed through the bulkhead behind us, crushed our seats against the control panel.

Silence. I moved my arms and legs, and they responded. I was alive and well. Dick was undoing his harness.

"No fucking life gear, huh, Dick?" I heard myself say. "No life gear? That's real smart, isn't it? That's real smart! Fucking pilot!"

"Shut up, Brian."

Through the windshield, I could see only the surface of the water. Hell, I thought, we're sinking nose first.

Dick pounded on his side window until it popped open. "Hurry up, boss, or you're going to be looking at fish out there."

He scrambled out the window and dropped from sight. I felt a surge of panic and scrambled out behind him. The water was two feet below the window, the tail of the DC-6 high. We swam to the tail and caught hold of the stabilizer. I had hardly any sense of the water temperature.

"What do you think?" I asked. There was no need to shout now. The silence was complete.

At that moment, the plane stopped sinking. Dick had clearly brought us back toward shore, and we'd ditched in the shallows.

"We may have hit bottom up front," he said. "Good if we have. That gives us a little time."

"What do you think we should do?"

"When we were dropping, I saw lights over there, to the west."

He heaved himself up on the horizontal stabilizer and stood up. "Yeah, yeah. I can see 'em."

"How far?"

"I dunno. Few miles. We can head there or wait here and hope someone saw the crash."

"Somebody'll come for sure."

Dick sat down and then slipped back into the water, which was now warmer than the air. "Yeah, but I have no idea how long until this thing goes under."

I could just make out his boyish face in the dark. "Shit," I said. "You're asking me to make another decision? I don't want to move from here, and I don't want to stay here. It's dark, man. You're the pilot. You call it and I'm with you."

"Okay, I'm for getting out of here and swimming for the lights. It can't be more than a couple of hours' swim."

"A couple of hours? Jesus Christ, Dick, how the fuck am I going to swim for a couple of hours, man?"

"I don't know, Brian. What else do you have in mind?"

"Oh God, God, God, God, God, God!"

He looked at me with disbelief. "Snap the fuck out of it, man. We're going to make it, and that's all there is to it. Now snap out of it!"

"Hey!" I said. "Those are my lines!"

For a moment we bobbed together in the still water. I thought of sharks.

"Fucking fuck, Dick," I finally said. "If I drown—and I've always been afraid of drowning—I'm going to come back and haunt the fucking shit out of that fucking cheapskate Jerry, and if I don't fucking drown, I'm going to fucking make him wish I did."

"So?"

"Let's go."

From time to time, I would tire. I just could not go on. I'd flip over on my back and kick my feet ever so lightly, not making much headway. Then I'd think of sharks, and energy would surge through me once again and I'd be good for another little while. Fear was my enemy and my friend. Every moment it threatened to kill me, and every time it rescued me from myself. I swam long past the point that would have marked the end for me under any other circumstances, long past what I would have called exhaustion. I did not pause to bargain with God. When I needed to, I evoked the terrible jaws that could reach up from the dark depths below me and tear my entrails out. That was enough.

Toward the end of the second hour, I was lifted on a slight swell and saw the lights. "Lights!" I called.

"You still there?" was all Dick said.

They were fishermen. Two boats. We shouted, and they shouted back, their voices full of amazement and alarm. They immediately started their engines, and one boat was alongside us in moments. Several arms reached down, hauled us up and onto the deck, wrapped us in tarps used to cover the catch. They were Indians, friends of Billy G., needless to say.

We beached on the shore of the Guajira Peninsula, and one of the four men ran off for help. Within an hour we were in Billy's kitchen, sipping hot, sweet coffee.

We were stuck in Colombia with no way out except through normal channels. Dick, amazingly, had everything he needed in a waterproof money belt, but I had no identification papers, no passport, no entry visa, nothing. I was, obviously, about to become another opportunity for some enterprising Colombians to make thousands of Yankee dollars getting some gringo out of a jam.

Sleep came in fits the first night. I woke every hour or so with sharks coming up through the mattress. I stayed in bed all of the next day, and when I finally awoke on the second day I felt much better. Billy handed me the morning paper. There, on the front page, was a photograph of the tail of the plane sticking out of the water. The headline read: "Planeload of Cocaine Down Off the Coast." Of course, cocaine made a better headline. There was no mention of pot whatsoever. The story claimed there were two, maybe three Americans aboard, and the authorities said they had had little chance of survival. Good. I was probably dead. That was a help. Apparently the military, in cooperation with officials from the United States, were going to dive on the wreckage later that morning. The plane's ID number had been taped over. A military source— a Major Fernandes—was quoted as saying that the first thing they would do was remove this tape so that the ownership of the plane could be checked out in the United States. The suspect pilots had been seen in and around Riohacha during the previous week. Police would be asking residents of the area what, if anything, they knew of these people.

The town was crawling with American cops, said Billy. It wasn't safe to go outside at all. He was afraid word had gotten out that we had been rescued. He didn't want to take any chances.

Later in the afternoon, Major Fernandes arrived. He was excited, but not in any way threatening. He had accompanied the dive team and the American officials to the wreckage site. The plane was starting to sink fast as air trapped in the fuselage escaped. They'd figured they had about half a day at best, but they hadn't been in the water more than a couple of minutes before a shark attacked one of the divers, removing his arm at the elbow. They'd rushed him to shore, and by the time they'd taken care of him, it had been too late to return to the site that day. Their plan was to head out first thing the following morning. Major Fernandes would keep us posted.

The next day came news that by the time the new dive team got out there, the hungry Caribbean had swallowed the evidence whole. The newspapers assured their readers that, beyond any shadow of a doubt, the plane had carried a multi-ton shipment of cocaine bound for Florida. Two Americans and one Colombian were said to have drowned in the wreckage.

Now it was official. I was dead. Perhaps it would not be quite so difficult to get out of Colombia, after all. Dick decided to move out to Barranquilla, where he would arrange for an entry visa to be forged to his requirements.

"Hey, copilot," he said, standing in the doorway. "Don't forget what you've learned."

"How could I? What about you?"

"Me too. Never make the same mistake twice. That's my new motto."

We laughed and he was gone.

Nearly everyone I was connected with in the States would have gone underground until the heat lifted. I really didn't want to drag Yvonne into this mess, but I needed to ask someone to help me, and she did have the option of saying no.

I lay low for two weeks. Riohacha was running with American and Colombian police asking everyone they could about the rumors of the gringos seen in the area before the crash. As was the Colombian way, the cops were unable to get a straight answer from anyone, and we had Major Fernandes keeping us tuned in to the investigation. In Colombia and Jamaica, there were always military and police personnel willing to help people in trouble, usually for a price, but sometimes because they simply liked being around the action.

After two weeks, I ventured into the town, to the overseas calling center, with assurances from Major Fernandes that all was clear. As I strolled into the center, I could feel the eyes of the locals on me from every direction. They knew me, though;

they'd been protecting me during the investigation that had just ended. As I walked into the telephone office, no one said a thing to me, but there was an unspoken "*gracias*" sent from me to them and an unspoken "*no hay problema*" from them to me.

I asked the operator for Yvonne's number in Florida. One ring, two, four.

"Hello?"

"Yvonne, I'm so glad you're there."

"Brian! Is that you?"

"Yes."

"I'm so glad to hear from you. I had no idea what was going on. Everyone's disappeared. I was beginning to wonder if you were alive or dead. I hated it. I . . ."

"Yvonne, I'm okay. I'm not dead, news reports to the contrary. But listen, Yvonne, I'll fill you in later, as soon as we're together, okay?"

"Okay."

"All right, then, listen carefully. Do you remember where I used to go dirt biking with Bob?"

"Out by the dunes, wasn't it?"

"Right, good. Now, listen. Just beyond there, along the same road, there's a grove of trees on your right. Do you know them?"

"No, not specifically. I'm sure that I can find them."

"Good. Okay. Now, if you walk about halfway past that grove, you will see a path made by dirt bikes there. Take the path until it forks and then go right. You following me?"

"Yes. Take the right fork. Go on."

"Then, about a hundred yards down, you'll see a fallen tree trunk on your left. You can only walk on one side of this trunk, and about halfway along the trunk, if you dig there, you'll hit a small metal safe box at about two feet. Would you go see if you can find that for me?"

"Of course I will."

"I want you to take Jimmy with you from the bar. I trust him not to say anything, and I don't want you to go alone. Plus, the key is at Bob's house, and Bob's not around. You'll need help to force the box open. I think Jimmy'll be able to muscle it open with the right tools. Is that okay with you?"

"It's okay with me. But I won't be able to do it until tomorrow. I have to work tonight. I'm just getting ready to go."

"Thanks, Yvonne, thanks a lot. Is Jimmy bartending tonight?"

"Yeah, he is. I'll talk to him when I get there. Don't worry, we'll get it done."

"I'll call you tomorrow at 2 p.m., okay?"

"Brian, don't worry. It's okay with me."

This box contained all my identification and money. I needed it if I was to get out of this jam.

By the time I spoke to Yvonne at two the next afternoon, she had the box. She thought she could get a few days off work. I asked her to take the Canadian passport, driver's license, and $5,000 and go to Miami, where she could buy an open return and catch the following day's afternoon flight on Avianca to Barranquilla. Santiago would pick her up, and I asked her to wear the blue top we'd bought together and carry the saddle purse I had brought her from Colombia. She said she needed a vacation anyway.

I was beginning to feel that I might, after all, get out of the country without going to prison or being killed. Santiago was working on getting someone to stamp my passport as though I had come into the country legitimately, but I still needed an entry permit, which was not going to be as easy as getting the passport fixed. But this was Colombia, and anything that could be had anywhere could be had in Colombia for a price. Santiago was in Barranquilla, taking care of it as only he could.

At four o'clock the following afternoon, Santiago picked Yvonne up in Barranquilla, and at eight that night we were sitting across from each other, enjoying dinner in Riohacha.

———

Santiago was able to have a rubber stamp fabricated that duplicated the one used by Immigration officers. We stamped my passport to read as though I had arrived a couple of weeks earlier. The job of duplicating the entry visa was turned over to a friend of Santiago's, who owned a printing company.

While my paperwork was being worked on by capable hands, Yvonne and I toured the peninsula. Although I did not yet have my visa, I had an official-looking document provided for me by Major Fernandes that would cover me anywhere within his jurisdiction on the Guajira. Yvonne and I toured the same sights I had first seen with Billy, as well as the salt mine strip. I told her the story and showed her the newspaper articles, including the one telling of my drowning. It was an idyllic interval. Then Santiago called and said we needed to be in Barranquilla the following day.

That night, I bid an emotional and drunken good-bye to Billy G., Maria, and their family.

The visa was absolutely perfect, indistinguishable from Yvonne's. Another impeccable Colombian forgery; they were—and probably still are—the world's undisputed best forgers, capable of duplicating almost anything.

Our next step was to get the official seal on the visa. Santiago had made arrangements with someone who claimed to be Barranquilla's chief of operations of the DAS (the *Departamento Administrativo de Seguridad*, Colombia's FBI) to use his official seal, which was the same as that required. The price would be $1,000. I was immediately concerned. Why was it so cheap? It would have been a bargain at $10,000. "Are they setting me up?" I wondered.

"No, no." Santiago shook his head. "No, this guy knows our story. He figured out you were the pilot or somebody like that.

He's seen the story in all the papers. It was part of the deal that he meet this *hombre*."

Now I was truly worried. But Santiago knew this country, and I had to trust his instincts and contacts.

The following day we drove into a wealthy district of Barranquilla. From the road, we couldn't see the house. It was surrounded by a seven-foot-high wall with broken glass embedded in the top. We parked and walked to the entryway, where a camera pointed down at us. Santiago rang the bell, and a voice in English bid us welcome and asked us to come in. I wondered if I would come out of this place in handcuffs, or dead.

Señor Carrera was a gentle, stooped person with soft hands and a soft manner. He wanted to know all the details of my story. When I finished my tale, I sat in silence, waiting for the trap to spring. Instead, he said he needed to charge me something for his service, but it was not an excessive departure tax, as he put it, because he felt I had gone through enough as it was. The $1,000 changed hands. He sealed and signed my visa and shook my hand.

Santiago drove Yvonne and me to the airport for our flight to the States. In the main terminal, to my surprise, was Major Fernandes. He greeted me loudly from across the hall. "*Señor! Señor Zorro!*" His broad face was wide with smiles. "Now you are leaving safely, and we are sad to say *adiós!*"

"I know I've been fun, Major."

"So good to know you and meet you. So very glad. Such *buen negocio*, with you and your friends. Many more! Many more!"

Santiago shook my hand. "*Adiós, amigo*," he said gruffly. "Next time, better airplane, right?"

"More thinking, less doing," I said.

He smiled, then winked and walked away as they called our flight.

TWENTY-SIX

SPRINGFIELD'S BEEN IN THE HOLE for the last sixty days for spinning out, acting out, flipping out. Now he's going home tomorrow morning. He's walking around, saying good-bye to everyone. I grasp his hand. "Hey, Bill, good luck, man."

"Thanks, Brian, I'm gonna need it, that's for sure. They expect me to live with my parents for three years. That'll kill them. Still, I've always lived with them. Oh well, good-bye."

"Good-bye, Bill. Don't come back."

Good-bye. Good-bye. No barking, now, Bill. No clucking like a chicken. No quacking like a duck. Good-bye. Good luck. Gone.

Not quite. I bump into him by the phones. He's telling someone he's considered by the court to be schizophrenic.

"Do you think you're schizophrenic, Bill?" I ask.

"Brian, some say I am, some say I'm not. I'll say I'm fifty-fifty."

"Where you from, Brian?"

"Santa Barbara. Busted out of Seattle."

"Banks?"

"Nope, pot."

"Pot, huh? What'd ya get?"

"Ten."

"Next time do banks."

"What?"

"I used to deal, speed mostly, quarter-gram to quarter-pound, but I decided to try banks. Forty-one later, here I am, six years."

"Six years for forty-one banks?"

"That's right."

"How'd you get caught?"

"Paranoid. You know speed, man—you see the enemy everywhere. I followed the FBI right into a job one day."

Los Cubanos are back. José moved out from the bed under me today. He's found a place on the second tier. Now I have a *Cubano* bunkie. The noise level has jumped. Four of them are standing around my bunk as I write. One, a known shit disturber, is telling the others that I have too much locker space and that I need to change the way I store my property. He doesn't think I understand what they are saying. The others seem more cautious. I don't feel comfortable, even with my locker locked, even with me standing next to it. The smoke is unbelievable. They are screaming from one end of the freeway to the other. People are screaming at them from the other tiers.

"Shut up!"

"Shaddup!"

"Shut the fuck up, Cuba!"

"You Cuba motherfuckers! Shut the fuck up, motherfucking fuckers!"

"Hey, O'Dea, how you be?"

"All right, Cuba. Welcome back, man. How are you?"

"Yeah. Thanks, Bria, mang."

They are so glad to be free again.

"Hey, Brian."

"Hi, Dean."

Dean, thirty years, ecstasy.

"I'm looking for a spiritually directed book. Harry says you've got the library."

"I've got a few in my locker. Let me get them, and you can pick a couple."

He chooses *The Seat of the Soul* by Gary Zukav and *Jesus Lived in India* by Holger Kersten.

"How's your living area with the return of *los Cubanos,* Dean?"

"Noisy, but we've got a pretty good corner where I am now."

"Who's in it with you?"

"Mark and Rosenberg and one other guy I don't think you know, Cummings, a murder-mutilator. He killed some guy and chopped off his hands and feet and head and put them together on a hill without the torso. They never did find the torso. Some kind of white supremacist."

"How much time did he get?"

"Six years. Manslaughter. They couldn't find the torso."

The *Cubanos* are much more subdued today, having recovered from the initial elation of their release into a lesser confinement. I am about ready to make myself available for whatever service I have been assigned to this place for, gradually releasing myself from the limitations of anger and hostility. Until now, I have been thoroughly entangled in each person's battle for justice, fair treatment, fair play amidst so much hypocrisy and injustice. I'll be wiped out if I continue like that. It does nothing to help the situation, even exacerbates it somewhat. I have to discover how I fit into the solution.

"Count! Counting B Range!"

The drug of choice in here is heroin, but most of the piss tests seem to be conducted on pot smokers. It's easy to spot the heroin users, but rarely do they have any trouble with the cops. Somehow they're able to get their hands on heroin and needles and not get caught. The penalty for bringing drugs in through the visiting room is five years added on to your sentence, yet people do it every day. Prison is no treatment for drug addiction. Those who choose drugs choose them over everything else in life, up to and including life itself.

"Hey, Aaron, what's the difference between Folsom and here?"

"A big, big, difference, Brian. The clientele there is much heavier. Half these people here are goin' 'round tellin' shit on other guys. They don't tolerate that shit there, man. Snitch wouldn't last two hours in the yard. Somebody'd stick somethin' in you quicker'n shit, man. Last year this school principal from Fresno showed up on a child molestin' beef. He wasn't in the yard six hours 'fore someone pinged his head with a hammer. He looked good and dead when they carried him off. Snitches, kid fuckers, they don't make it there, man. And this little shit— like cuttin' in the line at chow—they don't tolerate that shit there either. In that joint, you mind your own business, keep away from the cops, and keep your mouth shut, you do okay."

To the novice, walking in the yard for the first time, seeing all the *chulos* with their hairnets and the groups of mean-looking blacks, whites, beiges, this place looks like Folsom or San Quentin, or Marion or Leavenworth. But with time I see that Terminal Island is fairly mild, as prisons go. The hardest part about being here is deeper than being behind walls—it's being in my mind.

Night. Bob Bitchin, loan shark from A unit, is threatening another man in our area.

"You best just shut the fuck up, man! You got seven days from the 26th of August to pay me. You lied to me, mother-fucker! Just keep your lyin' motherfuckin' mouth shut. Seven fuckin' days from the 26th, man, or else."

He knows how to pick on people smaller and physically weaker than himself.

Harry watches with me. "He's a loan shark, Brian. Other guy owed him thirty-six bucks and was supposed to pay him last week, and the week before. Bitchin says he lied and now the debt is doubled. Best to stay out of that stuff, man. Just ignore it. You can't help, and they're snakes anyway. Money for drugs. Dirty situation. Forget it."

Still feel that silent scream raging through me like a tidal wave looking for a shore. Lot of work to do on my acceptance level. Everyone in this place looks like a cartoon today.

"My name is Brian. I'm an alcoholic. Yesterday I had three and a half years sober."

The AA meetings are once a week. The Aryan *chulo* Jimmy speaks up.

"My name is Jimmy. I'm an alcoholic and an addict. I've been in this stinkin' system since I was twelve years old, and I'm forty-six today. Most of those years I've been in one prison or another. This is the first nine months clean I've had since I was nine years old. I know stayin' sober means a chance at stayin' out of prison, and I know this is my last shot. I don't know nothin' else but bein' locked up, and I wanna know somethin' else for a change. I want to live, I want to walk free, eat what I want when I want, sleep where I want with whoever I want. I don't want nobody tellin' me what to do no more, don't want nobody lookin' up my butt or checkin' my piss. I want my life back, and I'm gonna have it this time. Thanks for helpin' me out."

All around, guys nod assent. They ought to know.

TWENTY-SEVEN

I HAVE A CHILD, MARRY, AND SETTLE ON A LEGITIMATE OCCUPATION BUT DEVELOP POOR HABITS

THE DC-6 was at the bottom of the bay at Barranquilla, and my credibility—and credit—was down there with it. I retreated to the U.S. With the help of my friend Bob in Gainesville, Florida, I got some funds together for some small-time trading in the Caribbean. I got in touch with Santiago and Juan, and we agreed to meet in Martinique to plan a truly successful campaign. I arrived in the spring of 1976 and settled in to wait for them. They didn't show.

I was staying in a half-baked hotel where the only thing that worked was the cash register. In due course, I didn't have enough money left to pay the hotel bill or buy a ticket out of there. I couldn't think where to turn. Jerry was out of the question. Santiago was unreachable. At last, my thoughts gravitated with reluctance to my brother Chris—a truly good man. I'd beaten him up financially many times, but he, like the rest of my family, was still there for me. I phoned him, and he said okay. I gave him the name of a bank in Martinique, and waited it out under the watchful gazes of the hotel staff. They weren't overlooking the growing bill. Chris's money took almost two weeks to arrive. By the time it got there and I'd paid the old bill, I was in just as much trouble as when I called him. The staff was keeping an increasingly beady eye on my luggage.

That was when I thought to call Terry Fields, the LA lawyer, remembering the last thing he'd said to me when we parted in Jamaica during the Super Soul fiasco. "Give me a call," he'd said. "Come to LA. Get out of this place. This is bullshit." Hey, he was right.

I phoned Terry. He answered the phone himself.

"Um, Terry," I said. "It's Brian O'Dea. Remember me?"

There was a little pause. "Yeah, Brian. Hi."

Whew.

"Look, Terry, I had a couple of things going on further south, but I'm in Martinique right now and, actually, I've got no money. I need to get out of here, and I was wondering if you could help me out."

"What do you want to do, exactly?"

"I was thinking I could come to LA and see what I could put together. You know, something good."

There was another pause.

"Okay, Brian. Call me back in an hour."

I called back.

"Go to the Bank of France in Fort-de-France tomorrow at noon," he said. "Ask to see Jacques Davos."

"Terry, shit, I really appreciate this, man. But please, please don't send me money through the bank. I did that already, and it took two weeks. The fact is, man, they've got a guy watching me at the hotel, you know, making sure I'm not smuggling my stuff out of the room one sock at a time. I hate—"

"Brian?"

"I hate to trouble you about this."

"Brian? Did you call me or did I call you?"

"Um . . . I called you."

"That's right. Go to that bank tomorrow morning and ask for Jacques Davos."

"Okay, Terry. Okay."

I went the next day and Jacques Davos gave me $5,000. Fuckin-ay, I thought as I walked back out into the sunshine with my pocket bulging, I'm talking to the right guy here.

I telephoned my old friend Margaret in LA, and she said I could crash on the couch in the apartment she shared with another woman. I bought a ticket and departed without delay.

I arrived in LA on November 15, 1976, and after a while made the acquaintance of a group of people who were moving money offshore for wealthy clients. My job was to show up at various banks with $9,000 in cash in a briefcase ($10,000 was the limit for undeclared transfers) and buy a cashier's check in favor of some offshore company. I'd do the rounds until I'd taken care of the whole amount—usually a few hundred thousand—and carry the checks back to their offices.

With time, I was back into the South American coke business in a small way—not my preferred calling, to be sure, but neither could I remain a bagman indefinitely. Juan and Santiago had finally resurfaced. I'd take a few runners with me down to Colombia, and they'd run the coke in false-bottomed suitcases into Guadeloupe or Martinique or St. Martin. I'd take the coke out and burn the suitcases in the wilderness to get rid of the evidence. Other runners would take the stuff on to Miami and other U.S. ports.

I began to meet more people in LA and moved out of Margaret's and in with a guy who had Neil Young's old house in Topanga Canyon. I was sleeping in Neil's old studio, and one afternoon a young woman dropped by.

"Hey," she said. "I've got to introduce you to this friend of mine. I think you'd really dig her."

The friend was Suzi Foreman, and she lived at the other end of Topanga Canyon. At thirty, she was older than me—I was twenty-eight—and a free and gentle spirit, a hippie, dark-skinned with long dark hair. Her father, Joe, was a Cherokee Indian, and Margaret, her mother, was a white American. They lived in the essentially rural Chatsworth Lake area up in the San Fernando Valley, at the north end of Topanga Canyon Boulevard. Suzi and her mother were community boosters whose Chatsworth Lake Citizens Committee attempted to prevent the encroachment of development on this beautiful preserve in the Santa Susana Mountains. Joe was a delightful man, who'd given up his engineering position at Rocketdyne and returned to carpentry. He liked to build houses in the neighborhood, and he'd go on kindness binges and give them away to the tenants. One day he gave six away.

Suzi was a haircutter who had a good clientele, movie stars and the like. When I met her, she was making a lot of money. She was a partier, yes, but a sweet and modest partier. In no time, I'd thrown her boyfriend out and moved in with her. Some months later, she got pregnant.

Meanwhile, through my old roommate Margaret, I met people who worked at Yellowfingers, an LA restaurant popular with old dealers, and through Yellowfingers I began to establish some excellent connections. One of them was Darryl, who was the engineer at a company called Far Out Productions, which produced records for Jimi Hendrix and Eric Burdon and the group War. Darryl and his buddy, when they weren't doing real work, had become part-time chemistry apprentices. They showed me something astonishing: coke is soluble in methanol, and that solution can be soaked into any fabric or paper. The methanol evaporates instantly, and the coke is embedded in the fabric. If you later soak the fabric in methanol, the coke will redissolve into solution and you can flash-evaporate the solution and find yourself left with pure coke. Unless a customs officer pawing through a shipment of ponchos should suddenly and unexpectedly pick his nose, the drug was undetectable.

With Darryl looking after the chemistry back in the States, Santiago and I bought a farm in Colombia. We called it *La Finca* ("the ranch")—almost five hundred acres, near a place named Los Llanos ("the plains"), a spectacular six-hour drive outside of Bogotá. The last hour and a half of that drive was through farmers' fields until, all of a sudden, you came upon a gate. I was never able to find the place myself, even after I'd been there ten times. Our living quarters at *La Finca* consisted of posts in the ground that held up a thatched roof—no walls—and our furniture consisted of hammocks. Around us, a vast plain was dotted with cattle, crisscrossed with brooks and relieved here and there by twelve-foot anthills and scattered oases of palms. In one of these oases, we made a clearing for our open, thatched-roofed lab.

In Ecuador, operators turned the coca leaf into coca paste. We brought the paste in from Ecuador and ran it through a fairly sophisticated purification process based entirely on gravity and chemicals and supervised by a Colombian chemist recruited by Santiago.

When we weren't at *La Finca*, I stayed with Santiago and his family in Bogotá. This was not as amusing as one might think. Santiago wasn't really a party guy and, from his perspective, there was probably little percentage in broadening my Colombian social network. Neither was I inclined to wander the streets looking for a good time. That was something I had learned not to do in Colombia.

I was in downtown Bogotá one morning to change money at the Banco Nacional. A grand staircase leads to a gymnasium-sized room encircled by tellers, filled with hundreds of people. I looked across a sea of heads and spotted a head at least a foot farther from the floor than every other head in the room. It belonged to Gary O'Brien of New-foundland, late of Jamaica. I had once been the man's scout leader and, at another point, his partner by association with Will Shears, Gary Sexton, and crew. There he was, down there doing exactly the same thing I was doing, hooked up with Juan, the very connection I had bequeathed to his group. They were working out of the west Colombian sea-port of Buenaventura.

If there hadn't been the best of histories between Gary and myself, well, what the hell, it wasn't the worst. I was soon a frequent, if not daily, guest at the apartment where he and his wife lived and, sharing similar cultural and personal inclina-tions, we fell to drinking, snorting coke, and smoking dope from noon until midnight every day. In the back of our minds there may have been—may have been—a vague sense that we were carrying excess to, well, excess. Certainly I experienced real alarm one evening, after doing a forty of rum, a few joints, and several fat lines, when the contents of my skull began to slosh back and forth. I shook my head in an attempt to clear it, but the utensils hanging on the kitchen wall started to dance. I felt a spurt of alarm. I'd finally gone over the top. I looked across the table, and the terror in Gary's eyes reflected my own. The dishes in the cupboard began to shake and clatter. I remembered the deadly nightshade and those days lost in hell. I opened my mouth but made no sound. The sloshing in my head stopped suddenly.

"Hey!" I heard the voice of Gary's wife from the living room. "Hey. Earthquake, eh?"

Gary and I stared at one another in wonder. We were from Newfoundland. We didn't know from earthquakes. We burst into laughter.

"Shit," Gary said.

"Shit," I said.

"Want a beer?" Gary asked.

It was only an earthquake. We'd thought it was something serious.

Suzi and I lived in her house in Chatsworth, built in 1925 of retired telegraph poles and railway ties—the stitches and threads of the pioneer West. The house had been a gift from her father. I bought the property around the house for us. Here in Chatsworth, I would take delivery of the ponchos. I had a lab set up in my garage for extraction. When the methanol was dissolved and the product dried, the result was a flat white powder. One final step was required to arrive at crystallized cocaine: the powder had to be redissolved in the smallest amount of methanol to make a solution that was in turn soluble in ether. We then poured the ether solution into glass vessels and added a crystal of pure cocaine. The dissolved coke precipitated out onto the glass walls, and the liquid could be poured away. The atmosphere was dense with the smell of ether and cigarette smoke. I gave no thought whatsoever to the kingdom come I was begging to be blown to.

While I was working away in the garage one night, humming and smoking amidst the reek of ether, I happened to look out the front door. There were three cop cars in my driveway. For a moment, I stood in a sort of daze. My God, I thought, I'm busted. In a flurry of panic, I began to dismantle my little factory—a hopeless task. There was nothing I could do, and I stood still in the center of the room, paralyzed. I went back to the door and looked out. They were handing out a ticket to somebody down at the end of my driveway. We owned a little antique store there, and the police often used my parking lot.

"This is ridiculous," I thought. "I've got to stop bringing work home."

I moved the lab into the mountains outside of San Diego, to a town called Julian. It was about a hundred yards from a

Salvation Army camp for San Diego's inner-city kids and fully
enclosed by trees. I spent weeks in there, surrounded by ether,
crystallizing coke and smoking cigarettes. I'd be keeping
twenty-five-gallon jugs of ether company, then I'd feel a bit
hungry. I'd pop some toast in the toaster and light a cigarette.
I simply assumed I was invincible.

I was more wary, though, of other dangers. One day in 1977,
I picked up a copy of *High Times* magazine, and right there on
the cover was a story about smuggling coke in fabric and
washing it in methanol. At that moment, I knew my serious
cocaine career was over again. My passport was full of Colombian in and out stamps, and it was time to retire it. And there
was a further omen: I couldn't reach Santiago. It would be
a long while, in fact, before I was to meet the craggy-faced
Indian again. Unbeknownst to me, he'd just flown into
Martinique on papers that the authorities deemed to be false,
and in this way he drew a breathtaking seven years in the most
primitive conditions the island could offer.

I started middling quantities of pot out of Tucson, Arizona,
with guys from Nebraska. We hired people to go up to Nebraska and harvest a bunch of Nebraskan no-high, wild hemp
that had been used for rope-making in the Second World War.
It grew at the side of the roads, and they charged us $10 a kilo,
delivered. We'd cut good stuff with it and turn $100 worth of
weed into $1,000. It seemed to make sense.

In this desultory, coke-snorting, inattentive manner, I made
my living until our son, Cheyenne, was born, on September
29, 1977. Time for a new beginning.

Suzi would cut my hair, which was then long and blond, and
she used a moisturizer called Tri. It was the first time I'd ever
encountered a hair product I could actually feel working. She
would talk about how healthy it was for the hair, and I started

buying the stuff from her. In the throes of career redemption, I suggested we go down to this company, Tri, which was in LA, talk to them, get the rights to this product, take it to Canada and sell it.

We set up an appointment, went in to the Tri office, and made a deal. The sales manager at Tri was a great guy named John Paul Jones De Joria. He loved my idea and backed me all the way. In no time I'd arranged the money and bought a bunch of product. I put it in my van, and Cheyenne and Suzi and I drove up to Vancouver. This was it. I was almost out of the business, almost going straight.

In Canada, I started knocking on doors. I was convinced I could sell this hair moisturizer because I believed in it, because I was persuasive and persistent, and because it didn't bother me to hear no. This last quality was especially important because I heard an awful lot of no's. For eight months, we slogged the streets, making our calls with Cheyenne in his stroller. Suzi could talk the hair talk. I could talk the sales talk. But these Vancouver hair people were hard cases.

I wanted to produce Tri in Canada, but until I got the volume up, I had to import it. Fortunately, John Paul and I had set up a system for importing Tri that would entail paying less duty. I opened a U.S. company that bought the product from Tri for, say, a dollar. My U.S. company then sold it to my Canadian company for twenty-five cents and took a seventy-five cent loss on the sale. The importing Canadian company paid duty on the twenty-five cents. The American company could write off the loss for three years.

Then, as part of a power push at Tri, John Paul was fired. This was the best thing that could have happened to the man, but at the time it seemed lousy. He started sleeping on my couch while he planned to start his own company, John Paul Mitchell Hair Product Systems. I loaned him $15,000 for this business, and he wanted me to join him. I said no, I couldn't, because I was doing Tri. Today, John Paul is worth over $1 billion (I presume), and he wears it well.

The new people at Tri wanted to promote their product in a big way, and it happened then that I bumped into CI on the street in Vancouver. He and I went way back to St. John's. His sister had been a girlfriend of one of the Montego Bay Newfie team. She had gone on to marry a now wealthy young man known to have run a few loads and to have escaped trouble time and again while those around him copped a variety of sentences. This guy was under a shadow of suspicion, and CI, his brother-in-law, was also known to be occasionally active in the smuggling field.

CI greeted me on Robson Street. "Hey, Brian," he said. "Hey, CI."

He was a big, heavy, swarthy, bearded man, a bit of an over-indulgent pig, in fact, although I was no stranger to overindul-gence myself.

We went into Joe's for coffee, and right away he told me he'd recently been busted for pot and was out on bail. Perhaps the family luck had run out. I told him about Tri, and it turned out he had money and wanted to participate.

Together, with the cooperation of the new Tri management in LA, we laid out a plan to take over the hair-product market in Vancouver. It cost a lot of money. I mortgaged our house in California, and CI put in the rest—in all, $1 million. We bought air time on local pop radio stations, and a billboard at every major intersection in Vancouver became a Tri bill-board. We put on a $100-a-ticket invitation-only show for a thousand of the best stylists in the city. Five thousand people showed up at the Four Seasons Hotel. We used closed-circuit TVs everywhere in the hotel to drive home the fact that this was a spectacular show.

The business leapt from $3,000 or $4,000 a month—with me closing 20 percent of the contacts I saw on a $90 opening order—to $100,000 a month, closing 100 percent of the people I saw on opening orders of $800. Everybody was talking Tri. Meanwhile, CI's dope case got dropped and, most astonishingly, they gave him his money back. That was one for the books, though it was the sort of thing that seemed to have become a tradition in his family.

I pulled into a gas station on the King George Highway in Vancouver. It was 1979. Suzi and I were still driving the '67 Dodge Tradesman van we'd brought up from California—carpeted, with a couch in the back. Cheyenne was sitting on a little IKEA stool between the front seats. There were two guys filling a Dodge in front of us: sports jackets, shirts with no ties, hair just over the ears, casual but not quite hip. One of them looked at me. He had the kind of face that wanted to know more about me.

"What do you think those guys do?" I asked Suzi.

She smiled. "Yeah, right."

The Dodge pulled out and disappeared. I got out and put gas in the car.

Down the road about two hundred yards, the two guys in the Dodge pulled us over. Man, I thought, how can one man be so right?

"What's goin' on?" I asked. "Why're you pulling me over?"

The older of the two looked at me, stone-faced. "We want to check you out," he said.

"Hey," I said. "There's no reasonable cause."

"This isn't the States," he said. "Let me see your driver's license."

I handed him my license.

"You're a Canadian."

"Yes, I am."

"You can't be driving a car here with U.S. plates. We're seizing this van right now."

"Whoa," I said. "That's just bullshit. I'm married to this American sitting right here."

"Get out of the car, sir. Get out now."

There was a lot of threatening mumbling and looking through stuff. In the end, they made me trade places with Suzi. We pulled back onto the highway.

"Suzi," I said. "This is the start of something no good."

I had sixteen employees out selling and working in the office. Two days after they'd stopped the van, fifteen cops walked in and ripped the place apart. They came up with the books for my American company and, in the fullness of time, charged me with conspiracy to defraud the Canadian government of import duties. A court date was set.

On my way to court three months later, I pulled out of my driveway, about fifteen miles from the courthouse, which was in White Rock, B.C. I was late, and I was extremely anxious. I stopped at a stop sign. The guy in front of me didn't move. I blew my horn and he—the infantile prick—gave me the finger. I gave him the finger back, and he pulled over, and I pulled up next to him, and he was, yes, the prosecutor in my case. For a wild moment, we stared at one another.

Finally I spoke. "Fuck you," I said and went on, freaking all the way.

I walked in alone. CI had left the district some time before. The prosecution had two of my secretaries—women who really cared about me—sitting there with cops on either side of them. I thought, wow, I'm fucked. And there were the people who owned Tri in the U.S., also seated between cops. When their turn came, they explained that it was John Paul who'd done it, yer honor, and he was no longer with the company. They had no idea what sort of structure this O'Dea had set up.

That's why they'd come all the way up here to testify against him, the only guy in the world to put a million bucks in their business.

One by one, everybody got up to say I had conspired to defraud the Canadian government. It didn't matter that I hadn't, in fact, conspired to defraud the Canadian government, that I was following a legitimate American business practice that allows a company to take a loss for years. It didn't matter that, in the United States, what I did with my own product was my own corporate business. Really, nothing mattered at all: I was to be hammered.

They offered me a deal: plead guilty to evasion of custom and excise duties and I'd have six months to pay a $25,000 fine—$1,000 a week. The alternative was six months in prison. My business was shut down. Make up my mind.

The guys who'd pulled me over had run a make on me and turned up my 1972 conviction in Newfoundland. It was obvious to them I was using hair products as a cover for a drug operation. That's why fifteen cops could hit my office.

Some choice.

TWENTY-EIGHT

I'VE SEEN ONLY three guys walk out through the front gates of this place under their own steam. Everybody else goes to another facility, on a chain, in a bright orange jumpsuit.

Suddenly, today, Sam shows up on the range in a new pair of Levi's, a blue cotton shirt with a collar from the seventies, new Nikes, and a big smile. He lopes over to me. "I'm goin' home, homey. They finally saw the light. Hey, I'm gonna miss you, homeboy!"

I stared at him. I thought he must be joking. Then I knew he wasn't. "I'll miss you too, Sam."

"Hey, fuck it, homey, I'll come up to Canada an' see you. You're gettin' outta here in a minute too."

"To God's ear, Inkman."

"Homey, listen. Give my gun to Phil, will ya?"

"Don't drop that fucking thing on me, *amigo*."

"Come on, homey. It's just a tattoo gun. Look at me—I'm goin' home or somewhere, an' I had that motherfucker in my house here for years. Just give it to Phil. He's gonna come by lookin' for me later. Tell him I'll get a number to him."

I take the tattoo gun. Sam's looking pretty good. No junk for a while.

"I'm goin' straight, homey. I got the blue thread, man. I'm on the way, man, the way."

"Right. The invisible way."

"That's it, homey. Good-bye. I love ya."

His skin is clear, wrinkle-free, and pale. His hair is tamer than usual, even brushed. Maybe he's right.

He throws me a peace sign and disappears through the door I came in by.

Simmonds, the recreation boss, has given me a dirt space to create a garden behind the basketball area.

Brian Daniels warns me to be careful. "You want to make part of it a Zen garden, right, Brian? Be careful. Change the name to Japanese-style garden. If they think you're going to start some meditation-type stuff here, they'll kill it. Don't forget, man, the folks running this place are fundamentalist Christians. Meditation and spiritual uplifting are Father Bill's territory, and he's already refused to allocate time for a meditation group in the chapel. It's too subversive for him. When you get your garden looking real good, one of two things is going to happen. Either they'll have you tear it up and move it somewhere for the warden, or inmates won't be allowed to go into it. Take at least a year to build it the way you want it. Do it nice and slow, make it a project, don't fuck yourself out of it by finishing it."

I spend the morning digging up my garden, turning the soil, getting ready for fertilizer. My unworked hands rebel, and I have huge broken blisters on my palms.

Mark and I paint the doors in one of the recreation buildings because the Ninth Circuit judges—three hundred of them, including my judge—are going to do a little tour. Presumably, they occasionally experience some curiosity about horror, long to see the condemned cooking in the inferno as they sip their drinks at the warden's cocktail party. Dante reserved the eighth level of hell for such hypocrites.

"Hey, Brian, see that black guy out there in the hole exercise yard?"

"Yeah."

"You know who he is?"

"The prisoner or the cop?"

"The prisoner."

"No, who is he?"

"He was an assistant federal prosecutor. Probably prosecuted fifty coke cases—guys doin' time here."

"Oh yeah? What's he here for?"

"Sellin' coke, of course."

"Guess he'll never get into the population."

"Ha ha. He'd be one dead ex–assistant federal prosecutor. And he's not the only one either, just one they caught. That cop lieutenant you don't like? I know he gets fucked up on coke—a sloppy drunk and a coke freak, the motherfucker. He's the worst in the joint if he thinks you're doin' anything. He's the first there with the piss-test bottle. Prick."

I feel like such a coward. I just can't settle down and do this thing. I know the only thing I can change here is how I look at it, yet I resist changing my outlook for fear of falling into some "just-do-the-time" role. Am I behaving like a crybaby? Am I a weak link in this process, or is this just a natural stage in the progression of internment?

Cards hit the table. Cubans sing songs to one another. The TVs rage. Men wander up and down in boxer shorts, flexing muscles and smoking cigarettes. The shower's running, toilet flushing. A couple of guys dance around each other, pretend boxing that could lose its pretense at any second.

Stud is standing across from me. He's holding a magazine. "Okay, buddy, listen to this. Am I borin' you with all these great statistics, buddy? Okay, okay, okay, listen. You don't mind if I eat in front of you, do you, buddy? Okay, okay. Murder: 23,380 last year, 64 every day, buddy, 2.6 every hour, buddy. How about cars stolen? Okay, buddy, you ready for this? Okay, 1.4 million last year. Okay, 3,864 every day, 160 every hour, 2.67 cars stolen every minute, one every twenty-two seconds. Rape, buddy, an' they say only one in eight is reported, but we're only dealin' with the ones the government figures, buddy—rape, 120,000 last year, 329 every day, 13.7 every hour, one every three minutes in this lawless country, buddy, no wonder these fuckin' jails are full of these lops, buddy. No fuckin' wonder bein' a cop sucks, with the streets like that. Can't be a cop with a felony, buddy, can't join the military either. Big deal, huh, buddy? Who wants to join them, anyway? All right, buddy, gotta go, okay? Gotta go to bed. Y'know how many cars are made in the United States each year, buddy? Thirteen million plus, buddy. Lots more cars to get stolen. Okay, buddy, gotta go, okay? G'night."

"Recount! Let's go! Stand up! Recount!"

"Asshole!"

"Recounting!"

"Go to night school, asshole!"

"Fuck you!"

Five hours later, another recount—most likely the same computer error that hasn't been rectified. Uh-oh, third recount. They can't seem to get it straight.

Now we have a squadron of cops here, counting us one more time. The numbers never change. They finally go around to each person and do a picture-card count. We are accounted for.

———

There's an officer in charge of tools. He sits in a tool building all day and does no work. Every time I've been to his tool shed, he's been on the phone talking to his girlfriend.

"Listen, O'Dea, that's the third time you been back here for tools. You can't be doin' that. I got other work to do."

"I'm sure you do, boss, but this garden building stuff's new to me, boss. It's still kind of hit and miss, so I'm not sure what tools I'm going to need until I'm into the job. I'm learning."

"Don't learn on my time, O'Dea. Send someone who knows what they're doin' to get tools for you, but you can't be buggin' me like that."

"Sure thing, boss."

After a long, muddy morning in the garden, my blisters are starting to understand what's happening. So are the plants, which were brought in by the landscaping crew. None of them suffer too much from their travels and transplanting. Their shock was minimal, like our shocks when transplanted into this soil. Shock and fear, and when the fear finally subsided, when I began to notice that the only thing to fear here was myself, my mind, there was another layer: resistance to being here. Now I am simply a choice away from letting go of it. Somehow, I am able to find glimpses of my purpose in being here.

Another lesson in powerlessness. This whole journey is going to take its own time. I spent the last half hour in the chapel doing meditation. I am so tired most of the time, I nearly fell off my chair while I was om-ing. I prayed for an accepting heart. Now it's 9:10 p.m., and my heart seems a little more accepting, my load a little lighter.

This is a bit-by-bit process.

"Counting B Range! Counting!"

TWENTY-NINE

I HAVE LESS FUN BUT FIND JESUS

BACK IN CALIFORNIA, I met Bill and Kris Shaffer at Terry's place in Laurel Canyon in the Hollywood Hills. The younger brother, Kris, was a lady-killer with long auburn hair and a tiny strip of beard under his lower lip, a spitter. He was the nautical end of the Shaffer brothers' empire, a sailor-adventurer and the man with the foreign contacts. Bill was the slim, blue-eyed business Machiavellian, formidable if joyless. He had recently completed a year living in a tent on the roof of his mansion, smoking base brought up to him by hookers. When I met him, we talked awhile, then he invited me around to his house. I had to walk sideways inside because the place was furnished wall-to-wall and floor-to-ceiling with boxes of Thai sticks.

The Shaffers combined shrewdness with madness in a way that attracted me. I started making a tiny living doing some work with Bill, middling some pot, moving some stuff. I also took up moving money again for people who needed to have their wealth offshore. This time I hired people, gave them $100,000 or $200,000 apiece and sent them out to the banks, where they'd buy the cashier's checks for, say, $8,752.63, made out to such-and-such a company. I'd put the checks in my pocket and fly to, say, the Cayman Islands and deposit them.

Actually, it wasn't illegal to fly boxes of money into the Caymans. The problem was that the Caymans had customs inspections and everybody got to see your money. For that reason, we would on occasion fly cash by private jet to St. Martin, an island that offered the advantage of no customs. A car would drive out onto the runway and take off the luggage and drive into town while we went through Immigration. We'd go to a bank on the French side of St. Martin, and the bank would accept the money and give me a check for it. They charged a 1 percent fee. We'd take the check and fly it into the Caymans. By these means and others, I paid off the fine.

Then, all of a sudden, after years of doing coke, it stopped being fun. Somehow, though, I couldn't stop doing it. My relationship with Suzi was on and off, good and bad. When I'd go off on a coke binge, it wouldn't involve her, but eventually she started doing coke with me, trying to keep up with me. It broke her. Late in 1979 she entered a recovery hospital in Pasadena. Cheyenne was just two and was staying with Suzi's mother. I'd show up at the hospital in a limousine after being up for two days, high on coke. The staff told her I was the problem, not her, and she was nuts if she went home to me.

"No," I said. "No, babe, that's it. I'm straight now. That's it. Come on home, babe."

"You're crazy if you go with him," they said.

She came home with me, and soon enough we were doing coke again. By the time our daughter, Cherokee, was born in 1980, I'd started disappearing for three, four, five days at a time. I'd chase coke out into the night, night after night. I'd leave my wife and my kids, not phone home, show up five days later, a broken rag. I'm sorry, I'm sorry, I'm so sorry, I won't do it again. Blah, blah, blah.

I grew increasingly unreliable in business, and at one point I wound up dealing with CI again—always an indication of bad judgment on my part.

"You're an asshole!" I screamed at him on the phone after some piece of mendacious behavior. Really, I'd never forgiven him for splitting when the heat was on me at Tri. I slammed down the phone. A minute later, it rang again. It was him.

"Asshole, eh?"

"That's right, CI. A-s-s-h-o-l-e."

"I'll show you who's an asshole, asshole!"

He hung up. Boy, I was scraping the bottom of the barrel.

We went up to our country place at Lake Nacimiento near Paso Robles and hung out for a few days. Cranked on coke, I drove out into the land in my dune buggy under a blazing sun. I lost track of time and sustained a sunburn more terrible than the one I'd caught in Bogotá years before. By the time I was back in Chatsworth, I was in almost unbearable pain. Blisters the size of racket balls rose from my shins and ankles. Soon I was unable to walk and was confined to bed. I used crutches to hobble to the bathroom.

I woke up. It was the middle of the afternoon. CI's greasy, ugly face was inches from mine.

"Asshole, right?" he said. He stepped back. Behind him was a goon just as ugly, but genuinely mean-looking.

"Hey," said the goon. "He's already paid me to break your arm but, listen, fella, I gotta tell ya, I may not be able to stop myself."

My gut clenched in fear.

"Who's Mr. Tough Guy now?" asked CI.

Jeez, I thought, that's a dumb thing to say. I said, "Go ahead, buddy, take your best shot."

Because what he and his goon didn't know was that in the desk behind them I had an antique revolver. I'd been shooting

it out the window out of sheer boredom just a few hours earlier, and I knew there were two shells left in the cylinder.
They were going to hurt me, yes, and then I was going to blow
them away.

"Get up, asshole!" CI said.

"I can't," I said. "Look at my leg."

They looked.

"Shit. Ugly," the goon said.

Then CI picked up one of my crutches and used it to rip
open my blisters. I screamed in agony, and at that very moment Suzi rushed in the door with my daughter, Cherokee.

"Hey!" the goon turned to CI. "Hey! I said no kids or
women!"

Suzi didn't wait to sort out good from bad, not that it took
much sorting. She started smashing CI with her fists.

"Hey! Hey!" CI yelled.

"I'm outta here," said the goon. He turned and was gone. CI
followed him, Suzi still pounding his back.

Thus passed five unhappy years.

One evening in 1984 I opened the door and there was
Santiago, back from the past, with his years in a Martinique
prison behind him. Santiago knew no other life than the one
we had shared. He showed me a diabolically clever way of
filling the corrugations in cardboard boxes with cocaine. This
was how he was going to ship his product into New York, and
I would look after it from there. This we did—just once, but
successfully—and then he disappeared again, and I have never
seen or heard from him since. Maybe he retired to a real
ranch, as he always wanted to do.

The secondary effect of the New York deal was that I was
now in direct possession of the *clavo*—the stash—and could
stoke my sickness to white heat. My world came apart entirely: I was broke, untrustworthy in business, absent from my

life. I struggled without success to put down the coke. Suzi struggled too, though with somewhat greater success.

In October of that year, she came back from a trip to Oregon with some money and tried to keep a bit of it for herself. My insane coke mind convulsed in fury. I screamed and ranted. I broke furniture. I had fifty handguns stashed all around the house, including a machine gun with a silencer on it.

Suzi looked at me, and her eyes were cold. If she was afraid, she didn't show it. "Brian," she said. "You do something about this now—right now—or I'm out of here."

"You're out of here?" I shouted. "You're out of here? I'm out of here! Fuck you! Fuck you! Fuck you!"

That was as good as I could do.

I stormed out of the house, left my wife and children, and tore over to this coke dealer's house—that's where I went when I needed support. A blonde girl who'd just left her husband two days earlier showed up. We sat talking in the dealer's living room, and by later that day I was staying at her place, and this swiftly became living at her place.

Suzi took the kids, left our house empty—a fitting emblem of our lives—and moved out of LA. She wouldn't allow further contact between us. I kept trying to play the middle man in little dope deals, and then, six months later, I was sitting alone in a diner, thinking about getting hold of some coke and thinking how much I didn't want to. I can't do any more of this, I said. I called one of Suzi's girlfriends and begged her to have Suzi contact me, talk to me. The next afternoon, Suzi called.

"I just want to get sober," I said. "I just want to get some help and get our lives back together. Just help me do that, help me find some way to get sober."

She was living in an apartment with the kids in a little beachside community outside Santa Barbara. Two days later, she called me. "I've found a hospital in Santa Barbara," she said. "I found this hospital called Pinecrest. They'll take you, and I've got a place for you. Meet me Wednesday at the Barber's Grill in Santa Barbara, and I'll take you in there."

On Wednesday I pulled my white Firebird up in front of the hospital. Suzi was with me, hanging in there. We sat in silence.

"You know what?" I said. "I haven't done any coke today and, you know, I can handle this now."

"Handle what?"

"My life."

"What are you saying?"

"Really. I'm okay."

She looked at me. I couldn't read her expression.

"I'm going in there," she said and got out of the car.

I sat out in front of the hospital in the car. All my clothes were in the backseat. I listened to the radio. I didn't think about much. An ad came on. The announcer asked if I was confused about coke.

"Are you having a hard time?" he wondered. "Want to stop? Think you can and then you can't?"

"That's right," I said.

"There is a way," he said.

"I just don't know what it is." I said. "It's hard."

"At Pinecrest Hospital in Santa Barbara, professional practitioners and counselors will put you firmly on the pathway back to your life. They'll help you—as they've helped so many others—understand yourself and your addiction. Most importantly, they'll give you the tools you need to say goodbye to coke forever."

"Where is that?"

"That's Pinecrest Hospital in Santa Barbara."

I reached into the backseat and grabbed my clothes.

I was there for the twenty-eight-day intensive program. I went to lectures, therapy sessions, AA meetings, CA (Cocaine

Anonymous) meetings, self-esteem courses. I started feeling real good, what they call the pink cloud. Everything was great, there was no more work to do, there was nothing underlying anything. You just stopped using the damn drugs and your problem was solved. Suzi came to visit me with the kids every day or so. I did my time and was ready for the street. I had my motorcycle brought up to the hospital.

I couldn't understand why nobody felt good about letting me out of the hospital, but, hey, that was their business, wasn't it? I waved a warm good-bye to all, strolled out to the parking lot, climbed onto my motorcycle, kicked it into life, revved the engine a few times, tore out of the lot into the street, and— bam!—a truck hit me twice, once with the front wheel and once with the back wheel, in the head and down the side, ripping the skin off. I lay unconscious on the crosswalk to another hospital just across the street.

I woke up in a bed. There were a bunch of people standing around me: my counselor and various people who'd been in recovery with me. I didn't recognize them. Unfortunately, I'd lost all recollection of the previous month, making it a very poor investment, indeed. However, since the addiction-recovery hospital was also a regular hospital, the staff of the second hospital sent me back across the street to recover from my injuries and do the addiction program again. I was there for another month.

Finally, on the sixtieth day, my poor wife came to pick me up so we could be together again. We drove back to the little apartment she'd been living in on the beach. She had a big bag of pot under the bed, and the kids were out playing on the beach. I pulled out the pot and rolled a joint and fired up that joint, and cracked a beer and chugged that beer.

"You know what?" I said. "I think this is going to work."

"Yeah," Suzi said. "I think so too. You seem so much better."

After six months of this, I knew I was recovered and could afford to let my guard down enough to do a line—a line, for God's sake, just a little line—and from that day on, I had my face so far into that bag of coke I couldn't hope to get it out. It was like I'd been in that bag the whole time. Now I did coke—all of it, all the time. I disappeared for days again, I stopped showing up in my life again for anything but cocaine, became again the brute in my own home, again the unreliable dealer. Occasionally, people who'd known me when I was supplying them would front me small amounts of coke, mainly out of pity. They knew their chances of getting their money back were slim.

Early 1985. I was sitting alone at the end of the railway tie barrier that separated the two lanes of my driveway. I was looking out at the mountains, doing nothing at all, something I was doing more and more often.

A big orange Cadillac pulled up in front of our antique store, the Log Cabin Mercantile. A man, stout, with a pencil moustache, jumped out. He had a sort of Florida-sounding twang: "Hey, mister! How are you?" There was a question!

"All right," I said.

"Hey," he said. "My name's Paul Halloran. I'm the new preacher down here at Chatsworth Lake Chapel. You're Brian, right? Suzi's husband?"

"That's right," I said.

"Great to meet you, Brian. I know Joe and Margaret, Suzi's parents. I just knew I had to come down and talk to you. They said we'd have a lot in common. We're the same age, aren't we, about? I just wanted to stop by and say hi. Hi, Brian."

"Thanks for doing that."

He laughed a little, and I thought, who is this creep? He kept eyeing me without saying anything more. I felt uncomfortable.

"Hey, Brian," he said. "Your life is not in good shape, is it?" He looked right at me and I felt I had to look back.

"You know," I heard myself say, "it really isn't."

"What's the problem, Brian?"

"It's fucking everything."

"Well, what do you really mean?"

"Coke. I don't know what to do. I'm stuck."

"I might be able to help you out, Brian."

"Oh yeah?"

"I might have an idea. Would you like to listen?"

"I'm listening."

"Brian, why don't you accept Jesus Christ as your Lord and Savior right now, right here, right this very second."

He looked at me. His eyes seemed very bright and close. At first I didn't know how to reply. Finally, I did reply.

"Are you kidding?" I asked. "What the fuck is that? You're talking to me about Jesus Christ as my Lord and Savior? What does that mean?"

"All you have to do is trust, Brian. It's as simple as that. You step out in faith right this moment—right this moment know that Jesus Christ died for you. For you, Brian O'Dea! For you!"

"I don't know what that means."

"He died for you, Brian, so you could be reborn. You accept that, accept that this very moment, right this very moment, and see what happens, Brian."

"This moment?"

"Here's the deal, Brian. Either your life starts to get better from this second or it doesn't. Either this works or it doesn't. Am I right, yes or no?"

"Yeah, you're right, I suppose."

"If it works, fantastic. If it doesn't, you've lost nothing. Am I right?"

"Yeah, I guess."

"You have nothing to lose, Brian. Just say yes."

"Just say yes?"

"Just say yes to Christ, Brian, this very second."

"This very second."
"Just say yes this very second."
"Yes," I said.
"I accept Jesus Christ as my Lord and Savior."
"I accept Jesus Christ as my Lord and Savior."

In that instant, I was transformed, jolted by Jesus, clobbered by Christ—body, mind, and spirit. I was then and there reborn as a Christian fan, an instant Christian cheerleader. All my best efforts to that point had brought my life to these lows. Here, now, was a guy telling me that my best efforts weren't the key. If it didn't work, I could walk away. At that moment I lost my island status; an isthmus was built between me and the rest of the world. I was at last free from the bondage of myself, and I knew then and there that I was happier.

From that moment on, if you saw me coming and you weren't prepared to accept Jesus as your personal Savior, you had better get out of my way, because I was going to talk to you about Jesus Christ. I was obnoxious for Jesus, an honest-to-God believer in the Son of God, and I wanted to tell you about it. It's just fucking unbelievable how this works, I'd tell my Jewish friends. I have the answer.

And, having made such a blind leap in God's direction, having wagged my tail for Jesus, He chose to throw me—well, a bone.

My friend Barry Levinson had been running Zip-Kit, a vending machine refurbishing business in the San Fernando Valley, and doing quite well. He was a tall, gentle, good-natured man with his own demons, but he'd proved a good friend and loyal partner. Now he asked me to come in with him on an opportunity, and together we'd see if we could put something together. He didn't want to spend the rest of his life recoining cigarette machines. He knew that if I could only focus, I'd make things happen.

Barry had met this guy, Ken Kolb, who'd been living in Green River, Utah, for some years and had developed a passion for collecting dinosaur bones, working some of the agatized ones into striking jewelry. Barry and I got to brainstorming, and we developed a packaging and marketing program that would throw bucks at the National Geographic Society with every sale. We acquired thirty tons of these broken bones and were ready to rumble. This was the idea that would set us free, and it was totally legitimate. All that was lacking was a few hundred thousand dollars.

I went off to see Bill and Kris Shaffer. I'd lost contact with them during my cocaine decline, but I reckoned we were still friends. First and foremost, I had to tell them the big news: Jesus Christ had died on the cross for them. If they would just accept Christ into their hearts that moment, their whole lives would change, just as mine had. And, oh yeah, I needed $250,000 to market dinosaur bones as jewelry.

As tough as nails and, in their own special ways, as mad as hatters, Bill and Kris listened. They'd always liked my chutzpah, a quality they admired in others, no matter what failings others may have had. Now, through an act of faith perhaps, they believed in these dinosaur bones, perhaps more than they believed in Christ, and they decided then and there that they were going to make these dinosaur bones work, even if O'Dea was born again.

THIRTY

THERE'S A NEW GUY in the bunk next to me, and he reminds me of what my own first few days were like. He's sleeping now, as he slept most of today, yesterday, and the day before. The first defense against being slammed in here is sleep. No matter how long the sleep lasts, there is still a tiredness that cannot be removed by sleep, just the passage of time, the passage of time. As I'm getting into my locker, he wakes, shouts a Spanish obscenity at me for disturbing him, then realizes his error and rolls over, muttering apologetically, and slips back off to sleep.

"*Cuenta! Cuenta!* Counting B Range! Counting! Stand down! Four o'clock count!"

"Did you hear about Jesse?"

"What about him?"

"He got rolled up. The lieutenant came in and ripped his house apart, and then they rolled him up, SHU-box time. He had the horse tied up in his cell."

"These people would rather do dope than live. Jail is not the answer, Ricardo."

"My cellie is gonna get a move soon too. They're gonna shake him down too, and that'll be it for him. Shit, man, I got thirty years, I don't wanna spend my time worryin' about a junkie cellie. As soon as he goes, you move in, Brian, okay?"

"Okay, Ricardo, okay."

Russell is busy making one of his giant beaded Buddhas, four feet square and consisting of hundreds of thousands of beads. He sells these works for as much as $30,000.

"Russell, do I see you meditating in the south yard sometimes?"

"Yeah, it's kinda tough, but I've got to do it somewhere."

"Why don't we talk to Father Bill about getting meditation time in the chapel?"

"Hey, Brian. I did already. You know what it's like. I told him we had thirty people who want to meditate and suggested 1:30 p.m. every day in the chapel. He said 'No no, they'd have to take off work.' I suggested that they already let guys off work for Catholic affairs. 'That's different,' he says. 'No, I'm just not doing that.' I used to go to the chapel on my own at 1:30, and he told me I had to stop. I said it didn't make sense: he was in his office and the building was open. He said that, even though he was there, technically, there was no supervision, so I had to stop coming to meditate."

"How much time are you doing, Russell?"

"Ten years, new law. Eight years, eleven months total on ten."

"Coke?"

"Pot. I had 144 three-inch pot plants growing. The probation officer doing my presentence report started to lecture me on the evils of pot. She was twenty-five years old. I said, 'Excuse me, but you're much too young and inexperienced to lecture me on anything.' She said, 'Oh yeah? You'll see,' and she recommended that the court give me thirty-five years.

"The first year was hard but, you know, when I see Ben with seventy, Cornbread with fifty, Mark with fifty, Larry with the rest of his life—actually, all these guys have life sentences for pot—I feel fortunate. It doesn't make it right, but the best way for me to do my time is to choose feeling good, not bad."

"I'm lucky, getting ten, old law."

"I've been in almost two years, and you'll be out before me, Brian. Yet we both got ten years. Ten years under the new law is the same as fifteen years, old law. This whole way of treating people has never worked and never will, yet they continue to do it."

"Gotta go, Russell. See you tomorrow."

"All right, Brian, g'night. See ya tomorrow."

The evening soups are cooking, cards hitting the tables, money changing hands.

"Counting B Range! Counting!"

THIRTY-ONE

I EMBARK UPON A BIG ADVENTURE BUT UNWISELY MAKE AN ENEMY

THE DINOSAUR BONES were looking good, very good, and Jesus Christ was my Savior. Things were so good, in fact—and I was feeling so good about them—that when the telephone rang on the morning of June 10, 1985, and I picked it up and it was CI, I didn't hang up immediately.

"Hey, Brian," he said—you could still hear his Newfie accent—"Hey, it's me."

That's when I didn't hang up.

"Hey, CI."

"Hey, Brian, listen, I know you and me, we've had our problems in the past and our issues, like, but I have an opportunity here, and I need your connections and your connections need me."

"I know it's great, whatever it is."

"Hear me out, Brian."

"CI, I'm putting my life onto another track right now."

"Brian, I have without a doubt the best off-load situation you could imagine. If you can just get in touch with your guys and come and take a look at it, I just know this would be perfect for them."

I said, yeah, yeah, I'd talk to my people, and I got off the phone. CI. Phew. Last thing I needed. Just when the dinosaur bones were looking good. I forgot to mention his call to the Shaffer brothers.

June 17, 1985. CI called back. I said I'd speak to them, and again I didn't. .

June 24, 1985. CI called a third time, and I was a little exasperated.

"Hey," I said. "I must tell you the truth, buddy. I'm trying to get out of this business, and I don't want to do this anymore. I've got a real business opportunity that I've presented to my connections. I'm getting money from them to do this dinosaur thing, and I don't want to interfere with it by talking about a dope deal. You know what I mean? I just want to keep going with my thing."

"Okay, Brian. You sure?"

"I'm sure, buddy."

July 2, 1985. He called again.

"Okay," I said. "I'll tell you what I'll do. I'll mention it to them one time only. I'm having a meeting with them in a couple of days. I'll tell them about it once, and that's it. If they're interested, fine. If not, you know that's all I got for you."

I used to meet people at this place called the Iverson Movie Ranch. My friend Bob Sherman owned it, and I could take people there any time. I don't know how big the ranch was, but Bob had about thirty acres fenced in and a big California Spanish–style house. He had a museum in there filled with mineral samples from all over the world and butterflies and bugs and lopped-off heads of African game that the previous owner of the ranch had brought back from big-game safaris.

The original *Ben-Hur* was shot at the ranch, and all the *Lone Rangers*, the *Hopalong Cassidys*, and hundreds of other movies. There was a vineyard and a nine-hole golf course and all-natural rock and flagstone barbecue areas. I called the Shaffers, and we agreed to meet at the ranch.

July 6, 1985. Bill and Kris had a limousine—a stretch yellow taxi—that they'd given to a friend of theirs, and he was their driver. After the meeting, they were going down the driveway in this limousine when suddenly I remembered the CI thing. I ran about half a mile across the golf course and waved them down. Kris rolled down the window.

"Hey, look. I forgot. There's this guy who's not really a friend of mine but I've known him all my life. He called me. He's up in Washington in Anacortes in the San Juan Islands. Anyway, he tells me he has this incredible off-loading situation. The connections, the people, the locals, the whole thing. I told him I'd tell you about it. That's all. I mean, if you were interested, then, you know, we could take a look at it. If not, not. That's it."

Kris turned and looked at Bill, then looked back at me. "Hop in," he said.

That afternoon we were on a plane to Washington.

It was everything CI said it was. He was involved with a guy up there named Tony Franolovich, whose father was an admiral in the Yugoslav navy during the Second World War. Appearing to be a Nazi sympathizer, he had actually been an American mole, so when the writing was on the wall for the Nazis, he pulled a boat into Split, Croatia, where he picked up anybody who wanted to go. The next stop was Ellis Island, from where they were immediately deported to a refugee camp in Venezuela. In Venezuela, a priest, learning that Tony's father was an American spy, had someone from the

American embassy come over, and the Franolovichs were soon living happily ever after in Anacortes, Washington. They became fishermen and leading figures in the huge Croatian community there.

I liked Tony right away: big boy, big habits, big heart, with black hair and a black moustache to match. He was captain of his family's boat, the *St. Peter*, a fifty-four-foot-long seiner, and most importantly, he was the godson of the owner of a dry dock and shipyard facility that covered a chunk of private waterfront on this beautiful island. Anacortes was a picturesque farming, fishing, oil, and timber town on Fidalgo Island, the easternmost of the San Juan Islands. As a callow dope dealer, I was still able to respond to the place. It produced the best oysters in the world, Penn Cove selects, and in April the commercial fields of daffodils and tulips stretched as far as the eye could see. The shipyard consisted of a half-dozen immense green wooden buildings filled with equally immense machinery for the construction of yachts and fishing boats. The interiors were vast, haunting. Pacific Northwest timber beams arched overhead, and the heavy floors were reliable but eerily creaky. When I looked up, I could see five or six stories of boats arrayed above me.

"How are you going to get that boat down from there?"

Tony's godfather laughed. "Don't worry, my friend. This is my yard. Anything can happen."

And did.

It was, indeed, the ideal off-load place. We could run the boat in here and tie off—no one would know, business as usual, as far as anyone was concerned. There was a private driveway down which our trucks could come into the vast yard and load up without anyone seeing. The Shaffers loved it, and I couldn't help but love it, and I let myself believe that CI would be okay.

We flew back to California. The Shaffers and I talked about the opportunity and decided we'd take it. We agreed that their end of this thing would be the other side of the world—Southeast Asia, Europe—and my end would be this side of the world, once the cargo hit the Bering Sea. We also agreed that we all had a demon with coke and we were each of us trying to leave it alone. Coke makes you completely unreliable. We resolved that anybody who did coke was out of the deal. Everybody who subsequently came in agreed to these terms. In the end, there were 110 of us working on this thing from one end of the world to the other, and every one of us had previously done coke.

August 1985. I went back up to Washington, and the Shaffers set off to organize in Southeast Asia, where they were dealing with a senator in Thailand whom we called Tony the Thai. Tony the Thai arranged through some friends of his in Australia to purchase seventy-five tons of pot from military personnel in Vietnam. Meanwhile, a group of English guys had a boat we called the *Misty*. Its job was to pick up the load in Vietnam and bring it over to us in the Bering Sea. We had people in Hong Kong who were there to keep our connections open in Southeast Asia, because at the time it was easier to live in Hong Kong than it was in Vietnam or Thailand and drew less attention. Bill and Kris Shaffer now started to raise millions of dollars of other people's money to do this thing—ultimately $10 million, maybe more than that.

December 1985–February 1986. We needed a bigger vessel. I went with Tony to the Seattle waterfront and leased the *Cathy B*, a hundred-foot tender, a sweetheart of a boat. She was actually built as a troop and equipment carrier during the last war. Tony hired the crew—people he knew, including two of his nephews. Using guys in their early twenties represented a risk, though, because, if the shit hit the fan, they might not be able to resist the threats and pressures.

We spent the next months putting the boat together while I made arrangements to transport the product from Washington to California. I needed trucks. It was time to level with Barry, my partner in the dinosaur-bone business.

"Barry," I said, "let's drop this fucking dinosaur thing, buddy, and focus on doing this. How'd you like to start a fishing company?"

Dangling the vastness of this operation before Barry was like offering candy to a child. Like me, Barry was perpetually in pursuit of that which would set him free and, as I did, he felt that money, enough money, would accomplish this. Barry had a friend whose son owned a trucking company. This son figured out what we were trying to do, so he took our first $30,000 cash down payment and disappeared. We had to go off and lease other trucks. I put cash into Zip-Kit, the vending machine company Barry managed for a couple of modestly shady goodfellas, and with Zip-Kit as the front, we leased five 44-foot brand-new Peterbilt tractor trailers, painted them all with Zip-Kit Inc. on the sides and put them on the road immediately.

March 1986. We didn't know precisely when we were going to get the shipment. I realized I needed somebody up in Washington on the boats, somebody who could keep an eye on what was going on, somebody who could keep me informed, someone who knew me and whom I knew well. I didn't know Tony well, and I didn't trust CI. I thought of Frank Graf, a friend of mine in Cleveland, a brilliant mechanical engineer. We'd met through Suzi and done a little casual business together. He'd formerly built racing engines—engine carburation was his specialty. Now sixty years old, his long hair graying, he was living in Cleveland, building and collecting his own cars. He was as loyal as a pit bull. I phoned him.

"Hey Frank, will you come out here? We got this thing going on, and if you'd come out and get on these boats and just keep your eye on things for me, I'd be incredibly grateful. You can live with Tony and CI up on Mercer Island. It's a very ritzy part of Seattle. They have a condo there."

It sounded right to Frank, and he was aboard as chief engineer.

April 4, 1986. I was down in Los Angeles building the trucking company, hiring drivers, and getting guys into trucking school. I got a phone call from Frank.

"Brian, I got to tell you this. I hate to be the one to phone you about it, but, you know, I'm concerned. CI came home the other night at three in the morning in a limousine with a couple of hookers. They had a bag of coke, and they were just fucking crazy. But, Bri, this Mercer Island place, we can't be doing this here."

CI. Shit. If there was going to be a problem, this is where it would start.

"All right, Frank. I'll take care of it."

I hung up and did nothing, hoped I wouldn't hear anything further.

April 14, 1986. Frank phoned me again.

"Brian, it happened again last night. You've got to do something about this."

"I'll get to it, Frank," I said. "I really will. Just keep your eye on him."

April 20, 1986. I got another call.

"Look," Frank said, "it happened again, and I'm just calling to tell you, I'm out of here."

"What do you mean?"

"I'm out. This is too dangerous for an old mechanic like me."

"Shit, Frank, please. I'm sorry. Just stay there, okay? I'll come right up. I promise."

———

April 22, 1986. I gathered some friends, substantial guys, and flew up to Seattle. We went over to the condo just after lunch. There was CI, still in his underwear, scratching his nuts and looking hungover. We sat him down at the kitchen table and explained that he had to go on permanent leave.

"What the fuck are you talking about, Brian? Leave where?"

"Leave here, CI."

"For where?"

"For your fucking brother-in-law's in Florida."

"I'm not going there. Why would I go to his place? This is my fucking deal, Bri. Don't start pushing me around. This is my deal."

"That's right. It's your deal, and you go anywhere you want and do anything you want. Go blow your fucking nose out with as much coke as you can get and butt-fuck every hooker on the East Coast. Just get out of here and don't show your face until this thing is over."

"You're trying to fuck me, O'Dea!" He was up out of his chair, and he looked scared and dangerous at the same time. I was glad I wasn't there alone.

"You're fucking yourself, CI. When it's over, you'll get your money. Until then, if we see you around here, forget about it, it's over."

"What? Just like that?"

"Just like that. This afternoon."

"You're fucking me!"

"Nobody's fucking you, CI. We're not like you. You get out of here, and you'll be taken care of."

"You're fucking me!"

But he was gone by four.

———

May 1986. I started sending truckers up and down Highway 5 from Los Angeles to Seattle. Every couple of weeks they'd drive up and then they'd drive back and then they'd drive up and then they'd drive back. We had to know the road conditions at all times and the procedures at the inspection stations. We couldn't afford any problems at the stations. Everybody had to know how to keep their log. You can't send a truck up and down the road with nothing in it all the time, or with the same waybill. You need new waybills every time you go. The inspectors read your log, they read your waybill to see what you're carrying. We bought a load of cedar shakes in Oregon, and we filled our new trucks one at a time with shakes. We had our own dummy companies and our own dummy waybills, and we sent that same load of cedar shakes up and down and up and down that road a hundred times in all these trucks, changing waybills every trip.

June 1986. We set a safe house up in Seattle that was operated by Phyllis, a friend of one of the guys. In this house was a safe phone. The only people who knew about this place were those who needed to know. Phyllis had everybody's cell phone numbers. If anything went wrong, we arranged to call her and she'd get everybody in touch with everybody else.

For more general purposes, all of us on land in North America had pagers. The pagers had 800 numbers, and if one of us wanted to talk to somebody else in the group, we'd page them from a pay phone. Pay phones in the 1980s had telephone numbers and ringers, so we could phone in on them. All of us in the lead of this operation had a $500 box of quarters that we would use at pay phones.

Our cell phones, on the other hand, were strictly for emergencies, and we tried to keep away from them as much as possible. These were early days for the cell phone, anyway, and the things almost filled a briefcase. I had the first

Mitsubishi portable, and it was a five-pounder that you had to hold up to your ear with both hands. Cost me $3,000.

At the same time, we needed a safe way to communicate with our boats at sea. In Anacortes, we moved a thirty-four-foot motor home into a campground and put a so-called single side band radio in it that was capable of transmitting all over the world. It needed power and a huge, long antenna. There would be so much current in the antenna, anyone who touched it during a transmission would be fried. We ran a wire from the truck up through a tree, then ran a 150-foot antenna horizontally through the trees of the campground. With this, we could communicate with the *Misty* in the South China Sea and with the fishing boats off Alaska. Of course, we had to keep the California boys away from the campground because they all stood out too much. I was the sole California guy in Tony's life. Locals believed I was there to finance the expansion of his fishing business.

Single sideband is reserved for licensed radio amateurs, but anyone with a receiver can listen in, and there are government agencies all over the world constantly monitoring single side-band transmissions. We couldn't risk communicating in plain language, and there were no war-surplus Enigma machines or twenty-first-century computer algorithms to rely on. But we had the ingenuity born of long experience. I bought a bunch of new 1985 Webster's dictionaries, and everybody got one. If a boat captain wanted to send a message to Anacortes saying, "Pick up load, present longitude, present latitude, estimate arrive Tuesday," he'd look up the word "pick" in his dictionary and find it on page 759. It would be the thirty-second entry on that page. He'd do that for every word. Then he'd contact the home base and request a number of parts. "Check part 759-32," he'd say, then, "Check part 1080-61," and so on. The home base would reply in a similar fashion.

———

July 1986. The boats were now at sea, fishing. The *Cathy B* was a tender. Fishing boats—herring fishers, say—wouldn't bring their catch on board, they'd just bring it into a net and close the net, and then the tender would come by and vacuum out the net. The *Cathy B* ran fish up and down for fishermen, and the *St. Peter* fished herring. For a whole season, we appeared to all the world to be running a successful fishing business.

We knew that the stuff would come over from Asia in kilo blocks in plastic shrink wrap. We'd have to take the load off the *Misty* in the Bering Sea, then go up into a fjord and hide while we did quality control, graded every single package, and entered it into a computer. We would know exactly what we had and what each package would sell for. We'd know this was the triple-A that would go for $1,150; this, the double-A that would sell for $1,125; this, the standard grade that would go for $1,000. We would know exactly to the dime what the revenue would be on the load. Then we would have to re–shrink-wrap it and put it in wet-lock fish boxes so that the load looked just like any other load of fish that had been wet-lock boxed at sea. When all that was done, the *Cathy B* would come out of the fjord and head straight down for Anacortes.

September 1, 1986. My birthday. We got the word that the *Cathy B* was coming in. We had spotter planes looking at Coast Guard activity. I went out on the dock and waited. At about eleven in the morning, the *Cathy B* chugged around the spit and into Anacortes harbor. I could see Frank Graf on the deck. Slowly, the *Cathy* drew in and docked. Frank and Tony and I shook hands.

Frank was laughing. "When we pulled up to the dock, and everybody's in the bushes, waiting to see if everything is okay, and I see nobody standing there but you, Brian, I knew everything was okay."

We didn't make any big deal about it. We backed the trailers one by one up to the boat and started boom loading. In three hours, everything was on the trucks, and the trucks were on the road, with a car following each truck. They were off to our sorting and distribution facility at an olive ranch in Lindsay, California.

With the twenty-five-ton off-load completed, the crew was just yippee-ki-yay. I got them an ounce of coke, and we cruised over to Friday Harbor, where we partied up a storm, snorting our fucking brains out, inviting everybody from the bars onto the boat. Poor Tony, he started smoking coke, then he started injecting coke. I couldn't find him. I went down to the engine room and tripped over him in the dark. He was lying on the floor in the engine room, hiding out. That's how bad that shit is. At last, a couple of us came to our senses. We still had all the Thai boxes down in the hold. We hadn't even bothered to dump them in the ocean. That was something I should have done, and didn't. We pulled everybody out of Friday Harbor, dumped the boxes at sea and washed down the boat.

September 10, 1986. I went down to California to help with the distribution of the pot and the movement of the money. About half of the pot was actually distributed out of New York, where I picked up millions of dollars from strangers on Manhattan streetcorners with suitcases full of cash. I brought it back to the west coast, where we had a couple of stash houses that ended up stacked floor-to-ceiling with boxes and boxes of cash. All the while, we were organizing the second load.

October 17, 1986. CI showed up at Tony's house in Anacortes.
"Hey, CI. How are you?" Tony invited him in.
"Okay, okay." He looked around. "Where's O'Dea?"
"Brian? He's not here. I think he's in California."

"Okay, okay. Anyway, I just came for my dough."

"Uh-huh?"

"So?"

"Well, I don't have money here, CI."

"When can you get it?"

"I don't really know, CI."

"Well, get on the fucking phone and find out about it. I want my money. I want my first installment right now, and that's a million bucks. At least a million."

"Okay, I'll give them a call."

"When?"

"Uh, tonight. Can't call before tonight."

"I'll see you tomorrow, then, Tony."

"Good, CI. Yeah, good."

Tony called. No one wanted to give CI any money at all until the whole deal was done, but least of all did we want to give him enough money to go out and get nuts with and draw attention to himself. We did want to keep him down while we were pulling the next part of the load together. Tony suggested we give him fifty grand. I thought this might be a problem and said so, but the others thought it best.

October 18, 1986. CI was back. Tony had made sure he was not at home alone.

"CI, look, there's a lot going down right now, and nobody's getting any money until the whole deal is done."

"Don't shit me, Tony."

"I'm not shitting you. Nobody's seeing any real money until we're done."

CI stood silent a moment. He made a little laugh.

"But look, CI, the guys have authorized me to give you some walking-around money for now. Sort of on my account. So that's what this is." He went in the closet and brought out a bag and put it on the table.

"What's in there?" CI asked.

"Fifty grand."

CI didn't say or do anything for about a minute. Then he picked up the bag. "I'm being fucked in the ass," he said.

"No, you ain't, CI," said Tony.

"I know what it feels like," said CI.

From Tony's place, he went straight downtown to the Seattle DEA's office. He walked in and introduced himself. "Here's fifty grand," he said. "There's a whole lot more where that came from, and I can tell you where it's coming from and who's involved." CI . . . Confidential Informant.

THIRTY-TWO

I'M UP ON THE THIRD TIER. Phil, a decent guy but a loser Aryan type
nonetheless, is teaching me how to crochet a guitar strap fash-
ioned from Camel cigarette packs. I hear voices in the next
cell.

"Hey, Bobby, hand me the scarf or tie me off, will ya?"

"Jesus, Buddha, why don't you shout it out or somethin',
man? Shut the fuck up. Fuckin' Silva and Lawrence are working tonight, man, two of the worst cops in the fuckin' joint, an'
you're shoutin' at me. You got a fuckin' death wish or
somethin'? Keep it down."

"All right, gentlemen! Nobody moves! Put that down, King.
Down, I said! Get the lieutenant on the radio, Lawrence."

"Roger."

"Okay, Buddha, over here. Put your hands behind your
back. Sit down, King."

"Yeah, Lieutenant, Silva here. We got a situation on the
third tier, here in J. Need some help. Got four to go."

"Roger, Silva, right away."

Thus, four prisoners qualify to wear brown jumpsuits and get
an hour of air a day—the SHU's standard allotment. Imagine

their need, imagine their pain, imagine their fear. How does this world deal with that? Why, punishment, of course, even harsher than before. How can they ever recover, how can they ever let go? How can they ever love? How can they ever learn another way? This is the way, this is the way it was for them. Mess up, get beat up. Beaten little boys who know nothing else. Little boys handcuffed in the SHU box now, little boys handcuffed.

"Hey, O'Dea." Another recruiter from the third tier, Aryan sector.

"Yeah, Shorty."

"You know Buddha went to the hole last night, don't ya?"

"Yeah, I know."

"You wanna move up?"

"No, thanks. I'm fine right here. Thanks, though."

"You like it here on the motherfuckin' freeway, man?"

"Yeah."

"You're fuckin' crazy, man."

Just as Rivas, the good black hack, says, "You move up there, it won't make no difference, 'cause you'll end up like them."

"Hey, Brian!" Voice from above.

"Yeah. Who's that? Where are you?"

"Billy, up here."

"Hey, Billy, what's up?"

"You gonna move up here?"

"Don't think so, Billy. I'm fine here for now."

"A couple of guys are holdin' their extra bunk open for ya."

"Thanks for thinking of me, Bill."

One of the four guys shooting up in the next cell is HIV-positive, and all of them know it. The price they are willing to pay is an agonizing death.

Now the hacks are rolling up another. The hacks say it comes in spurts. This guy's gone for fighting.

I sit on my bunk writing, surrounded by *Cubanos* chirping up a storm. Good and lonely boys, a dozen or so of them, all listening to the same radio station through their headphones, singing along loudly, moving, dancing, singing together, laughing at once, then crooning along, full of expression, lost from the poison for a few moments, then laughing. Lost children.

Mark says, "Can you picture a dozen of us in a Cuban jail with our headphones on, singing some song together, dancing and crooning?"

No.

During the night they roll up three more for smoking pot. After all the action in the unit over the past few days, they still smoke pot in here, where it can be smelled and where a shot in SHU takes away so much precious time.

"Red, get over here."

"Wha's up, Lieutenant?"

"What the fuck you got under there, man?"

"Whaddaya mean, Sullivan?"

"Right, Red, open the fuckin' coat."

"Okay."

"Uh-huh, 'nuf fuckin' sugar to make a gallon of pruno. Let's have a look in yer house there, Red."

That's the last of Red, our thirteenth SHU victim in forty-eight hours. They want the freeway to disappear during the visit of the Ninth Circuit judges. They're filling up the hole with guys from this unit. Don't want to appear overcrowded.

"You know, O'Dea, the guy who trained me as a guard opened my eyes up to a lot of stuff."

"What was that, Mr. Rivas?"

"He showed me what I didn't want to be. We'd be walkin' along the yard, and he'd stop someone just walkin' by an' say,

'Hey, you, get against that wall,' for no reason. He'd get lit up an' shake 'em down jus' for fun. Fuck that. I knew right then that was how I wasn't gonna be. Them guys are the ones who couldn't make it on the street, who wanted to be tough guys but could only pick on small people. An' that's what they do here."

"Count! Recount!"

The card game resumes. The TVs flare. Spanish, Cuban, and English mix. The shuffling of a deck of cards. Soup's on, snacks munched. The Hare Krishna heroin smuggler with a five-year sentence moves next to me.

"I had my fuckin' locker broken into yesterday, man. They took everything, including my photo album. Why the fuck would anyone want my photos and a two-dollar album?"

Must be a lot of karma hooked up with using a religious organization as a front for smuggling heroin.

I'm paying my price now and not later for the choices I've made. The good thing about this journey is that, when I get out of here, I will once again have a clean slate.

"Boss, I just can't make this garden grow without water. You've got to get me a hose."

"Can't you borrow one somewhere?"

"From where, boss?"

"Look, O'Dea, I been doin' my best, but these people work here act like they own shit 'round here. They think that the gov'ment hose is their hose. See, people here don't use common sense. Seems that's a gov'ment affliction. I was fightin' in Vietnam, duckin' bullets, an' they was somewhere arguin' 'bout what kinda table to sit down at. You know what I mean, O'Dea? Well, it's the same mentality here."

"I get you, boss, but I still need a hose."

———

I meet Paul at the inside iron pile in the south pile.

"How's your time going, Paul?"

"Okay. I try not to be bitter about the hypocrisy, but some days it's tough."

"How much time are you doing, Paul?"

"Twenty-seven."

"Twenty-seven years."

"That's right."

"Coke?"

"Pot. Actually, I got fifteen years for the pot and twelve years for obstruction of justice. I was in international waters on a ship flying a foreign flag, but the Coast Guard still wanted to board me. I wouldn't even come out on deck, or answer them on the radio. They fired a few shots across my bow, and I kept on going. There was nothing I could do, so I burned the boat. They gave me twelve years for burning my own boat, a foreign-registered vessel in international waters. They said they had permission to board from the country of registry. They got that permission four hours after the boat went down."

"So they got you on conspiracy?"

"Yeah, they got one of my crew, a Kiwi, and threatened him with the rest of his life in jail, and he couldn't hold out. I didn't blame him, but I'm doing twenty-seven years, and he got out after eighteen months. I'm trying to get the twelve-year obstruction thrown out. Gotta keep up the hope, Brian. Twenty-seven years, new law, means I gotta serve around twenty-three years. Can't do that, man. It's a life sentence for guys like us. We'll all be here until we're in our seventies. Can't do that, man. I'm going home long before that."

"You sure are, Paul. You sure are, man."

THIRTY-THREE

I LOSE JESUS BUT MAKE A FORTUNE

I WENT HOME to Newfoundland in February 1987, and while I was there I visited Scott Stirling. I didn't really know him all that well. I'd done the talk show at his father's radio station when I was a kid, and now Scott was running the station. He and his wife lived in a fine house in St. John's, up by the golf course. They had their own indoor-outdoor pool and a tennis court. I went up to the place, and while I was there, I explained to Scott, as I explained to everyone, that he had to be born again.

When I was leaving, he put his hand on my shoulder at the door. "I can tell you're a seeker, just like me," he said.

What he meant by that was a mystery because, as far as I was concerned, I had sought and I had found. There was no building to be done now: the building was there, done, this was it. Yet I admired Scott and his success and his presence. So when he said he'd like to give me a book to read, a book called *Nine Faces of Christ: Quest of the True Initiate*, I could only nod. "Perfect. Thanks."

I took the book and read it on the plane out of Newfoundland. It was by Eugene E. Whitworth of Great Western University in San Francisco and was written as the autobiography of a guy named Joshua, who was Jesus Christ. Before the plane touched down in LA, this book had ripped the fundamentalism out of me. It turned Jesus Christ from a thing into a human being, and in the process it stole my answers and left me with questions I couldn't cope with. My defenses were down, but for the moment, I shut my mind to the void.

April 1987. This load was to be much bigger, so we bought a 160-foot vessel, the *Stormbird*, formerly an oil-rig supply boat. We spent $1 million outfitting it and building a shelter deck where people could work on the product unseen and out of the elements. It was also—somewhat incidentally—an effective fishing machine.

July 1987. The first load had been twenty-five tons, and the second load was to be fifty tons. Almost a year had passed. We were busy with distribution, and the careful organization of the second shipment in Asia took a lot more time, money, everything, than we'd anticipated. The whole project was paying off, and everybody wanted more money. We wanted more too, and we worked hard.

August 1987. A couple of our guys were worried we were being watched. No one was sure. The evidence was vague, disconnected, hard to pinpoint. The same car, not a neighbor's, parked on the street day after day, a guy reading behind the wheel. Some funny stuff on the phones. We sometimes speculated that this, whatever it was, might be coming from our old pal CI. I got in touch with those same substantial friends who had told him to leave the first time. We arranged to meet him at a hotel cafeteria, and we sat down and had a chat with him.

"Jesus, CI," I said. "This is getting to be, like, an overhead, having to keep traveling here and there to talk to you."

"Never mind spending money on traveling, Brian. How about paying me my share of this operation?"

"You'll get your share. Why wouldn't you? If you didn't, why, next thing we know, you might be knocking on the DEA's door and we'd have people parked outside our houses, you know, studying the racing forms and peeking at us from under their fucking fedoras."

"What the hell are you trying to say? I'd rat you out?"

"We're worried, CI. That's all. More worried than you need to be."

"That's bullshit. That's total bullshit. You think I'd do something like that? You're crazy. All I want is my money."

Al, who was with me, piped up. "Yeah, but if it was you, buddy, you know what would happen? You know?"

It was entirely rhetorical, of course. It was CI, and nothing ever did happen to him, and the DEA was recording the entire conversation.

September 1987. We lost sight of CI at this point, and nothing alarming arose. Our suspicions ebbed. The Shaffers were fairly high-profile guys—they were showing up north too much, and maybe they were drawing the heat. We dropped the matter and kept working. We did take some measures to increase security, however. Every one of us on the ground now had a police scanner that could pick up the local police transmissions. The problem with our scanners was that we had no idea what frequencies the DEA or the FBI or any of the feds used for their transmissions. We couldn't uncover this critical information.

September 18, 1987. We brought a guy up from San Diego who was actually on bail and soon to be convicted. But this poor fellow was also a radio expert, and he had a spectrum analyzer able to isolate the transmission frequencies of the federal government agencies. Now we could program into our scanners the DEA, FBI, and ATF frequencies. It was important to know what the other side was doing, especially when they knew what we were doing. Especially when we didn't know that they knew what we were doing.

September 28, 1987. We'd picked the load up from the *Misty*, and now the boats, including the *Stormbird*, were up in the fjord. We had three crews going through this fifty-ton load, sorting it out, repackaging it, putting it all in wet-lock fish boxes, getting ready to come back into Anacortes. Again we were on the radios, using the dictionaries.

This time, though, we all had a bunch of money in our pockets and were living well. We decided it was important that Tony and Bobby Mack, his first mate, fly down to have a chat with us about the particulars of the off-load. Our planning needed to be precise, and everybody needed to be on the same page. Tony and Bobby flew down, and I picked them up at the Seattle airport, ninety miles south of Anacortes. We turned onto Highway 5 and headed back up to Anacortes. About twenty miles from the harbor, my scanner lit up and turned on.

"Uh, yeah, a brown Suburban. We're right behind it. We should be pulling up into Anacortes in about twenty minutes." It was the DEA's frequency, and I was driving a brown Suburban. I looked in my rearview mirror and saw a car with antennas following me.

"It's the DEA," I said.

Tony looked around. "Oh no. Oh shit," is all he said.

My insides were frozen with fear. I gradually pulled away from the vehicle tailing us until it was finally out of sight. I turned off Highway 5. I drove for six hours. During that time, every car on the highway was a cop car. Every car I saw coming at me, behind me, on another street, parked a mile away, was

a cop car. The farmer on the tractor was a cop, the fisherman on
the boat was a cop; they were all watching me. I raced along
every dirt road. For two hours, we didn't say a word to one
another.

Finally, Tony broke the silence. "What are we going to do,
Brian?"

"Shit. I don't know what the fuck we're going to do. We're
going to drive."

"Where are we going?"

"How the fuck do I know?"

We had a fifty-ton load in Alaska. We had three crews at
work up there. The cops were following me. I didn't know
who they'd already picked up. I didn't know how far this had
gotten.

We didn't speak for another two hours.

"You okay, Brian?" Tony asked.

"I'm fucking freaked," I said.

We were silent for two hours more. Finally, we were almost
in Spokane, as far away from a port as you can get in Washington. I stopped at a pay phone and called the safe house.
Phyllis answered.

"Oh, thank God," she said. "There've been four groups of
you today who've been followed, and I've heard from everybody but you, and we were all worried that you were gone."

"Well, I'm not quite gone yet."

"Okay, so here's the plan. Everybody is to meet at the
campground tomorrow at four. Can you be there?"

"I don't see why not. If we drive all day tomorrow, we
should just about make it."

September 29, 1987. Independently, each of us arranged for
new vehicles and made it to the campground, shaken but
ready to put up a fight. There were Tony and Bobby; Gordon
Booth, who worked for the Shaffer brothers as their on-the-

spot man in Washington; Bill and Kris Shaffer themselves; Terry Restall, the English guy who had the boats over in Southeast Asia; and me.

After some discussion, we could sort out several hard or probable facts. First, they knew. Second, we now knew that they knew. Third, they didn't know that we knew that they knew.

We needed further intelligence. The Shaffer brothers threw in their connection with a lawyer named Howard Weitzman in Los Angeles, a lawyer to the stars and the money. Howard knew a guy named Steve Swanson, who was a former DEA agent and had become a private investigator. The Shaffers immediately hired Steve Swanson to find out what the DEA knew.

In the meantime, we decided to stay perfectly still. Everybody would go underground while this guy Swanson went to work.

When the meeting was over, Tony and I went for a walk under the stars.

"Shit, Bri, I don't know if this worth it. I mean, for the money."

"Yeah, well, let's ask ourselves again after we've got the money."

October 3, 1987. Swanson reported back. Certainly the DEA didn't know that we knew they were on to us. They knew nothing about our trucking company. They thought the pot was staying in Washington. That was good news. Bad news: they knew the identity of each of our vessels, and they were looking for them hard, with aircraft flying up and down the inside passage. They knew we were on the load, and they knew that the other boat, the *Misty*, had gone back. The Coast Guard and Navy were all involved—everybody was involved— but it was, first and foremost, a DEA thing.

They didn't know about our trucking, which was the one thing CI didn't know about. So it was him. We talked it over carefully. It was a question of either throwing the load overboard and coming home and letting them find nothing, or trying to pull it off. We decided we would try to pull it off.

October 7, 1987. We went to a friend—Skip, he was called—who had a boat named the *Blue Dolphin.* He was in an old ramshackle office down at the Birmingham Pier. We offered him $300,000 to loan us his boat for the weekend.

He looked at us with this sort of flat expression, a sort of sub-twinkle. "Just the weekend, huh?"

"Yeah, just, like, to take it for a weekend spin."

"Won't go too fast, will ya?"

"Oh God, no. We'd be very respectful of her."

"I wouldn't want her going too fast."

"Oh no. We wouldn't go speeding around in it, no way. No waterskiing or shit like that."

This was a two-hundred-foot ship. It normally carried down smaller boats from Alaska and often carried a deck full of Indian boats up to fish Alaskan waters.

"Make sure you bring her back," Skip said.

October 11, 1987. We were listening to the feds doing flyovers, listening to their communications, talking about looking for us, talking about not seeing us. We put our crew on the *Blue Dolphin* and sent it north to pick up the load off the boats that were hiding in the fjord.

October 14, 1987. The *Dolphin* slipped into the fjord, and the crews transferred the load. She put out again and turned south.

October 16, 1987. The feds were watching Anacortes. Nothing could happen in Anacortes that these guys wouldn't see. We met at night—Bill, Kris, Gordon, Tony, Bobby, and me—and decided on a plan. It would be business as usual. The *Dolphin* would put into a regular harbor—the least perfect off-load location imaginable. By anyone.

October 17, 1987. In the early hours of Saturday morning, Tony was off the Washington coast near Seattle. We radioed our boats that were hiding out in the Alaska fjord. They pulled out into open waters and tied off together like they were doing something. The scanners lit up. "We got 'em! We got 'em!" they cried. Wow, they were keen.

At 6 a.m., Tony pulled the *Dolphin* into the harbor at Bellingham, Washington, north of Seattle, a major port and home of the University of Washington. I was driving around downtown before the ship came in, sizing up all the coffee shops and looking at the people in there. To me, everybody looked like a cop.

The trucks were hidden. With them were ancillary trucks, forklifts, and all the required equipment, all carefully organized and waiting. I was starting to freak again. "This is going to im-fucking-plode," I kept muttering, "the moment that boat pulls in here."

The ship came into berth. I drove down and got out of my car. I was the only one on the wharf again. Frank was waving to me from the bridge. He knew it was all right because I was there. I was less sure.

We pulled a truck down immediately and backed it in. There was a coffee shop window with a good view of what we were doing, and there were people in there watching us. Because each truck had four pallets of cedar in the back as camouflage, we had to use the forklifts to take the cedar off. The back of the trucks smelled like cedar because they'd had nothing but cedar in them for two years. If someone opened the back doors, he'd be hit with an immediate smell of aromatic cedar. We started sliding wet-lock boxes out and throwing the boxes up onto a conveyor belt that carried them into the back of the trucks. We spilled a box filled with fish under the conveyor so that it looked like the box had fallen off and broken. All the boxes looked the same but only one or two had salmon. The rest were filled with what we called brown carp.

Now some guys who had been watching us from the restaurant started coming down to talk to us. So we just picked the fish up off the ground and gave everybody a nice salmon, and they were delighted. Off they went, with a thank you very much.

As we filled each truck, we forklifted the four pallets of cedar back into place. Nobody thought it strange. In five hours—Saturday morning from six to eleven—we off-loaded the entire ship in front of God and downtown Bellingham. Every truck was off to California.

As our boats crossed the Canada–U.S. border in the Inside Passage, all hell broke loose. Helicopters and boats and ships and airplanes were everywhere. The Navy, the Coast Guard, the ATF, the DEA, the LMNOP, QRS, TUV. Every initial in the United States security-agency lexicon was there. They scrambled aboard with shouts of triumph. There was coffee and doughnuts waiting for them, but there wasn't so much as a joint. A lot of red herring. They'd been had, and they were very angry men, very angry, indeed. But it was done and it was gone.

December 1987. We felt pretty smug about the whole thing, though in my heart of hearts I just couldn't believe they'd let it go. But you have to hope for the best, and so we lived our lives. For the next several months, I stayed in a motor home and moved pot and money from coast to coast. Never had a single problem. Did it on the street corners of New York City. Did it with strangers and no guns in sight. At the end of the day, we did just under $200 million in business.

The only money that was lost in the entire affair was internally. One of the Hawaiians who worked at the ranch in the distribution facility was running $2 million up to San Francisco one day and disappeared. He was never heard from again. Left a family behind in Hawaii and probably just absconded with the dough. Bizarre, but hey, what was two million lousy bucks?

THIRTY-FOUR

RICARDO FINDS ME in the garden.

"Hey, Brian, you gotta come back to the unit. They're killin' the freeway. They don't want all those bodies in the hallway when the judges come through next week. They were gonna put you upstairs with the Aryan boys, but Rivas an' me stopped that. I got you a room with a real quiet *Cubano*. You move in with him for a while. As soon as Chino moves out of my cell, you're in with me. Okay?"

And so I'm in Cell 9 on the lower tier, B side of J unit. The bed is a hard one—no spring, just a metal slab, but I hope for better sleep. It certainly feels cozier in here than on the freeway. My locker space has been cut in half, and the space is quite small for two people—eight feet by ten feet, with a metal toilet and sink, but it will be just fine.

At my request, Counselor Jenkins is looking at my file.

"Pot case, huh? You think they want another doper in Canada, O'Dea?"

"I've been clean and sober for three years."

"And you smuggled pot clean and sober?"

"I got clean in '88, and I was working in drug and alcohol rehabilitation until I came here in July."

"You mean you got busted after you got straight, and after you were helping people get straight, and they still sent you to prison? What the fuck? Lemme look at your jacket. Shit, man, you're right. What are they thinking of? Okay, O'Dea, let's see what we can do to get you out of here. Each step of the process, you come to me first and I'll get it rolling. Write up the application form on the weekend, and I'll get a sentence computation sheet for you on Monday and we'll do a team progress report on you. I'll push that through. We'll see if we can't get your application out of here next week."

"You're all right, Jenkins, thanks."

Gunther Russbacher was a CIA pilot who says he flew George H. W. Bush to Paris during his secret Iran-Contra negotiations.

"Hey, Gunther, nice to see you."

"Well, enjoy it, O'Dea, 'cause this is it. I'm out of here today."

"Off to Washington to the Congressional hearing?"

"With a few stops on the way. Worst of all, Louisiana. Somehow I just don't feel safe. I'm one of three out of a group of twelve of us in the CIA who are still alive, and something doesn't feel good about this trip. Maybe I'm just paranoid."

"Like you don't have good reason. My friend Bruce says he's surprised you're still alive. If they take you down, Gunther, come back and haunt the bastards."

"Nice knowing you, O'Dea. You've been one of the brighter lights in my journey through this inferno."

"Thanks, Gunther. I wish you well."

A little later, I spot him from across the yard, hands cuffed together attached to a chain around his waist as he is led to

God knows where, pale and frightened-looking, with a tentative smile on his face as he walks headlong into the fire. Goodbye, Gunther. You were a CIA agent but, by being here, you somehow became a better, more heart-centered person. It's hard not to become more compassionate here. So much injustice, so much pain, so much loneliness, so much fear, so much despair, so much fellowship.

Four *Cubanos* are making a rice-with-chicken-and-bananas dish in the unit's microwave. They're talking away in their singsong clippity-clop way, making the best of it. They are brothers and share what they have with one another. They seem to enjoy having me around, but I still have a sense of not quite belonging. They look at me sometimes like I'm pretty stupid, and they talk about me and chuckle. It's okay.

I'm sleeping in a cell for the first time since 1973. The bed is a metal sheet with a two-inch mattress on top. There is a sense of privacy in here that I didn't have in the freeway, a few feet away. These three walls, and a ceiling that's touchable, give me an enclosed feeling. Of course, the front is completely open, just bars like we all expect a cell to have. The door is a section of the bars that slides back. It used to lock, but none of the cells lock anymore. Inmates are always free to move about on the tier. It's as quiet as it's been since I got here. Not a sound on the tier. Think I'll take the opportunity to meditate.

Black guys down the hall talking about their baseball game. Fantastico, a small *Cubano*, lights a cigarette and examines the tats on his arms. One of them must be fairly new, judging by the way he constantly checks it out. Cards hit the table somewhere to the right of me, a cross-cultural game with English and Spanish expletives thrown about freely. James walks back and forth in front of my cell like a duck in a shooting gallery, munching on a nutty cookie.

"Count time! Get off those bunks and on the floor! *Cuenta!*
Stand up! *Cuenta!*"

As my favorite author, Robert Anton Wilson, says about
men like this guard: "He has a face that hasn't liked anything
it has looked on in his life."

"Count time!"

Fantastico sits on the edge of his bed, reading a novella.
Humberto sings a plaintive ballad in his cell, next to mine.
Spanish TV bleeds a romance film through the screen. Faron,
my cellie, is taking a nap. And me, I write and write and write.
Toward the One, the perfection of love, harmony and beauty,
the only being, united with all the illuminated souls who form
the embodiment of the Master, the Spirit of Guidance.

I wait between the visiting room door and my house during
the last calls for visits, but I'm not included. You must stay
close to the unit or the visiting room when a visit is expected,
because they won't look for you. That increases the anticipation level. As the hours fall through the cracks, the heart beats
faster and hotter, the feeling of loneliness and pain increases,
the feeling of utter powerlessness is magnified a hundredfold.
We are the warehoused, and many pay besides us—our children, our families and friends. The people who pay the taxes
get little for their bucks from this system.

Suzi told me she was coming at last and bringing the kids.
I've been waiting here for hours. They don't necessarily tell
you when you have a visitor. Anyway, no visit.

I need to let go completely. I know there is no room for
moods here, but I am feeling somewhat defeated. My eyes
hurt, lump in my throat, shoulders slumped, hollow gut. My
body feels like it's being pulled toward the earth. I don't even
want to rebel anymore.

In for the night. Count is underway. I walk down south, watch a ball game, come back by my unit, sit outside in the yard and observe the parade of stars. The junkies are pulling one another aside for furtive discussions: forty gimmicks are missing from the hospital, and both sides are on the hunt for them—cops and junkies. Gamblers collect or pay up on tonight's softball game, Cubans sing and dance, scholars go to and from Chapman College classes, born-again Christians scream in tongues from the chapel, the sun sets through the concertina wire, legal beagles slide in and out of the library, black brothers jam hoops on the north yard basketball court, Mexicans play handball, gangbangers cruise in mobs with their headphones on, gangsta rappers program their minds, pot smugglers eat ice cream by the vending machines, Aryans throw weight on the iron pile, older guys throw bocce balls with the Mafia crowd near our garden. The Mafia guys love the garden. The prisoner rock-and-roll band screams out from the auditorium while Lieutenant Prick lurks outside our unit, waiting on someone in particular.

"Baclaan, get over here."

"Whaddaya want, Lieutenant?"

"What do you think I want? Hold up the wall."

And he rifles Baclaan's body with the desire of a brownshirt.

"Get in that shower and strip."

"What the fuck?"

"Get the fuck in there before we move to SHU and do this!"

Baclaan goes. His clothes come off piece by piece, and with each piece another fragment of his already minuscule power is removed from him until he is standing there naked, bent over, holding the cheeks of his ass open and coughing a most powerless cough.

"Get dressed and get outta here."

"Fuck you."

"What did you say?"

"I said, thank you."

Injustice is so commonplace, you notice it less. First frightening and shocking, then so frequent you let it roll on by without protest or exclamation of any kind.

He/she got here today and is now outside the unit, trying to hustle Manny.

"Hey, handsome. Mmm, mmm, good."

"How are you doin', cutie?"

"All right. Better if I could have you, gorgeous."

"I'm in your unit."

"Oooh, I'll see you tonight, handsome."

Looks so fragile, but doesn't act that way. He/she's walking the yard with some of the other boy/girls. They're showing her around. What kind of life must it be?

My head touches the ceiling when I sit here on my bunk. Directly in front of me is my locker, on top of the Cuban Faron's locker. To the right, on the floor, is the steel toilet with no seat, and on the wall to the right of it is the sink. To the left are the bars. Derek stops and looks in.

"What happened to your stomach, Derek?"

"Oh, that. Shot a few times. It wasn't much, though, small caliber, 25-millimeter. Anyway, I was knocked out when they shot me, so I really didn't feel it. I was just a kid—member of one of the Pala Blanca. We're one the oldest gangs in LA, started in the 1930s and still alive. Every one of us, man, we're cold-blooded killers, man. Anyone can kill, but not everyone can kill in cold blood. I don't give anyone trouble. I joke with the fools here. I give everyone the respect they deserve. But I'm a cold-blooded killer. You can tell us, man. We have a dress code, a look, a demeanor. American-born Latinos. It's no problem to spot us. You see us in the yard, Brian. Sometime I'll tell you some stories for your book."

He drifts off. Mark comes over. "You know what he did to get here, Brian?"

"No, Mark, what?"

"He unloaded his shotgun into two pot dealers—brothers—then threw them overboard. One died, the other floated, holding onto his dead brother for sixteen hours at sea, got rescued and testified against him. Derek's going to be released after fifteen years. They weren't the first people he killed either. I think he told me his first hit was when he was thirteen."

"What must've come before that?"

"No shit. Hey, lookit there. The new he/she with her entourage. Damn, look at those guys chasing her, like flies on shit. A nurse in the hospital today told me that one of them is HIV-positive. See that Cuban, the black one with the other he/she? He's HIV-positive, too, got it from her since he's been here. They don't care. For that, they'll take AIDS. Did you hear about the one with the tits, Kim? They found her and another Cuban behind a TV stand, up in education, both with their pants down. They're in the SHU box for a while. She has AIDS too. They usually let the sex shots out of the hole after a couple of days. Smoking some reefer is way heavier than spreading AIDS around here."

THIRTY-FIVE

I HAVE ONLY ONE LOVE, AND IT BREAKS MY HEART

I HAD A WALK-IN CLOSET built on the back of our house, attached to my bedroom. The walls were constructed of river rock, the floor of flagstones. When I pushed a button on the wall, the floor slid open to reveal a recess about one foot deep by three feet square. Little by little, I filled the space with currency of every denomination. Millions of dollars flowed through that little river-rock room. For the first time in a long time, our bills were promptly paid.

Mom and Dad and I had long been reconciled, and now I could afford to show them how well I was doing. I flew them out to California repeatedly, put them up in the best hotels, took them out to the best restaurants. They didn't really know what I'd been doing, and they didn't really ask.

Meanwhile, the logistics of moving the product from one place to another were less onerous than importing it had been, and I had a lot more time on my hands. For me, this proved a complication. Over the next year, I ran truckloads of pot to the East Coast, and money back from there to LA. We usually loaded the trucks at Bob Sherman's ranch, where we could transfer loads from one truck to another without drawing attention to ourselves. The house was behind locked gates and guarded by vicious dogs. Bob himself would often accompany me on the trip to the East Coast to pick up money, and then drive back with me. We got the drive from New York to LA down to under forty hours, downtown Manhattan to Bob's driveway. Some cocaine was required to achieve this time, needless to say, and more cocaine was required for the later runs. As a matter of momentum, we would extend our use of coke beyond the actual trip, and this extension also grew with time. The coke became less the tool it took to stay awake across the country and more the monkey it had been not so long before.

Bob's wife couldn't wait to see me come, carrying the bag. She loved coke as much as I did. At first I'd pull into Bob's driveway, say a brief hi, get in my car and head home. After a very few months this became pulling into the driveway, going up to the house and sitting on the couches and beds in that house day after day. It became forty hours across the country and ninety-six hours hiding out at Bob's.

My life consisted of trips from home to various theme parks with the kids, interspersed with trips carrying dope or loot, and coke binges. I had a deal with the Shaffers that would have seen them pay me fifty bucks a pound for everything my distribution guys handled. But I couldn't be bothered to pursue it, and I thereby lost out on millions of dollars. The inevitable endgame was underway: powerlessness over just about everything.

While I was busy hoping Suzi would look the other way, she was busy in our closet. She bought hundreds of thousands of dollars' worth of stock for our antique store, which hadn't been open for years and would never be properly opened. I had to buy two shipping containers to hold the stuff. She couldn't help herself when it came to money, and what she didn't spend I was snorting and giving away. I started with a few million in cash, but I just couldn't say no when people showed up needing to borrow $50,000 or $100,000 or so.

The property holder of the acreage surrounding Paul Halloran's little chapel down the street threatened to sell. My perspective as a Christian had altered profoundly, but my spiritual life was alive and well. In my continuing negotiations with God, I came up with some money for the Reverend Halloran, and his church bought the land.

The present held no allure, the future held everything and nothing. I had arrived again at that place where I was willing to trade all I loved and all who loved me for my renewed affair with coke. I knew there was nothing good about doing coke, other than the anticipation of doing it—that delicious time between the decision to do it and its arrival in my body, that magical time of allure and compulsion to fulfill. I chased what was no longer there, chased it into a dark cave alone, a cave where you paid a fortune in rent.

I knew there was a hammer and it was going to fall. I never let the thought of that hammer linger long enough to put words to it, but it carried such weight, I knew without words. I knew I couldn't take this shit with me much further. And when I bought that final kilo under the pretense of showing it as a sample, I knew it was going to take a lot of work to get through.

During this time, our group threw some remarkable parties at the Iverson Ranch. Tony would fly in with fish still wiggling and make the sushi right there on the spot. The setting, the food, the drink, the women—it was all empty and wonderful. It was at one of these parties that I introduced my old buddy John Paul—he of Paul Mitchell hair products—to Bill Shaffer, and they remain friends to this day. John Paul, in turn, introduced me to a man who said his name was James Dalco. James had a warehouse full of coke, and eventually I went to see it. I was awestruck. I told myself I needed a kilo as a sample. I left the premises knowing this was going to be a time to remember later in life, the beginning of a transition, the pushing off from the shore, the crossing over.

I secreted the kilo in a carpet roll in my garage. Once or twice it occurred to me that this was awfully like my hiding a pack of my mom's cigarettes in our garage when I was ten. But for the moment, the worst thing would be for Suzi to get her hands on coke. That's all it would have taken for both of us to die quickly, hiding in the garage from our children. Searing our brains out.

Suzi didn't want to know that I was losing it again, and she ignored the signs. She ignored the hours I spent in the garage, my not coming to bed, my constantly blocked nasal passages, my generally quiet, unfriendly manner.

I returned to LA from a money trip to New York. I drove to the ranch and had Bob sneak over to my house and nab my *clavo* from the garage. For three or four days, his wife and I stayed awake, rambling through the giant house and grounds, stepping outside only after the sun had gone down. We became vampires, living in an unfulfillable fantasy world of perverted sex that never happened, a world that must remain indescribable to those who have not felt that need for constant provocation, constant stopping, chasing, almost catching, touching momentarily, letting go, chasing, almost catching, Bob peeking in through the window, just as sick in his own special way. He had watched his wife have affair after affair with one young guy after another. Even I saw a couple of those gas jockeys come and go. Yet she was essentially a generous soul, and we were all—even me, in some sense—still born-again Christians of one stripe or another. She did manage to go outside now and again to have a look around.

But I had begun my descent. Cocaine had shimmered before me like a threshold to some undefined future, and that threshold, lingered at too long, was turning to hot coals. When that happens, those at the threshold must feel those coals or die in a bid to escape them. Few experience both.

After three days in the main house, I could take no more intrusion on my passionate embrace of the drug. My drug and I needed to be alone. I retired to the guest house and asked Bob to look in from time to time.

Around me was a sprawling green lawn with dips and curves that led to hidden patios cut into rock, waterfalls, ponds. The air was warm, the skies clear. Insects chirped in the bushes and birds sang in the trees. I snuck past all this and down to the guest house. I brought with me my bag, a couple of cartons of smokes, a bottle of rum, a case of beer, a few jugs of wine. I secured every curtain.

Suzi began driving by the gates. She blew her horn and screamed at the top of her lungs. "Fuck you, O'Dea! I know you're in there!"

I crouched in the guest house and peeked through the curtains toward the road.

"Fuck you! Fuck you, you bastard, O'Dea!"

Sometimes her voice was broken by sobs. After a few days, she stopped coming by.

I would reach into my bag and shovel a gathering of powder in the general direction of my nose. My heart would race in my chest. My mind would run on toward oblivion. I lit cigarette after cigarette, and the matches made a lurid flare in the darkened room. Now I knew only fear, nothing under it or over it, a sole and soulless fear.

On the fifth day the trees in the yard shook with malice in the wind. Night fell and the wind was gone. Ah, night. Thirst. Wine from the jug. I clutched my bag, held it tight. Ah, night.

Light. Shit. The sun. I peeked from the curtains at the trees. They shifted toward me and I closed the curtains tight, held them to the frames. Lay on the couch, got up, lay down. Ah, night.

The seventh day. There's that sun. Oh, Suzi. Fucking Suzi. Thirsty. How many smokes? Some. Where's Bob? I don't want to see Bob. How's the bag? Good, plenty in the bag. Where's the sun? Don't look. Don't look at the trees. The curtains glow. Evening.

That fucking sun! Oh Jesus Christ, I gotta go home. Jesus, help me! Fuck! Where's the bag, fuck, where's the bag? Oh, here it is, in my hand.

Settle down, settle down. Suzi, fucking Suzi. Oh Jesus Christ, what am I going to do? Jesus! Fucking Suzi!

Did I drink all that rum? Where's that rum? Oh God, who the fuck's that? Who is that? It's you, you fucked-up fuck. No! Yes, you! It's a fucking mirror, asshole! Oh yeah. I was going to take that mirror down. When was that I was going to do that? Yesterday. Yesterday? What the fuck? Which yesterday? I'm going to look out those fucking curtains. Just one fucking peek, okay? Okay, boy, one peek. Oh, Jesus, fucking bright. Fuck, I'm in trouble. Another day. I got to go home. Hey, look. Look at that fucking tree, will you! It's Suzi. Ha ha. Oh boy, chum, you been up too long. Wipe those eyes. No, look! Look! Her friend, right? And her car, and the kids. Look, there's the kids!

Oh Jesus. Fall down on the floor and slither away from the window. Get away from that window, boy. Nothing but sand worms out there. Stand up, boy, stand up! I'm trying. Stand up, boy! Oh, hey, hey, wait a minute, something's got hold of my chest. Never mind! Stand up, you creep! Stand up! Oh, something's got me, man, something's got my chest, man! Stand up, you shit! What the . . . fuck, man? What's that . . . thing . . . in me, man? Stand up, you piece of shit!

Bob found me unconscious on the floor, and an ambulance took me to the cardiac unit of a nearby hospital. This was a day before my fortieth birthday.

THIRTY-SIX

TWO *CUBANOS* are burned out of their cells. The burned-out go to the hole—protective custody.

The likely explanation is that two white guys were sent to the hole on a drug beef and lost their cell. The cell went to the Cubans. The white guys get out and want their cell back, but it doesn't work that way. They have to wait for one to come available. Until then, they sleep in the hallway. They hate that, so they go burn out the Cubans in their room. The Cubans end up in the hole and are treated no differently from those who are in the hole for disciplinary reasons. The white guys get their room back.

"Fuckin' Cuban, man."

"Motherfuckin' toad."

"Motherfuckin' white-ass motherfucker."

"Stupid fuckin' Mexican."

"When you've been down long enough, Brian, you'll see it just as we do, my friend. Don't think any differently."

"What's the conversation about, you two?"

"What do you mean, Lieutenant?"

"Well, you two look so engrossed in talking with one another, no one else around, just the two of you, I thought I'd join you. First I need to know what you're talkin' about, though, so I can join in. So, what are you talkin' about?"

"Well, Brian and me, we're just talkin' about ending this conversation, Lieutenant, which is what we're doin' right now. See you later, Brian."

"Yeah, Bill. See you later."

"Don't let me break up your little talk, now."

Finally I move into Ricardo's cell. This is the right thing. If men are to be trapped like animals in cages, let us be trapped with decent men.

Thunder and lightning punctuate the muggy afternoon. The TVs rage on in Spanish and English with exactly the same tone and inflections, the noise so overwhelming I'm unable to tell which is which. The thunder, though, is so settling.

Ricardo's friend, someone on the outside, commits suicide. One wonders why more people in here with these Buck Rogers release dates don't do the same thing. What exactly do they have to look forward to for the next twenty, thirty, forty years or more? Day after day of subjugation to an angry, hostile authority, constant humiliation and aggression, sphincter examinations, excretion testing, lousy food, censored mail and tape-recorded telephone conversations, two human beings living in a space built for one, loss of friendship with anyone on the outside. The friends forget you after a certain number of years, I'm told—actually, a mutual parting takes place as each stops writing to the other. The prisoner eventually reaches a place where there is nothing left to say.

The Ninth Circuit judges are here at last, examining their work, their caged animals. We're locked in the south yard all morning while they look around. Everyone in B unit is sent out; new furniture is put in for the tour. The judges tour B unit only. They ignore the freeway. They leave. The furniture is taken out.

One day I will be somewhere quiet, silent. One day I'll walk in the woods, kicking leaves up into the air, feeling the branches of fir trees dusting my skin, getting wet from the morning dew. One day I'll wake up next to you.

THIRTY-SEVEN

I LOSE A FAMILY AND GLIMPSE A TRUTH

EVENTUALLY they transferred me to Cottage Hospital, the rehab facility in Santa Barbara that used to be called the Pinecrest. I knew the place pretty well after my sixty-day visit in 1984. But during my first visit, it's fair to say I hadn't heard—not really heard—a single thing. Now, in 1988, after the heart attack, I came again for a month, and I heard everything as I listened to myself being described in others' stories.

This time I enrolled in a sponsor program, and I chose as my sponsor a guy named Doug Miller, who was leading a therapy group on Tuesday nights.

Every day I was on the phone to Suzi, begging her to bring the kids to see me.

"No, Brian. No." That was all she would say. She wasn't coming up, and she wasn't sending the kids up.

I'd been there for about two weeks when Cheyenne and Cherokee suddenly appeared in the doorway. Cheyenne was eleven then, and Cherokee was eight, two shaken children, always believing there was a way for their mom, whom they loved so much, and me—the father they wanted to love but were afraid of and didn't trust, and rightfully so—to get their acts together and come together. Their turmoil was the price of my choices.

They gave me an envelope from Suzi. On the envelope was an address in a little community called La Conchita, south of Santa Barbara, just a little strip along the beach on the Pacific Coast Highway. These children and I spent an hour holding one other and crying, and then said good-bye. I opened the envelope. Inside was a key. I phoned the cell phone in my truck. Suzi answered.

"Suzi, what's this? What's this in the envelope?"

"Brian, I don't want you to come home. I can't do this anymore. I've had enough. The kids have had enough. Just a minute, Brian, I've got to pass this idiot."

For a moment, I could hear only the sound of the truck.

"Brian?"

"Yeah?"

"I've rented you a place in La Conchita so when you get out you've got a place to stay. But that's it, Brian."

"What?"

"Consider us through."

She hung up.

I was both numb and filled with icy fear. I had no driver's license. I had no real American ID. I had no ability to do anything legitimate in the U.S. I'd always needed someone to front for me. Now, all of a sudden, I had two weeks; after that, I would cease to exist.

THIRTY-EIGHT

MIDNIGHT. A hack—a punch-drunk professional boxer—patrols.

"Hey, turn that light out in there!"

Pete Medina laughs from his bunk on the freeway. "Hey," he calls. "Two a.m.'s lights out, ain't it?"

"Get the fuck down from that fuckin' bunk! What's your fuckin' name, motherfucker?"

"Medina."

"Put it up against there, motherfucker!"

This guard pushes Pete into the bars of my cell. His face is pressed hard against the iron, distorted, grimacing, inches from me. He's almost naked. The cop, twice his size, starts to shake him down brutally.

"Hey, you tryin' to rip my shorts, man?"

"I'm gonna rip your motherfuckin' ass off, motherfucker."

A look of terror on Pete's face. He has known only one way of dealing with such terror—attack. I look into his eyes, see him struggling, hear him thinking, "About to get parole. Been down ten years. If I attack . . ."

The hack spins him around. My heart is pounding. I want to puke. I, too, am terrified. I want out of this madhouse; I want to get away from these dangerous people.

"Roll it up, little motherfucker! You gonna go to the motherfuckin' hole, that's where you're goin', motherfucker."

The cop is spitting and drooling, but there's another cop who looks shook up. He calls the first aside. They have words. Too many witnesses.

"All right, punk, I still think I should roll you up. Get back up there, turn out that fuckin' light, and shut the fuck up."

A load of new H, junk, jones, horse, scag, shit, heroin arrives in the yard, to the delight of the junkies. These people are serving time under the tough new law. They have nothing to lose. They have no good time that can be taken from them. No possibility of parole. They're willing to pay the price of a few weeks in the hole if they get caught.

On the freeway, a man who just got out of SHU, caught shooting H, is throwing up violently in the toilet. Someone helps him to his bunk outside my cell. His color is pale to see-through, ice packed in a towel on his head. He's just looking for the way out of here. Can I help? He wants to die, and perhaps the best I can do is let it happen. He's wearing a Terminal Island AA T-shirt.

A letter arrives without a return address. I open the envelope. Inside are photographs of Sam. It looks like he's in his own apartment. In some photos, he's holding a huge ball of blue wool. In the other photos, it's clear that he has strung the wool through the whole place. It stretches from lamps to doors to tables. And there's Sam again, holding the blue ball and smiling. He was as deep as any pool I've ever looked in. He understood all of those yearnings I feel. He's a junkie, a heroin addict, a tattooer, a bank robber, a seeker. I look for a long while at the pictures, and I look back in the envelope, but there's no written message. But I know that Sam is one of me.

Today they bring back the freeway in full form. Sixty new beds are delivered to the hallway in front of my cell and under the stairwells. I'm surprised it took so long. I walk by the staff bulletin board on the way to the library and see posted there, complete with photos, the best-dressed correctional officer of the month, the best-dressed uniformed officer of the month, the best-dressed supervisor of the month. They pile prisoners in here on top of one another, give us rags to wear. Drug addicts have no safe haven for recovery here, while the staff pat one another on the back for the sharpness of the crease in their uniforms.

"Shut the fuck up out there, you bunch of assholes! You think you are the only people here? Some of us work! Take your fuckin' game somewhere else, you bastards!"

"Fuck ju, mang . . . ju got a problem with us, mang? Ju weel see 'bout dat, mang. We play where we fuckin' please, mang. Ju got a problem, mang? Ju weel fuckin' see! Fuck ju, mang! Fuck ju!"

It's cold here this morning. No heat in this building. The upstairs has been condemned, due to asbestos, as has the south side of the building, both upstairs and down. In fact, this portion of the structure has also been condemned. The arm of government that oversees these things has chosen to look the other way. The institution responded to the asbestos problem by shutting down just a small part of one building when the inspection team came to inspect. I am told by the people who work in the powerhouse, which is the department responsible for water testing, that they invariably fudge the water tests to make it look as if the water here is fit for human and animal consumption. That's the way things are done.

———

They just came and took Ricardo, my cellie, to the hole. Out of nowhere. What can this mean? He told me earlier this morning that he went to the hack on duty and asked about the card-playing curfew. While he was talking to the cop, another prisoner overheard him and accused him of being a rat. Ricardo is not that. But when some of the chickenshits around here want to get rid of someone, they write a note saying that person is going to be killed or that person is involved with dope. They drop the note in any of the mailboxes. When the mail gets checked before it is sent out, the hacks find the note, and the victim is immediately sent to the hole "for protection."

I shout over the wall to Ricardo in the hole. He says a guy he had a disagreement with last month told the cop he was dealing in the yard. The guy did this yesterday, just before his release. So, today, they lock Ric up, along with five other inmates who've been having a dispute with this same scum. The investigation can go on indefinitely. If the cops aren't satisfied, they can keep these guys in the hole as long as they want.

"Count! Stand up! Let's go! Stand down!"

More news on Ricardo. One of the hacks told me what might be the real story.

"Isn't he the Mexican guy involved with Families Against Mandatory Minimum Sentences?"

"Yeah. I think his sister is one of the organizers."

"That's probably it. There's talk bureau-wide of a demonstration in all the prisons against mandatory minimum sentencing. Most likely that's what's going on."

If true, it's diesel therapy and rolling zip codes for Ricardo. They don't hesitate to ship you for something like that. A moving busload of chained human beings, pissing for the feds, eating baloney on dry white bread, lonely for families who have no idea where they are.

As I'm going across the yard tonight, I spot Ricardo. They're taking him to Receiving and Discharge, his hands cuffed behind his back. I run across.

"Hey, Ric! Hey, man! What's up?"

"I'm gone, Brian! Don't know why or where, but I'm gone. I love you, Brian. You're a great person, and you've helped me a lot, man. Thanks, man. It's been great knowing you."

"I love you too, Ric. I love you, brother. You're a light, man, don't ever let them dim it. I'll call your sister. So long, Ric."

"Change all this, Brian. You're the man. Change it for us!"

No, Ricardo, I'm not. No. I can't.

"Counting B Range! Counting!"

And again and again and again.

THIRTY-NINE

I LOSE IT ALL AND FIND MYSELF

I SAT IN THE TRUCK outside the empty apartment Suzi had rented for me. Here was the question: What was I, a man outside the law for twenty years, an illegal alien in the land of the free, a man who'd always been fronted by another, more legitimate person—what was I to do on my own?

I picked up my cell phone and dialed the phone company. A woman answered.

"Good morning. Pacific Western."

"Hi. My name's Brian O'Dea. I'm just moving into a new apartment in La Conchita, and I'd like to get a, you know, a proper land line in there. What do I do?"

"What's the address, Mr. O'Dea?"

I told her the address.

"That's fine, Mr. O'Dea. Would Tuesday be all right for you?"

"Yeah. Yeah, Tuesday would be good. Where do I go?"

There was a momentary pause. They were running something on me, I thought.

"You just stay there Tuesday morning, Mr. O'Dea, and we'll come and put your phone in."

"Oh, you'll come and put the phone in?"

"Tuesday morning."

"Really? Well, that's great, great. Thanks."

"Thanks for using Pacific Western, Mr. O'Dea."

I couldn't believe it. I'd been ducking this sort of thing my whole life. All of a sudden, I had a telephone in my name. A few minutes later, I had electricity. Within days, I had furniture. It was spectacular.

But I had nowhere to go and nobody to visit in a town where I knew no one. I knew only one thing for sure: I had to stay sober. I decided I needed to hang around the hospital in Santa Barbara. Everybody there was in worse shape than me by a country mile.

La Conchita was about thirty minutes out of Santa Barbara. Santa Barbara was a little town of seventy-five thousand, but it was on recovery the way a house might be on fire. In Santa Barbara, there were 180 AA meetings a week and fifty-two "anonymous" groups, more groups than you would find in a city the size of Toronto.

First thing every morning, I was up and into Santa Barbara to the AA clubhouse for the 6:30 meeting. Then I went right to the hospital, where I took breakfasts around to patients and sat and talked with people. Eventually, I became the chief volunteer. At lunchtime I'd go somewhere for an AA lunch meeting, then back to the hospital for a couple of hours, then to an afternoon meeting. Every day I thought, how am I going to stay sober today? How am I going to keep my life together today? Every day at AA meetings, I saw people who were in worse shape than I was—even people with years of sobriety. I needed desperately to be in places where I felt a sense of gratitude for being me.

If the last deal had been the most fun I'd ever had, these days in Santa Barbara were the most rewarding. Every day I felt I learned something. Every day brought its epiphany. Except when Suzi and I were fighting on the phone about who was right about whatever subject, I was loving being alive every single moment because, for the first time in my life, I was in service to my universal brother and sister. My motivation may have been a totally selfish and singular desire to stay sober, but I was in some way serving almost every person I knew, helping them overcome something. And I wasn't alone: everyone I hung with was doing the same thing. We were all on a common mission to help one another overcome.

If, in the past, I'd put my right leg in my pants first, now it had to be my left leg. I had no tools. I came with nothing. But the beauty was that everybody came that way. Nothing we had worked. We had nothing, and nothing was the perfect condition for getting well. Everybody was leveled to the lowest common denominator: nothing. Being nothing, we looked at others, and their lives meant something to us, and we, as a result, meant something to them. It was all intuition: following others who were in turn following us. It worked.

At the hospital, I led a group called Real Presence. Every Tuesday night, people would come out of that group on fire for themselves. Its success had nothing to do with me, although everyone tended to mistake the power of the group for the power of the group leader, whoever that happened to be. One of the participants was Rodney Utt. He'd come to the hospital to get sober, and I'd sat with him. He was a flat busted junkie, a man who'd done time in the early seventies for LSD out in Lompoc, a total hippie who'd been running a successful construction business until he'd got himself into a world of hurt with coke. He'd destroyed his family just as I had done, though his family had stuck with him. I loved Rodney, and I loved his family.

I also became friends with Dave Richo and Regina Jensen, both psychologists in Santa Barbara. Dave was the greatest teacher I'd ever known. I took his little book, *Letting the Light Through*, and sold ten thousand copies out of the trunk of my car to bookstores in southern California. Dave called me his "mentor" because I knew how to figure a living in a sense that was entirely different from his. Dave conducted a hugely popular class every Wednesday night at City College in Santa Barbara. Hundreds of people would line up to get in, and people were turned away all the time.

I made it my business to record these classes, then duplicated the tapes and sold them at the next class. I'd make $300, often $500 a week. I was becoming a well-known character in Santa Barbara, and meanwhile, everything I read and the people I was meeting were changing me, giving me a sense of acceptance, a sense of joy, that had no conditions attached but one: that you don't alter the given moment, but rather accept it. I had a sense of moving on, even though I wasn't moving anywhere or going anywhere or doing anything. I was stopped right where I was, paused, waiting for life to come with its next motion. I had an overwhelming sense of an impending future.

At Dave Richo's classes, I stationed myself at the front to do the recording. From there I could look down into the crowd, an advantage for a newly single, newly well man who was constantly on the lookout. I loved meeting people who were into this type of awareness and awakening, and if they were good-looking babes, well, all the better.

One December evening in 1989, fifteen months after my separation from Suzi, a woman entered the auditorium in the company of another woman, clearly her mother. The young woman was wearing long, loose white Indian pants. She was gorgeous, and she was at least six feet tall.

I turned to Doug Miller, my sponsor. "Doug, check her out."

Doug squinted across the crowd. "Shit," said Doug. "I don't want you messing with her. She's my type of codependent. I'll look into her case."

That was enough for me. I determined to mess with this woman immediately. My blond hair hung halfway down my back. I gave it a shake and set off.

"Hi," I said. "I'm Brian O'Dea."

I liked this opener because, if she'd heard of me, that was good, and if she hadn't, she might feel she should have.

"Yeah," she said. She looked back at the stage.

"I just wanted to say hi. I record the class here, and if, you know, if you need tapes, you can come and I'll sell you the tapes."

She looked back at me. She was quite a bit taller than me, and I had the unexpected impression that she didn't give a shit whether I was standing there or not.

"Yes, okay, thank you," she said. She looked back at the stage again.

At least she said yes, I thought, and melted away.

She showed up the next week, and I zoned in.

"Hey," I said. "Brian O'Dea. How are you?"

She nodded. Clearly she remembered me.

"Hey, how about going for a coffee after?"

"No, thanks."

I was going nowhere, and I knew she knew I knew. What to do?

"Thanks, though," she said. "Maybe sometime."

My heart skipped a beat.

She was there again the next week. I actually had sweaty palms.

"Hey, hi. Howzabout that coffee?"

She looked down at me and smiled. "Okay," she said.

Her name was Susannah. She was a clothing designer. She'd just quit her job as head designer for Carole Little, a well-known clothing company in LA. She had her own studio in a great building downtown with a bunch of artists. She came from a successful and artistic family.

I found an opportunity to drop in at the studio, then simply threw caution to the wind. There was a florist down the street. I instructed them to send a bouquet to her every day.

At the time, Susannah was seeing four men, but she did at least mention me to her stepfather.

"I don't know about that one," he said. "He sounds a little bit too much."

"Don't worry about him," she told him. "I'm having nothing to do with him. We just have coffee."

I did manage to get her to come up to my place one night after we'd been down at the Soujourner Café. Really, it was a terrific apartment. At night, you could stand on my deck and look out over the whole city of Santa Barbara. That night we stood there, looking, for a long while. The city below was spread out like the ocean.

"You ought to know," she said. "I'm not getting into any relationships around this town. You know that, don't you?"

"Are you kidding me?" I said. "I've just been devastated by a woman. What you see here is a ghost of my former self. I've been totally killed by a woman. The last thing I want is a relationship. You're a nice person, Susannah, and I like nice people. I just hope we can be friends."

"Yeah, that's what I want," she said.

Five minutes later, we were down on the floor, crawling all over each other.

So I had reason to be happy. If my money was gone, well, it had never made me happy. What I had instead was good work, good friends, and a wonderful woman I was falling in love with. Somehow, I'd taken the right path at last. Every day was a new day, and every day had its lesson.

"Danny?"

He was on a gurney in the back of the emergency room. The staff had given him some sort of oral sedative. He looked like they all did: skin gray, face unshaven, clothes stinking and stained. He was passing through that borderland between middle age and what lies beyond it. He was tall, his dark hair receding, his nose long and fine. With both arms, he gripped his body as a straitjacket would.

"Danny?"

"Yeah?" As in, "Who wants to know?" As in, "What can you do for me?" As in, "I'm in the wrong place. I'll come back later. I left the stove on."

"Hi, I'm Brian. I'm a drug addict." I reached out my hand.

"Yeah, right. Fuck off."

"What don't you believe? The Brian part or the addict part?"

"Fuck off."

"I am an addict, Danny, just one line from being in your shoes—that close, *señor*, that close in front of me, but quite a few days behind, thank whomever."

He shut his eyes.

"Feel like shit, huh?"

"What the fuck do you know? And get the fuck outta here, motherfucker, or give me something for the motherfucking pain, or just let me motherfucking go."

It was enough to make a person cry out loud. An otherwise beautiful person, a father, probably—a husband, a brother, a son—now a completely forsaken piece of human waste, owned by a habit, a habit he believed everything that could ever be good in his life was somehow worth surrendering for. All that was on his mind now was putting distance between me and him, him closer to the door, me closer to the wall. I put my arm around him. He started to sob like a baby. I felt no surprise. Instead, I wondered how much of my own children's sobbing I had missed because I was in this poor guy's condition. I wondered if I was trying to make up for that by hanging around the desperately needy. I wondered if I was still as desperately needy myself, just not so out-loud. My life seemed good. I seemed to have survived the mental and physical assault of coke. But I wondered if that hammer would ever fall, the one I kept waiting for. Maybe it wouldn't. In that case, what would I do with the life I'd been spared?

I realized I was crying too, my arms around this smelly wreck.

"It's too fucking hard, Dan, just too fucking hard altogether, I know. It's even too hard for me to understand how hard it really is, *amigo*. One thing I do know, though: somehow the pain goes away, at least the big pain in the bones you feel right now; that goes away soon, I swear."

"How the fuck would you know?" Danny sobbed. "Arggghhhhhhh!" he called into my shoulder. His pain reverberated in my marrow, and his tears filled the room.

The sedative finally kicked in. It would be a good time to head on up the hill to my apartment. My bike was chained outside the front of the hospital, and in ten minutes I could be kicking back in my hot tub, looking out over this wonderful little town. Santa Barbara had been good to me, so much better than I felt I deserved.

I got home and shut the door. Susannah had been there the night before, and our plates were still on the table. It was too late to call her. I was going to clean up, but, man, I was beat.

I thought I'd take that bath, but then decided I'd just undress, lie on my bed, shut my eyes for a moment.

I woke up and daylight was coming through the blinds. I thought about Danny. I'd better go back that morning, see how he was doing. Poor old bastard.

A hard knock on the door. Just from the knock, I knew this day was my day.

I got up, put on the bathrobe my friend Molly had made for me—a black and white thing—and went to open the door. There were venetian blinds on the windows. They were partly closed, but through the slats I could just see the hands and the handguns. I felt a strong desire to disappear. I opened the door. One guy held up a badge with one hand—a Drug Enforcement Agency star.

"My name is Gary Annunziata, and I'm with the Drug Enforcement Agency," he said. "Your name Brian O'Dea?"

"I wish it wasn't, but it is."

He nodded almost imperceptibly. "May we come in?"

"You've got the gun."

"That's right. You got any guns in there, Mr. O'Dea?"

"No."

"You sure about that?"

"I'm positive."

They came in.

"You know why we're here?"

"No, I don't."

The other cop, the bad cop, Doug, laughed. "Don't bullshit us, O'Dea," he said.

"I'm not into bullshitting anymore."

Doug snorted. "Let's get this straight, O'Dea. We know what you do. We know you work with drunks and dopers at the hospital. We know you do good. But this ain't about change or rehabilitation. This is about crushing your life, motherfucker. Now do the right thing."

But I'd beat them to it by years.

EPILOGUE

ON A SUNNY MORNING in September 1992, the call came across the loudspeakers, and I said my good-byes to men just like me, men serving sentences for smuggling pot, or conspiring to do so. Most of these poor souls had not had the good fortune to be tried in the Ninth Circuit, Western District of Washington State, and many had been hammered with terrible mandatory minimum sentences that would see them die inside.

"Go, homey!" they called from behind the lines of guards.

"Take us to Canada with you, homeboy!"

"Don't forget us, Brian!"

Tears of sadness and joy ran down my cheeks. I didn't care who saw. Finally unafraid of my surroundings or who surrounded me, I was going home to a home I had left so long ago, thankful at last that I was a Canadian.

Good-bye, my friends.

Put into orange jumpsuits, handcuffed and chained to the man behind us and the man in front of us, we were frisked, instructed, threatened, marched. We were bused to an Air Force runway, loaded on a jet for no one knew where. Up. Down.

Sacramento. Wait. More shackled men. The airline whose flights are always full. I'm terrified of suffering from thirst on the flights. I drink my fill. Up we go. A half-hour passes. Uh-oh. Must piss. But the shy bladder will never cooperate. Hold it. Impossible. Can't hold it. Have to go. Call a hack. He marches me, cuffed at the waist, to the john and stands there with his hand on my shoulder. He doesn't take the cuffs off. I struggle with my jumpsuit and manage to get my dick out. The plane lurches. I'm going to burst my bladder, I think. The guard tightens his grip. I shut my eyes and squeeze. A few life-saving drops escape.

"Take me back now," I say.

Down. Phoenix. Stripped, medicalized, another mattress on the floor.

Wait a minute. Hadn't someone said they thought Ricardo had been sent to Phoenix? I got up and walked out to the fence surrounding the holding pen for transportees. The desert twilight was already fading. There were twenty or thirty buildings scattered across a hundred acres.

"Ricardo!" I shouted. "Ricardo!"

A door opened twenty yards away, and a small man looked out.

"Homeboy?"

"Ricardo!"

He was on the cleaning crew for our building, and ten minutes later he was shaking my hand and doling out the candy bars and ice cream he knew I loved.

"Give Susannah a call for me," I said. "Just let her know where I am, that I'm all right."

"I will, Brian. Gotta go."

"Good-bye, my friend."

"Good-bye."

Ah, Ric, bright, bright light. He just had to fight the charges, didn't he? Couldn't plead guilty, because he believed he wasn't. So they thrilled him with thirty-five years.

Good-bye.

At 2 a.m., they woke me.

"O'Dea, get up! You're outta here!"

Stripped, processed, bused. Jet. Up. Down. Up. Down. Along the way, I met two guys who'd been on the road for two years, moved every two weeks. How grateful I felt, among these hopeless men. How fortunate. I was going home. Up. Down. Up. Down. Up. Down. The hell of Lewisburg. Up. Down. Up. Down. Northern New York State. Then, six weeks after Terminal Island, the bus to Canada. We crossed the bridge over the Thousand Islands, and the fall leaves were in full color. Sensory shock. How little color I had seen for fourteen months. I felt dizzy and nearly fainted. Tears rolled down my cheeks again, and I knew I was alive, knew I would be out of this nightmare before my official release in 1998. I knew that soon I'd be home.

From Millhaven, near Kingston, Ontario, I was quickly shuffled to Sainte-Anne-des-Plaines, Quebec, and from there to Springhill, near Amherst, Nova Scotia, where I unsuspectingly allowed myself to be elected chairman of the Inmate Committee. I discovered that the major difference between Canadian federal prisons and American federal prisons is the level of violence: Canadian prisons are far more violent. In Canada, the federal prisoners run the show.

A year later, I was flown to St. John's, Newfoundland, to take up residence four nights a week in a halfway house, a revolving door of break-and-enter artists, drunks, drug addicts, thieves, and assault-and-battery boys, mixed with the occasional murderer.

I took over a basement apartment in a house nearby that was owned by my parents. Susannah moved up from California, and my children, Cheyenne and Cherokee, now sixteen and thirteen, came to live with us there. I slept four nights each week at the halfway house, but spent my days and Friday, Saturday, and Sunday nights at home with my family.

It was impossible not to notice that somehow a miracle had happened: I was back home, in the town of my birth and among the people of my blood. It sometimes seems that we Newfies are destined to stand around looking inward at each other, huddled together as though around a fire for warmth, our backs to a dark and unknowable sea. We take this way of knowing with us, just as I took it with me everywhere I went: always the Newfie—changed perhaps, even to my brothers and sisters, by my cultivated American/Canadian accent—but a Newfie nonetheless. And now in Newfoundland.

Back in St. John's, the river of my youth beckoned me to walk beside it, where I once fell in so regularly. Every time I had walked by Rennie's River as a boy, Sliding Rock had beckoned me to its slippery surface, despite Mom's pleas. Then, clothes and all, I'd slip again—as good as accidentally—into its ruddy and polluted waters, never fearing or even knowing what infections lay waiting. Now, the proper burghers of St. John's have made Rennie's River pristine, but I'm too old to fall, having lost—or jettisoned—something between then and now that could release me.

It was a pollution suited to its time, of course, in a town polluted by the fear of sex, if not by sex itself. The church firmly, softly, reminded us of the inferiority of women, separated the children according to gender and swore its ordained teachers to vows of chastity that made the irrepressible imp of sex so attractive to just about everyone. The homes for pregnant women were crammed with shame-filled Catholic girls—children, really—and Mount Cashel was filled with their wanted or unwanted offspring. Everywhere there was dallying, diddling, dicking—all secret then, and much of it still.

As a product of that world, I had felt as a child that I was consigned to a hopelessly fallen state, and I took refuge in continual mendacity and constant bargaining. Then, as though hurled from a slingshot, I was out into the larger world, still ducking and weaving, then ricocheting into born-again Christianity, then plunging into chaos. I fled the discomfort of the present and the presence of my presence. I took to anything—and drugs are the obvious but not the only example—that took me away from the imperfect here and now. In sobriety, I have learned that the opposite of what I was doing probably works best. Being present in my actions is critical. Most of the time that may be an unattainable ideal, but it remains a worthy one. "Where I'm trying to get is here," Ram Dass said, "and when I'm trying to get there is now."

When I found a respite in the philosophy of the Sufis, it was not because they had the answers. Every authority I had encountered—and no one more than me—had possessed the answers. But the Sufis had only questions, and to have only the questions, as it turns out, suffices. I remain suspicious of most answers, but trust every question.

And so I was home, if only briefly. I began to receive invitations from around the province to speak at clubs and schools on my favorite theme: the consequences of choice. These invitations allowed me to travel, show Susannah the country and feel less incarcerated. I relished all this, which dovetailed with my view of myself. We were living on Susannah's savings, and I was passing my days in writing early versions of this book.

In prison, I had used Sufi teachings and a spiritual perspective to transform the grotesque injustice around me into something more useful and less painful. Now almost free—not a prisoner, a dealer, or an addict—I proudly regarded myself as still on the Spiritual Journey. I insisted everything had to have a spiritual reference point, and I had in my possession at all times the best possible solution to others' problems, and those of the planet in general. In other words, I had stopped growing. If I knew more and more, I became in that knowing more and more inert. The mundane world of making a living was to be left to others. I thought I had more important work to do. In fact, a great deal of learning did lie ahead. I was yet to discover that nothing was "spiritual"—or everything was.

Meanwhile, Susannah Lewis had chosen to make the inexplicable leap from being the head knitwear designer at a division of Liz Claiborne to being the partner of a man who'd been sentenced to ten years in federal prison, and she had traded Santa Barbara, California, for a cardboard-walled basement apartment in St. John's, Newfoundland. On October 9, 1993, Susannah and I married.

Shortly before Christmas 1994, two years after my arrival in St. John's, I attended my parole hearing. By now, I was longest-term resident in the halfway house. My case officer, who harbored some petty resentment for my calling him a chickenshit asshole when he reneged on his promise to support my application for accelerated release, now argued throughout the proceedings for a six-month extension and greater controls. The board thought otherwise, and I was free. Susannah took a job in Toronto, and I joined her there.

From time to time, I go home again. There are often years between trips, but flying into St. John's is always the same: hundreds of bobbing heads at the gate of the little airport, all vying for a better view of their loved ones. I always recognize many in that small sea of Newfoundland faces roiling before me, faces that look like those of my classmates, though they must be the children of those I once knew.

There's Dad, leaning against a pillar and on his cane at the same time, wearing his famous green hat of Irish tweed. I see him smiling, pushing his big frail frame in my direction, my kid brother Chris beside him. He reaches beyond me for my beautiful Susannah. And there comes Maddy, my mom— Johnny on her arm and wheeling her oxygen machine, its plastic tubing wrapped around her head—Mom, who's found a love for her errant boy that she never had when he was growing up, or if she had, she'd hidden it well. But somehow, all that's changed and now she loves him out loud and God help the person who would say a single word against him. There they are, then, my parents: frailer each time I see them, but miraculously more and more interested in their children.

"Sure, you shouldn't have come," I say. "We'd be home in a few minutes."

"I know, sweetie, but I had to come greet Susannah. What would she think? Hello, darling! How was your trip?"

"Great, Maddy," says Susannah, still shy with the O'Deas. "Thanks."

As soon as we're in the front door, Mom turns to my wife. "Dear, you come with me. I've been knitting this vest for Brian, and I'm having so much trouble with the directions. Who do you think writes them? Certainly not someone who speaks English."

As a knitwear designer, Susannah can't read a pattern to save her life. She knits from her mind out, creating on the fly. "I know," she reassures my mother. "That's why I never learned to read those things. Here, let me see your knitting."

My mother knew the day she met Susannah that she herself could die peacefully in the knowledge that her prodigal son was in the hands of a good knitter.

———

Prison may have awakened me to some of my more serious shortcomings, and even hinted at their origins, but it didn't take them from me. I might have gotten a glimpse of the whys, but as Dave Richo used to say, why is the question for children; how is the question for adults. I'm able to hide a lie in the why, an excuse, an easy forgiveness for a terrible act. How demands that I find a way to deal with it. Why is passive—information only, and speculation, usually—and asks nothing of me. It usually excuses me. Why takes me away from my examination of my behavior and into someone else's behavior, something I can do nothing about. How notices the why, but uses it as information only to get to the how of living.

Looking back over this manuscript, my life, I see the whys clearly enough, as clearly as I've seen other excuses in my life. If I ever choose to waste my life again, it will be because I dwelt on those whys.

"Your hypocrisy!" Now there's one of my favorite whys. "How could I live in a world of such hypocrisy? Your booze and tobacco are great, right? My pot's not, right? It's all right for the likes of the Seagrams—or even the O'Deas—to build their fortunes on the problems of others—and be hailed in the press as heroes. It's all right, isn't it? Meanwhile, pot smugglers and pot growers and ordinary users are feckless pariahs, right? Why? Why?"

As a tall figure in the little world of St. John's, Newfoundland, my father had been created in the familiar image of God the Father, that stern and unwavering God of the Old Testament. Revered by his people, he dispensed the sudsy manna that eased their suffering, yet he was wrathful toward the wayward, and far more of his wrath was pointed in my direction than elsewhere—not that I didn't give him some cause. His job, as he saw it, was not to deal with his son's tribulations but to scourge the sinners or, as gods so often do, ignore them. Why?

And on and on I could go. That's the trick of the why. I could get merrily lost in that funhouse and alienate even those who might effect the changes that I desire for the world.

Or the Christian Brother from St. Bon's. Now there's a why. I could grow seriously attached to him as the gatekeeper to all my destructive behavior. After all, I let him own the opening pages of this book.

Yet—oh, why again—why couldn't I go to my mother and my father and ask for their help, so long ago, when I needed it? Why couldn't I ask them? Why couldn't I ask? Instead, I spent thirty years protecting them—not least by my absence —when they should have protected me.

Just past my fortieth birthday, I came out of my room at the Cottage Hospital in Santa Barbara, where I had embarked on sobriety after a lifetime of its opposite. I went to a pay phone in the hospital corridor and called my mother.

"Did you know, Mom?"

"Know, dear?"

"Know what was happening to me? Then? When I was a kid?"

"I . . . I knew there was some change, dear. I knew some- thing changed."

"You let me down, Mom. You and Dad let me down."

"No, sweetie."

"But did you do anything?"

"Did I do . . . ?"

"Did you do anything to help me, Mom?"

There was a long silence.

"Mom?"

"You . . . you were such a brave little boy, Brian."

"Mom?"

"You were so brave."

Why?

In October 1995, I went home to St. John's and sat at my mom's bedside for days. I was often alone with her because my brothers and sisters had to be at work. During that time, I confessed to a whole raft of sins, whispered them into her dying ear.

Once I said to her, "Mom. It was me that burned the garage when I was a kid. It was an accident. I'm so sorry."

Mom squeezed my hand. "I always knew that, sweetie."

Those few days were the most sanctified of my life, and when she died two days after that absolution, eight of us were holding her: my brothers and sisters and me, our two aunts and our dad, each of us holding a part of her. I was at her feet.

Carnell's Funeral Home was on Kenmount Road, the original "road out of town," which seemed fitting enough. The wake was a huge affair, with hundreds and hundreds coming to pay their respects and have a last look at Maddy lying there pale, cold, and altogether gone. Dad sat in a chair at the head of the coffin; as the folks came and prayed by Maddy's coffin, they would move on to pay respects to him, John R., as he was affectionately known to his community. My brothers and sisters and I milled in the crowd and stood as a welcoming party in the hallway leading into the wake room, shaking hands, feeling the sympathy in the mourners' grips.

We were a fairly jovial group, reminiscing on our childhood, on Mom, having a wonderful time being together, something so rare at this stage of our lives: a celebration, a sad celebration filled with joy.

Just after supper on Sunday night, the evening before the actual funeral, Johnny—my older brother, lawyer, and Brian-bail-out artist—along with Chris, Judy, and Eileen, all Brian-bail-out artists, were standing in that hallway. People were trickling in before the evening rush. Rounding the corner and heading in our direction were a husband and wife we knew slightly, accompanied by a man who appeared to be a priest.

He was dressed in black with a Roman collar. He was altogether familiar, but all priests look somehow familiar to boys raised Catholic and fearful. As they drew close, they grew silent and tentative in their approach. I was standing against one wall, closest of my family to their approach. My brothers and sisters stood alongside me as we welcomed these new visitors.

I reached for the couple's hands. "Thanks for coming, ma'am. And thank you, sir."

I reached for the hand of their companion. "Welcome, Father," I said. I let go of his hand to welcome the next mourner. I stopped.

The hand.

This was no priest. This was the hand I knew too well, even forty years later. As I watched, he shook my father's hand. I stood, uncertain, then slipped into a room nearby and wept for a boy now vanished.

No. That man cannot have dominion over the last lines of this account.

How? How to turn that shit and all the other shit into something from which the flower that is my life can grow? That's the how that's worth investigating. Can all this introspection and retrospection answer that? I don't know. The whys still attempt their palace coups, but I've recently avoided relinquishing much of myself to them. Most of my time is spent in the how of today. There's not much time left to make it right.

Following the funeral, I came back to Toronto.

"Baby," I said to Susannah, "none of us are anything without family." On August 29, 1996, our son, Rufus O'Dea, was born, my third child. Perhaps this time I could be a good father, though that, of course, is all part of another life.

For now I have to leave the story in Newfoundland, where my brothers and I traveled together to Bell Island not long after the funeral. We stood looking out over the sea. A skin-blistering gale threatened to blow us across the escarpment. A two-hundred-foot drop separated us from the surging water. As we watched, brooks on their suicidal way to the sea below were blown back onto the tabletop landscape, spray freezing to the skin of our faces. So even the water seemed to be flung back to this rocky island, as though it was never allowed a full and complete departure, never allowed to find its resolution in the sea, blown back to form icicles on the stiff grass, blown back onto the trees, which reached westward but also failed to make it past this cliff.

Chris was squinting into the wind, sort of smiling. "Hey, Johnny!" he called. "Remember when they made Uncle Fabian the lieutenant governor of Newfoundland? Remember that party we had at Nanny and Grandpa's house?"

Johnny was nodding hard against the wind. "In that room we called the wake room."

"Right."

"Nanny and Grandpa were already dead."

"Right. And Dad made a toast and said, 'Father would have loved this.'"

"That's right."

"Yeah. Well, Mom and Dad would have loved this, wouldn't they? The three of us."

"Yes, they would," Johnny called.

He looked over at me, but I looked out to sea and pretended the wind was hurting my eyes.

ACKNOWLEDGMENTS

MY HEARTFELT THANKS TO:

SUSANNAH, you have laid the foundation upon which my life is possible.

Sally Lewis, a better mother-in-law could never be found for such a challenging son-in-law.

My brothers, Chris and John, my sisters, Eileen and Judy, who supported me through all the ups and downs, and continue to do so.

My children, Cheyenne and Cherokee, your continued belief in me as someone worth saving finally woke me from my slumber, thank you.

Doug Miller, your wise counsel prepared me for all this.

Russell Iadanza and friends, for paying all those phone bills for Susannah and me when I was "away."

Sonya Tone Utt, for copying and distributing these pages to my friends while I was "away," and for so much more.

Rodney Utt, your unconditional friendship, and preliminary experience and wisdom made me know I would be OK.

Dale Taylor, your visits were trips to a well for a thirsty man.

Charlotte Gusay for seeing the book in my words.

Jeannie Middle Class, you are my "Local Hero."

Neal Crosbie, for all the great artwork for my room in the big house, for the love and the friendship.

Regina Jensen, friend for life, bailer of the guilty.

Dave Richo, for your support in the gap.

Carol Frank, for putting Susannah up when she came to visit.

Canada Council for the Arts for the early development money.

Ned Pratt for the perfect photo.

Janis Spence, Kathy Hogan, and Helen Peters, who all worked with the earliest version of this manuscript, and helped me find my voice among the babble.

Mary at Trius, for typing her fingers to the bone.

Anne Spencer.

Deborah Harris, you led me to new places, all of them undiscovered parts of myself, some of which I wasn't ready to see.

Peggy Fisher for Kiloran McRae Lye, for Tecca Crosby, for Ian Brown, for Anne Collins, for the push in the right direction—an incredible lineage for which I am so grateful.

John and Anita Mallick for the great home in Paris that they share so freely with my family; and their daughter Alex, who has worked so hard to promote me and this book.

Robert Buckland for hearing my voice amid the cacophony, and being unafraid of it.

And finally, thank you to my brothers on the inside, who carried me over that frightening threshold and taught me to do my time.

PERSONAE

TO THE BEST OF MY KNOWLEDGE:

Dick Andrews. One-time colleague of Gary Sexton. Now living happily with his wife and children on Vancouver Island.

Mark Bartlett. Still number two in the Seattle USDA office, and still has a good word or two for Brian O'Dea, for whom he did not seek the death penalty.

The Christian Brother from St. Bons. Loved to work and play with young people. Retired and said to be living in Newfoundland. Wrote his own book.

John Paul Jones De Joria. A great hair guy. Living in Malibu and, by my strictly informal calculations, probably a billionaire. It looks good on him.

Derek. One-time belladonna fancier. Now has a hardware gig in Atlantic Canada. Rarely reads *Scientific American.*

Terry Fields. Canadian, eh. Left an unloving U.S. for his wife's homeland.

Suzi Foreman. My second wife and mother of Cheyenne and Cherokee. Still in LA.

Gary Fowler. Perhaps known to Gary Sexton, see below.

Tony Franolovich. Outstanding trawler captain, tempted into deeper waters. Eventually made up with the family and still fishing after all these years.

Frank Graf. Stout heart. Oldsmobile collector, honorable in the face of great adversity. Always preferred tranquil anonymity and still does.

Paul Halloran. Catalyst for my temporary conversion to Jesus. Still Christian, living in an Advent Christian Fellowship compound in Florida with his wife and many children. He brokers small insurance companies under an assumed name.

Regina Jensen. Best friend then and now. A psychologist with a thriving practice in Santa Ynez, California.

Jerry. Great fan of Kools. Didn't answer my recent e-mail.

Larry Layton. Former colleague of Jim Jones and a Terminal Island guy, a real sweetheart, free at last, thank God almighty, free at last.

Barry Levinson. Once a manufacturer of vending machines, and to this day a deviser of endless and inventive schemes. Remains one of my nearest and dearest friends.

Mark McFarlane. A Canadian at Terminal Island doing fifty years for coke. Got paroled and deported after doing ten. Now living on the west coast of Canada, doing well.

Doug Miller. My AA mentor and bandleader at my pre-prison party. Now works as a drug and alcohol counselor in Charlotte, North Carolina, and regrets not pursuing his music to the bitter end. He says, "Stay tuned!"

Eleanor Miller. Wife of my youth. She too was born again. Living in Newfoundland with her cats.

Gary O'Brien. Newfie dealer. He and I were shook up in Bogotá. Now a lawyer in Newfoundland.

Cherokee O'Dea. My daughter. Lives in Chatsworth, California, where she is pursuing a career as a photographer and film director.

Cheyenne O'Dea. My son. Is the father of my grandson, Conner, and is fishing with Captain Tony, whom you read about in these pages.

Chris O'Dea. Younger and loyal brother. Owns a real estate and auctioneering company in Newfoundland, a new career at fifty-something. Very successful.

Eileen O'Dea. My loved and loyal sister. Semiretired teacher. Divorced her husband and now lives alone in Nova Scotia. Happy and well.

John R. O'Dea. My father. Had a new knee put in but couldn't handle the recovery, so decided to die. I handed this manuscript in to the publisher on what would have been his ninetieth birthday.

Johnny O'Dea. Older and loyal brother. Successful lawyer in St. John's.

Judy O'Dea. My sister and Johnny's twin. Beautiful woman and friend, living well in many places.

Maddy O'Dea. My mother. Maddy is no longer in the building. Her earthly remains reside in a military cemetery right next to Dad's. Her spirit lives on in her grandson, Rufus, her parting gift to this earth.

The Preacher. Big man on that other island. I heard he coked himself into poverty.

Dave Richo. An important influence for me. Now teaching in San Francisco and, I suspect, being taught.

Gary Sexton. One time Newfoundland dope dealer who graduated to the Caribbean. After years on the road, finally home in the loving arms of his family.

Bill Shaffer. Once mad and shrewd, he met John Paul at a party we threw at the Iverson Ranch after the last deal. Now hangs with John Paul in LA. Made a movie in 2003, but it sank without a trace.

Kris Shaffer. Lady-killer and international boulevardier. Now living in LA.

Will Shears. Somewhere learning how to shout his story from the mountain top.

Bob Sherman and his wife, Debbie. Hostages in my coke demise. Sadly, they borrowed into oblivion and lost the ranch.

Joey Smallwood. First premier of Newfoundland and self-styled "Last Father of Confederation." Dead, dead at last!

Ricardo Vasquez. Friend and cellie on Terminal Island. Great soul, but no advantages. Still doing a ton of time back in Terminal Island, California.

Yvonne. Came to my aid in Colombia. Now in the fashion business in Germany.

DON'T KNOW AND DON'T NEED TO KNOW—
MY COLOMBIAN FRIENDS:

Major Fernandes. Knew an opportunity when he saw one.

Billy and Maria G. The man who would be chief and his good-hearted wife.

Juan. Hercule Poirot with a .38.

Santiago. Scary on the outside but decent on the inside.

LOST IN TIME:

CI. Aspirant leg-breaker and deal maker. Not snared in the Seattle roundup. He and I were destined to cross and cross again, but he seems to be avoiding me now.

Colin K. Finger counter extraordinaire.

Carrot. Jamaican friend. Go well.

The DC-6. Sorry, old girl.

Dick the Courier. He could fly and he could swim.

The *Fremad*. As pretty a boat as ever floated. Too bad we didn't go farther together.

Gentleman Bob. Gainesville businessman. Whatever he's doing, he's probably doing it well.

Sam King, a.k.a. Ink Slinger. Sam, where are you? Call me.

Donny Murray, a.k.a. the Syrian. Somebody apparently developed a petty resentment against Donny and emptied a revolver into him. He lived. While he was struggling to recover in hospital, visitors used a baseball bat to beat his bones to pulp. He survived that too. All long ago.

Richard. Jerry's partner. Ask Jerry.